Then Cam

MW00799600

Books by Gian J. Quasar

Then Came The Dawn
The Bermuda Triangle II
A Passage to Oblivion
Scarlet Autumn: Jack the Ripper
the Sea Ghost
Distant Horizons
HELL SHIP
SOMA
Recasting Bigfoot
They Flew into Oblivion
Into the Bermuda Triangle

THEN ★ CAME ★ THE ★ DAWN

THE SEARCH FOR AMELIA EARHART

THEN
and
NOW

GIAN J. QUASAR

Brodwyn, Moor & Doane

Quasar, Gian Julius

Then Came The Dawn

First Edition

Copyright © 2023 by Gian J. Quasar
All Rights Reserved

No part of this publication may be reproduced, broadcast, transmitted, distributed or displayed— except for brief quotations in reviews— without prior written permission.

Contents

A Foreword of Forewarning

This is not a biography of Amelia Earhart. This is, in its way, a biography of Amelia Earhart's disappearance. As a chronicle of discovery, this book cannot be an uncritical compilation that merely slops before the reader sundry claims and theories. This would only bloat the book with counterproductive assertions, the very ones that have reduced the fate of Amelia Earhart to a convoluted folklore of hearsay. Rather the purpose is to put in place the actual facts and then logically follow them as far as we can. The ultimate purpose of any quest, of course, is to attain the goal. Setting in place the solid facts of a true mystery is the first step toward its final solution.

The actual facts pertaining to the disappearance of Amelia Earhart have become only fragments lost within an aggregate of assertions that have been repeated oft enough until they have taken on the façade of truth. But the true facts are far more intriguing when cleared of the extemporanea of conspiracy theories, counter theories, and the cyclical reasoning that dominates such an *ad hoc* spectrum. Thus the goal here is to present the truth all in one volume. Its slim nature does not betray this goal; it is a reflection of it.

When head of the Max Planck Institute for Health, Gerd Gigarenzer said that the intuitional component of intelligence is not found in knowing what is important but in knowing what is *not important* so that it can be discarded from the equation. It is my hope the slimness of this volume reflects adherence to this wise insight.

Following this sagely approach, the biographical section of this book will be as thin as possible. The life of AE, as she liked to be called, insofar as she influenced aviation and insofar as she rose to unique fame in her time as "America's premier aviatrix," must be presented first for that which follows to make any sense. But I will keep it brief and to the point.

Biography is not "my thing" anyway. Mystery is my thing. To pursue and crack a captivating thriller! Thus the disappearance of Amelia Earhart rather than her life has drawn me to the case.

Perhaps my agnosticism is an advantage in this matter. I am neither a critic nor a fan of Amelia Earhart. I am not going to see her through rose-tinted spectacles. Nor do I have the need to denigrate an icon. I encapsulate the life of AE as it leads up to and motivates her final flight.

Her charisma and daring captivated a world and made her a fascinating symbol of progress. The sudden and unexpected snuffing out of such a luminary created much speculation about exactly what happened to her. It is not tragedy that holds our attention today. It is mystery.

Disappearance is different than destruction. It is to enter limbo, to forever remain alive but unapproachable. Her tomboyish face did not age before the camera. Her voice did not become shaky and quiver. She remains with us today, fresh, alive, frozen in her final smile and wave to those who adored her.

Then and now no one wanted to believe that the disappearance of the "foremost aviatrix" could be chalked up to running out of gas and going down at sea. Shortwave enthusiasts picked up messages for days after she vanished. The nation was led to believe she had initially survived on a desert island. Then the search was called off. The messages were declared a hoax. She faded from the front page with a question mark rather than a period.

From that initial question mark there have cascaded numerous questions. And like all questions, the answers must be honestly sought and finally be given. And this is where this volume will get investigative, where I have to take sides and reveal weaknesses and strengths in theories.

We've heard stories of a secret government spy mission, of things gone terribly awry in flight, of Japanese internment; cover up, of course; conspiracy, a must. We also heard the banal "crash and sink" can be the only logical conclusion. Facts have been used to support all of the above, but they are really only factoids regurgitated without applied context. This volume will not avoid them, but it will place them in context, for truth is always found within the context, not at the urging of a factoid.

After that final dawn over the Pacific Ocean the fame of Amelia Earhart has been passive to those who have searched for her. Legends have arisen that have intrigued us. Uncovered documents have contained statements that have shocked us.

Several clues have come together to instill the instinctive feeling there must be more to Amelia Earhart's disappearance than simply running out of fuel and crashing. It is time to finally weigh all of these concisely; to find their origins and to follow through to see which have merit and which do not. Thus the majority of this volume is devoted to that final dawn, and this final dawn can have little meaning without the life of Amelia Earhart having flown into it and having never returned.

PART I

Bitter Joy at Mountain Heights

Chapter 1

What the Publicist Ordered

Amelia Earhart was born in Atchison, Kansas, on July 24, 1897. From an early age her mother Amy Otis Earhart allowed her and her younger sister, Muriel, enough independence to develop on their own. Without being made to conform to the image of "good little girls," they became adventurous tomboys, with Amelia being the leader of the two. Psychologically, she was inventive and inquisitive, but also stubborn. Dabbling also became a character trait early in life, but it was the result of her searching mind and not flippancy of impulse.

An early example is seen during her teenage years in Chicago. She refused to attend the nearest high school to home because its chemistry lab was dirty and inadequate. She discovered Hyde Park High School had a much better lab, and so she walked much further to attend and graduate from this school, though she would eventually lose interest in chemistry.

By the age of 20 she had briefly attended a junior college in Pennsylvania, but a visit to her sister in Toronto, Canada, changed her career choice. Deeply moved by seeing the returning war wounded from the trenches, she took up nursing courses. She then tended many dying men and women from the strange Spanish Flu epidemic in 1918, and eventually fell ill herself with pneumonia and severe sinusitis.

By this time in her life she had developed an attractive and charming manner— well-spoken and determined yet without being pushy. She had a perky sparkle in mischievous eyes and rosy high cheekbones. With her hair newly bobbed, she was the caricature of a playful tomboy.

In everything Amelia Earhart was a contrast to "Moderns." Moderns were in vogue after The Great War. They were dissolute flappers on a bar stool, with ciggy dangling from parched lips. They had no dreams or ambitions. They were only rebels against the wholesome image of womanhood. In manner and appearance Amelia was a staid "good girl," but one with a revolutionary mindset. A woman didn't have to be just a wife and mother. She should think outside the box and be able to pursue her own dreams. She also didn't believe in stimulants of any kind. They were false and unnatural. She derived "intense pleasure" from physical exercise, a pleasure that could only be equaled, she would discover, by thrill. The thrill could not be an empty stimulant: she had to be experiencing something unique and fulfilling one of her goals.

By 1920, now 23 years old, she was living in Los Angeles, where her father, Edwin, and mother, Amy Otis, had moved. When the postwar economic boom hit America, she was still undecided on her course of life. But there was a savings account on her mother's side. She could be fancy poor for a while until she decided.

Thus she sought to finally sample something that had long excited her. It was late in December of 1920 that she drove through the orchards to the square cutout of fields in Long Beach. Near a wood, barnlike structure, in company of her father, she stood by a dusty biplane.

Servicing the cockpit was a woman in flight overalls precariously balanced on a ladder. She had ratty hair and a little grease on her face. Neta Snook was the only female flight instructor in the Los Angeles area. She flew out of Kinner Field, Long Beach, this long dusty airstrip set by a hangar and some outbuildings.

She looked over to her unexpected guests.

What stood before Neta was a young woman wearing a fashionable brown dress and matching jacket, high heels, with a scarf about her neck. She was a refreshing change from the Moderns or pretentious socialites. There was just something about Amelia. She was a dainty thing exuding good breeding and gentility.

Amelia asked her pointedly if she could teach her how to fly. Her charm was noteworthy, but it was clear that there wasn't much money to spend.

Neta agreed to teach her.

Amelia took her first flying lesson on January 2, 1921. It was in a heavy Curtis JN-4 Jenny, a standard biplane that had proven its worth in The Great War. It rose up under Neta's clutching fist on the stick and roared over the power lines. Opening up all around them were the checkerboard squares of lush citrus orchards. In the distance Los Angeles and Hollywood's Spanish stucco silhouette reclined under avenues of palms. Over their shoulder was the expanse of the vast Pacific, a blue calm sheet stretching into the endless thin haze. It would be a scene Amelia would see over and over, soon with her hand firmly clutching the stick.

Grinning exuberantly under large goggles, Amelia was becoming a pilot. She was experiencing the intense pleasure she craved, but it wasn't just from piloting. Flying was in its infancy, and aviation still needed pioneers. There was the ability to make a contribution and not just indulge in something whimsical. She soon bought an airplane for herself.

The Kinner Airster was a biplane manufactured by the field's manager and namesake, Bert Kinner. She bought a pretty yellow one and dubbed it "Canary." It was new, convenient, and lightweight. It was easier for Amelia to handle than the burly Jenny.

However, twice she crashed her bright "Canary." One time, they had taken off from Goodyear Field. The 3 cylinder Airster couldn't get enough speed to climb over the eucalyptus trees at the end of the field. Amelia pulled up, causing the plane to stall and plop down, breaking the prop and crushing the landing gear.

Like the vignette about Hyde Park High School, this incident also preserves for us one of Amelia's key character traits. Neta preserved the moment in her own writings. Still trying to recover her senses, she turned to see Amelia powdering her nose. Amelia's explanation— "We have to look good for the reporters."

Earhart wasn't vainglorious, but she was conscious of image. She was self-conscious of a gap in her front teeth—hence her "half smile"—and she was sensitive about what she viewed as her fat legs. In other words, she was conscious she was in a hobby that attracted the press and she was going to live up to its image of adventurous glamor.

Despite having a plane she felt comfortable with, Amelia still refused to solo. Neta had long urged her, but Amelia avoided an answer. "She'd look back at me with her winsome half smile, but she never committed herself."

Later, Amelia would write that she didn't think it wise to be soloing if she didn't know how to get out of any position that the airplane could get into. She wanted to learn stunting first— in other words, aerobatics, rolls, loops. This is an unusual assertion, but it fit Amelia's stubborn character and her quest for *substantive* thrill, not just aimless flying.

There is another and far more practical reason— flying was deadly. Amelia was attracted to flying because it was exciting, but she didn't court death. She admitted to two significant character traits, one a very visceral one, the other a flaw that followed. "Exercise of all kinds gave me intense pleasure. . . I might have been more skillful and graceful if I had learned the correct form in athletics. I could not get any instruction, so I just played and acquired a lot of bad habits."

Thrill of flying had easily surpassed exercise on the pleasure meter. Yet due to the deadly nature of flying, Amelia wanted the best instruction and not just her own acquired bad habits.

She went to a former Army pilot. Richard Motijo was her choice. Finally, after a rather long apprenticeship in Glendale, Amelia soloed and made a "thoroughly rotten landing," as she would later write. In any case, having graduated aerobatics she was in the perfect position to do performing.

Air shows were the place. They brought out the stars, the press and MovieTone news cameras. On December 17, 1921, Amelia was paired with screen star Aloysia McLintic at the Sierra Airdrome. Both performed aerobatics, with McLintic in a feisty Laird Swallow and Earhart in her bright yellow Canary. It was billed as the "Pacific Coast Ladies Derby."

Pursuing that "intense pleasure" had urged Amelia on in these early days, and her courage was undeniable. She took her yellow Canary up to 14,000 feet in the winter of 1922, briefly setting an altitude record for women.

Flying had introduced Amelia to "intense pleasure" on a much greater level than physical exercise. Now it also introduced her to another exciting world— the fashionable, celebrity world. Everybody who was anybody in Hollywood/Los Angeles was into flying. In the world of fast fashion, Amelia was becoming somebody, at least locally. With her charm and new social profile, she put Bert Kinner's little Long Beach airfield on the map. There she became the reigning star, and he used her image for advertising his new Kinner Airster. Not being rugged or powerful was given the spin of "lightweight" and "manageable." "A Lady's Plane was well as a Man's," declared the ad. That was smart advertising for a culture of money that slaved to fads.

Potential at cashing in on her fashionable image must have been seen, if not by Amelia than by her trendy friends. On August 8, 1922, the Los Angles *Examiner* declared that prestigious Vassar College "was prepared for its thrill of thrills. Some sunny day next fall a large and dusty airplane is due to pull a near-tailspin over its exclusive campus and, descending, to disgorge Miss Earhart, Los Angeles society girl-student aviatrix."

Of course, she didn't go, and probably had little intent. It was purely to get her recognized. Unfortunately, a puff piece about flying off to a name-brand college didn't advance her flying into any real income-generating vehicle.

Frankly, there was nothing to fly into. Amelia's fashionable hobby had wings but no legs. At present, air carrier service and other aspects of delivery were open to qualified pilots. Being a woman it would have been difficult for her to secure a job, but also she wasn't qualified. Air derbies and altitude records don't require one to really understand navigation and endurance. So far, Amelia had not had a single long flight.

The truth is she hadn't the money to sortie out on her own and garner long-distance experience. It took all of her money to maintain her plane for local flying. Susan Butler, her most voluminous biographer (*East to the Dawn*), presents a rather apt analogy of Amelia's expensive hobby, equating its upkeep to owning and maintaining a stable of polo ponies.

It was impossible for Earhart to advance far in her hobby given her present financial circumstances. Her most lucrative employ-

ment had been as a back office mail and file clerk at the telephone company. Even this income was eventually lost. At her
mother's request, she quit. Amy Otis wanted her to stay home
more and keep her company. Between her hobby and her work to
pay for her hobby they had little time together. Her mother's en-
ticement was impossible to refuse. She'd pay off her debt for buying the Airster (a whopping $2,000 — equivalent to $31,000 today).

However, the family bank, and thus Amelia's hobby, wouldn't
last long. She had advised her mother, who was by no means rich,
to invest in her friend Peter Barnes' gypsum mine. Building was
furious in the post war boom, and gypsum is an essential component of stucco/plaster. Amy Otis invested her savings. Amelia and
Edwin went to visit the mine only to watch Barnes drown in a
flood as he tried to get his truck out of the area. The mine was
wiped out. Their investment, all that remained of mother Amy's
stash, was literally down the drain.

Amidst personal tragedies there was still public recognition. In
June 1923 she was admitted to the Aeronautical Hall of Fame for
being "influential for advancing aeronautics." Ironically, soon
thereafter Amelia would have to sell her treasured Airster.

Now in the summer of 1923 she was down to the burlap —
completely tapped out. She had always been performing on borrowed time and money. When her bad business advice was heed-
ed by her mother, even the veneer was over.

She tried her hand at photography, but couldn't make money
at it either. Strangely, she set about to buy a truck with another
male friend and get into the building boom by trucking materials.
This was hardly what her society wannabe friends wanted, and
many dropped her.

The latter part of 1923 and 1924 are obscure in Amelia's background. One thing is certain: she hadn't prospered locally. She
had been hit by another severe sinus infection that needed surgery. This cost $500.00, which she definitely didn't have. Instead
of paying the bill, she bought a bright yellow Kissell car and
named it the "Yellow Peril." In this she casually drove her mother, Amy Otis, cross-country to the Boston area. Her sister Muriel
was teaching junior high in Medford, Massachusetts, and Amelia
opted for pre-Med at Columbia University. Her parents had di-
vorced, and it was time for the father to go his own way and for

the women to join up and get on with life.

Amelia may not have thought she gave up much in fleeing bill collectors eastward to Columbia U. Air Derbies had quickly become old hat. Her excitement level had reached a plateau, and she couldn't overcome the financial ceiling placed on her excitement quest.

But pre-Med didn't work out either. She had tasted a very different, exhilarating life already, quite a contrast to the humdrum of a university classroom and the biologic reality of anatomy.

Realizing that medicine wasn't her thing, Amelia wanted to get in MIT because they were forming a department of aeronautical engineering. This desire attests to her lasting interest in aviation or at least in the visceral excitement it gave her. She wanted to combine both business and the greatest pleasure she'd had, but it still remained beyond her financial ability.

Her next job was as a social worker at Denison House in Boston. Nothing more unglamorous can be imagined for the "society-girl" who was once written up in Hollywood as going to a girl's college to thrill the exclusive debutantes.

Despite her financial condition and the drollery of social work, Amelia still found opportunities for flying. . .at least as a passenger. Denison House had hit upon the happy idea of a fundraiser. No doubt with Amelia's enthusiastic advice, they agreed to let her drop passes over Boston as part of the fundraiser. Crocker Snow took her up on May 26, 1927.

The stunt came at the right time, of course. It had been less than a week since Charles Lindbergh had crossed the Atlantic solo and landed in Paris to world celebration. Locally in Boston the resulting news coverage from her flight got her name out in the street. For Boston, decidedly different from Hollywood, she was a solid citizen with a progressive hobby.

Close to a year goes by. Charles Lindbergh was still *the* national hero. Along with the exploits of Commander Byrd, Lindbergh's flight ushered in the new fad of adventure heroism. Individual courage was the soul of the new fad. These were not heroes of stunts but those who through their *individual* courage became vanguards in the realm of progress.

"Firsts" were naturally the cornerstones of success. Otherwise feats were merely costly endeavors with no promotional *i.e.* income value. Secrecy was also a must. If someone caught wind that a "first" was going to be attempted, they could jump the claim. This was part of the "business." Technically there may not have been money in flying, but there was money in "firsts." You could be promoted as a real life hero, and a lot of paying endorsements came with it. There was nothing like this in 1922 when Amelia reached to try and monetize her true passion.

As chance would have it, locally in Boston there was a key promoter in the world of aviation—Colonel Hilton Railey.

Byrd had sold his trimotor Fokker, which he had used on his polar expedition. It now idled in Boston harbor, purpose unknown. It was secretly being prepared for a special flight.

A new first was now to be prepared. A Mrs. Frederick Guest was going to back the flight. She would fly from America to England on the Fokker; if successful, becoming the first woman to cross the Atlantic. However, family urged her to find a replacement. It was simply too dangerous for the middle-aged and wealthy socialite. But the passenger, naturally, had to be a woman, otherwise there was no first involved. It was Railey's duty to find an appropriate candidate. He snuffled about contacts in Boston. A name was repeated. She was a social worker. This was honorable. In late April 1928 he called her at Denison House.

Receiver pushed up to her ear, Amelia listened to his pitch. He asked if she would like to do something "big for aviation."

"Yes!"

That it might be hazardous did not faze her. He asked her to come to his office.

Amelia came with friend, Marion Perkins. Railey was taken by Amelia's manner. Her cornflower eyes flashed with polite frankness. Her laugh was infectious, but she was conservative and formal. He studied her for a moment.

Wearing a brown wool dress, Amelia sat gently on the edge of her chair, only a few blond locks showing under her brown cloche hat. But what really struck Railey's eye was her resemblance to the most famous hero in America, Charles Lindbergh.

Finally, he asked: "Would you like to be the first woman to fly across the Atlantic?"

Amelia pondered but a moment. "Yes, sir, I certainly would."

Her decisive answer should not be taken lightly. After Lindbergh, the subsequent zeal to fly the Atlantic was shared by 18 aircraft and their crews, 4 including women. They weren't imbued with the zest for progress. It was for personal fame or national honor, and this probably explains why there were so many failures. None of those with women had been successful. Starting in the summer of 1927, the first attempt (with Lady Anne Savile) ended in her disappearance. Beauty contest winner Ruth Elder crashed in October and had to be rescued at sea. (Just for the attempt she and her co-pilot George Haldeman received a ticker tape parade in New York). Woodrow Wilson's niece, Frances Grayson, attempted on December 23, 1927, and also vanished. The Honorable Elsie MacKay left Lincolnshire in March 1928 with famed ace Walter Hinchliffe flying *Endeavor*, a black and gold Stinson Detroiter, en route to Mitchell Field, Long Island. Honorable Elsie and the great Hinchliffe were never seen again. Bits of wreckage later washed up in Ireland.

Now a month later it was to be tried yet again, and Amelia just found herself quickly in the running.

Railey now told her that she had to go to New York with him and meet the backers. He cautioned her that other women were being considered. Though this was true, it is highly unlikely that Railey was not going to completely endorse Earhart. Railey knew a good thing when he saw it. In fact, he believed he had found the perfect woman. "I felt that I had discovered not their norm but their sublimation."

To New York they went. She was, of course, chosen.

In her usual style of witty self-effacing she was to write:

> I found myself in a curious situation. If they did not like me at all or found me wanting in too many respects, I would be deprived of the trip. If they liked me too well, they might be loath to drown me. It was, therefore, necessary for me to maintain an attitude of impenetrable mediocrity.

In truth, Earhart's success was not due to being anodyne. She had the advantage of being a female Charles Lindbergh— wholesome Middle America with a tomboyish zest for adventure. She was exactly what a publicist would want.

The operation was underway, and it was made clear to her this was utmost secret. A hush-hush adventure was exciting for Amelia. She didn't even tell her own family what she was intending.

The dangers of violating secrecy were very real. In fact, it was via a leak that one of the most significant people entered the picture and then hijacked the expedition— George Palmer Putnam.

GP, as he was known on Madison Avenue, had a yen for all things adventurous. He had published Lindbergh and Byrd and any other adventurer he could get into his powerful publishing stable at Putnam & Sons.

Putnam was, in fact, the one responsible for setting Railey in motion to find a female candidate. Railey had visited Putnam in New York for an entirely different matter. During their conversation, Putnam mentioned he had heard that Byrd had sold his Fokker to a wealthy woman who intended to fly the Atlantic. He thought it would be "amusing to handle a stunt like that."

Somehow GP got more involved, even being entrusted by Mrs. Guest to find her replacement. Because this flight was to cement British-American relations, as Lindbergh's had done for French-American, Mrs. Guest had dubbed the Fokker *Friendship*. The flight, of course, had been intended for more symbolism than just being the conduit for the first woman to fly the Atlantic. So naturally when she had opted out, she had wanted the right sort of girl chosen in her place.

Both Railey and Putnam believed they had the right choice in Amelia. She was especially perfect for GP. She was eloquent, witty and self-effacing. She seemed well-bred and even better well-read. She had devoured books. She could also write. This was a potent combination. She could write a book and he could publish it. She was exactly what the über-publicist and adventure publisher wanted.

Ten years older than Amelia, GP had the appearance of New York's judgmental high society but the confident manner of a successful influencer. For one who fed off the adventurous nature of others, he had the appropriate features of a caged ferret waiting to break out of a clerk's aura. He dressed in fine, double-breasted pinstripe suits. His dark wavy hair was short and sometimes slick. His round glasses gave him an executive look and clearly fixed him in middle age. A weak chin, somewhat prim lips and flabby jowls, pinched nose— the effects of a ferret's excessive rooting—

yet he was convivial; everything one would expect from a vainglo-rious manipulator.

The *Friendship* lingered at Boston for weeks as they waited for weather to clear. In company of GP, Amelia visited the elite of the adventure world. She chatted with the Byrds and saw his plans for his Antarctic expedition. GP would take her driving in her Yellow Peril. At night they would attend Boston's theatres.

Despite knowing she was the cornerstone of the flight, she perhaps could not appreciate why she was being pampered by this New York heavyweight. She might have thought it was the book deal she knew was in the offing. But GP liked her. He had a very boyish nature, and this slim (118 pound) but tall blond girl seemed to have the same quality. He even saw flashes of a head-strong character. Considering their age difference, this quality may have excited him as youthful, even girlish vibrancy.

Amelia Earhart's charm was such that Hilton Railey also seemed to vie for her attention. Some thought it was budding ro-mance. Others thought it was fatherly protection. But it was clear Amelia was putting her faith in him. She personally asked him to walk her through what she must do in England. Railey accepted. He would leave by ship days before the flight in order to be in place. He would consider himself thereafter her unpaid manager until the "stunt," as Railey referred to the flight, was concluded.

Chapter 2

Unexpected Friendship

The *Friendship* took off on June 3, 1928. Boston Harbor shrank behind the misty sea spray streaming from the pontoons. Humming louder and louder, the trimotor stretched up to break the grasp of hazy dawn.

Flying gear covered every inch of Amelia— tight leather cap and goggles; fur collar of leather jacket tightly clasped around her neck. Flying gear covered everything, that is, except her big, satisfied smile. She was the image of an aviator. She held on in the back and watched the airspeed indicator. She was an adventurer in an adventurous age, but she was also now a potential pioneer.

History was not being made yet, however. Planes had traveled to Newfoundland before. Along here had disappeared Frances Grayson and her 3 companions in her Sikorsky amphibian *Dawn* the December before. This was a tragic reminder of the hazards that lay ahead.

The present hazard was the shroud of haze that had rolled in beneath them. Bill Stultz, the pilot, could only assume he was following the coastline north. Next to him mechanic "Slim" Gordon peered this way and that way, unable to make out any details.

It must have been a time of reflection for Amelia. We get a sense of her attitude from her "popping off" letters, as she called them. She had written them to her family just before she took off, and by now they had read them. To her father: "Hooray for the last grand adventure! I wish I had won, but it was worthwhile anyway. You know that. I have no faith we'll meet anywhere again, but I wish we might. Anyway, goodbye and good luck to you. Affectionately, your doter." The note to her mother is more revealing. "Even though I have lost, the adventure was worthwhile. Our family tends to be too secure. My life has really been very happy, and I didn't mind contemplating its end in the midst of it."

Read within the context of the tragedy that befell many of the 18 aircraft since Lindbergh, these letters truly reflect a dauntless attitude toward adventure. This same attitude is expressed in her own poem *Courage is the Price* where she writes that it is at "mountain heights where bitter joy can hear the sound of wings." The thrill of adventure did not come without the somewhat mitigating bitterness of danger.

Droning over what seemed an endless blanket of fog such sentiments must have replayed in her mind. There was certainly enough time. Bleakness blocked all from sight for over an hour and a half. Stultz finally dipped them down to 2,000 feet to get a glimpse. Through streaming fingers of parting haze, he recognized Fear Island, Nova Scotia.

Soon he made two large circles over their first destination— Halifax. Below, the citizens were immediately set in motion. The flight's purpose and takeoff had already been announced in Boston. Just as in the days when European ships made a lush Tahitian island in the Pacific, people came out in dories to greet the Fokker. Journalists stood by. There they all awaited the cracking of the fuselage door and the emergence of the strange people from the big city.

Amelia was a peach fuzz kid until she took off her cap and goggles. Her bobbed curls revealed a woman. Flashbulbs burst!

They encountered only a day's delay at Halifax due to weather. The next morning, the fliers successfully took off for Trepassey, their jump off port across the Atlantic. Only a small fishing port on the south shore of ragged Newfoundland, Trepassey greeted the Fokker with a dozen boats. If such an inanimate thing as a boat could show enthusiasm, these did. Each boatload was trying to rope the bird to tow it in. There was no need, since the Fokker could make its own way, chopping up the spray and dousing the welcoming committee as it motored closer to shore, there to anchor amidst the fawning flotilla. There was even a Paramount cameraman present to record the event.

Here they experienced their first let-down. The weather was soon nasty, as only the gray North Atlantic can be. The Fokker strained at its moorings while the three of them had nothing else to do but play cards at Deveraux House, their lodgings. They remained at Trepassey for 15 days.

Finally, on June 17, there was a break in the weather. It appeared it would only be a brief window. The billowing, huge clouds parted, the wind calmed somewhat. The sea turned blue again. The sun came through to sparkle the toupees of wet green grass on the rocky crags.

After 3 attempts, the pontoons of the *Friendship* finally lifted off the jagged swells. They were off, damage, if any, unknown to their undercarriage; one engine sputtered, still full of seawater. Like a fat albatross the red Fokker trimotor angled out to the gray horizon, choking, sputtering, but slowly climbing.

The rest is history, as they say. They braved the bleak and brutal North Atlantic. Hours into the flight they didn't know exactly where they were. But then there was land. The time had been 20 hours and 40 minutes. When they set down, it was at what seemed to be a British port. It was Burry Port, Wales. A constable, staid and officious, came out with others in a flotilla of boats.

"You be wantin' somethin'?"

"We've just come from America!" they declared triumphantly.

"Have ye now? Well, we wish ye welcome, I'm sure."

When it was finally understood why they were here, the welcoming committee formed. Amelia's presence was a particular triumph. The memory of the loss of the others was still fresh — Lady Anne Savile in the Fokker VII *Saint Raphael* and Honorable Elsie's loss in *Endeavor* with the great ace Walter Hinchliffe. The three of them were allowed to come to shore and the town went wild. They were international heroes.

Colonel Railey had been waiting for them at their actual destination, Southampton. When news came over that Americans had flown the Atlantic and landed in Wales, he was quickly off to meet them.

Railey got them hotel rooms. Amelia was given her own room, of course. He locked all the doors to keep the reporters and well-wishers away. He recalled that Amelia simply settled into the padded chair, threw a leg over the armrest and yawned.

"What's the matter? Aren't you excited?"

"Excited? No. It was a wonderful experience, but all I did was lie on the floor of the fuselage and take pictures of the clouds. We didn't see much of the ocean. Bill did all the flying. Had to. I was just baggage, like a sack of potatoes."

"What of it?" Railey replied like a true PR man. "You're still the first woman to fly the Atlantic and, what's more, the first woman pilot."

"Oh, well, maybe someday I'll try it alone."

This is the image Hilton Railey gives of the fledgling celebrity just the day before they were to fly to Southampton, there to meet Mrs. Guest and become superstars in England and the world. It is the image of an ambitious, *substantive* Amelia stoically lamenting her position as merely the hook for publicity.

As it would turn out no one was as dazzling at Southampton as Amelia Earhart. Her appearance and manner entranced the public. A gentle femininity was restored to her by the cloche hat and limp, flat dresses of the time. Her smile was broad and warm, her cheeks blushing, her speaking unpretentious.

Under Railey's tutelage she was the toast of London. The newspaper reporters flocked around her. When asked whether she'd like to meet the Prince of Wales, the most eligible bachelor in the world, the reporters made her response sound like a dumb American rube. "Wal, I sure am glad to be here, and gosh, I sure hope I'll meet the Prince of Wales."

A better insight into her true, captivating manner at this juncture is provided by Railey.

> As Miss Earhart's escort, I felt increasing pride in her natural manner, warmed, as it was, by humor and grace. Whether confronted by dozens of cameramen demanding over and over, "A great big smile, please!" or asked to wave to crowds (a gesture she used sparingly); whether laying a wreath at a Cenotaph or before a

statue of Edith Cavell; whether sipping tea with the Prime Minister and Lady Astor at the House of Commons or talking with Winston Churchill, she remained herself, serious, forthright, with no bunk in her makeup.

Despite the Grand Tour of who's who, Amelia was more interested in Lady Mary Heath. She had already set a record, a huge record. She had flown from Johannesburg, South Africa, to London— across the whole length of Africa, the exotic Dark Continent, and then over Europe. She had done so in her Avro Avian. Lady Mary took Amelia to see it at the field. It was a stronger plane than the Kinner Airster, with a larger fuel capacity. Amelia loved it. In a moment of excitement, Lady Mary offered it to her. Amelia accepted.

The hard-up social worker had bought a plane, apparently based on monies she would receive for making the flight. She latched it onto the deck of the USS *Roosevelt*, and the trio— Amelia, Stultz and Gordon— along with their chaperone Railey sailed home to New York City.

Amelia was clearly making a statement by buying the Avian. She wanted to be involved in aviation again, as more than just a "sack of potatoes," and certainly a lot more than just passé derbies. She was intending long flights.

The celebration at her return was phenomenal. There was even a ticker tape parade in New York City, the American equivalent of a lavish Roman triumph. Amelia was now truly world famous. The Press quickly dubbed her "Lady Lindy," though she hadn't piloted an inch of the Atlantic.

She was at the threshold of a truly grand adventure. Her value had exponentially increased. In London she excelled all their wildest dreams for promotion. Potential was everywhere now, and so was GP Putnam. He had Amelia stay at his house in Rye, New York, where his wife, Dorothy, acted as hostess. With him fawning at her shoulder, she wrote the book she had promised— *20 Hrs., 40 Min.*— and dedicated it to Dorothy.

Now the wisdom she had attained from understanding her own "bad habits" played a hand. Acclaim was satisfying for Amelia, but experience had proven disappointingly that it had no value to funding her flying. She needed the right person to monetize her hobby, and George Putnam seemed eager to help.

Syndicated rights to her story earned her $10,000. Endorsements for products ranging from canned rabbit to cigarette ads garnered her more. Within a few months she had netted $50,000 dollars. This was a huge amount of money, worth close to ¾ of a million in today's dollars. She also had 2 magazine offers to be an editor— this meant steady work and a writing gig. Her own megaphone! *Cosmopolitan* wasn't offended by her endorsing cigarettes (though she didn't smoke), so she took their offer (*McCall's* had withdrawn its offer after she endorsed cigarettes). She ditched social work and never looked back.

With a book coming out, with a position pending at a very influential woman's magazine, paid speaking engagements and endorsements, Amelia was maintaining her fame. But she was also becoming something else. She was becoming a brand.

Chapter 3

Brand Acronym

By her captivating character, Amelia Earhart deserved and earned her new found place of celebrity. . .except the one preeminent kudo that went with her name: "America's premier aviatrix." It was a false impression she was not responsible for. Her brief stint of fame in Los Angeles had been resurrected and it made good biography copy. Yet it was based on short hops and derby stunting, and she had never advanced beyond that level. Her current fame was based on being a passenger. Legitimacy as an aviation editor, influential speaker, and continuing recipient of endorsement money, wouldn't last long without new aviation triumphs.

Amelia was in a conundrum. She was in the perfect position to capitalize on the new craze of "firsts" except for the fact she wasn't a truly proficient pilot. There need be no explicit statement on her behalf that this dilemma weighed upon her. It is suggested by her next bold step: a solo cross-country flight from East coast to West. It was a woman's first. It was also a clever choice. With the Lady Lindy handle, she couldn't afford to take lessons in navigation else she would be exposed as largely an amateur. A cross-country flight was a wise compromise. She could hone her navigation and endurance skills, neither of which she had, and any mistakes she made would go largely unobserved.

Saturated by her fatalism and desire for adventure Amelia personally may not have fully accepted the dangers of her upcoming flight. But she no doubt knew she had found herself in that predicament she had come to recognize in youth— without proper instruction she learned on her own . . . and tended to acquire bad habits. Using road maps, she intended to follow roads, rivers, and railroad tracks.

Her first independent biographer, Paul Briand, who was devoted to her romanticized image (*Daughter of the Sky*, 1960), nevertheless had to concede that "Although she had never made such a flight before, her preparations, considering the distances involved, were happy-go-lucky and without design."

As her most ardent biographer, Briand perhaps could not see the significance of her own critical assessment of herself at this juncture in her budding career. She didn't know how to arrange long distance flights and, again, she couldn't take anyone into her confidence to teach her. He also couldn't fully see the daredevil quest for excitement in her. Essentially, he couldn't see that she had no choice but to blaze her own trail. . .and no fear about doing it; in essence, 'Hooray for another grand adventure!'

Being in close orbit, George Putnam was there to arrange publicity. Presently, it was good for his company as well, with her book still pending release. Yet it was becoming increasingly obvious that George was ready to echo her desires. And to one extent she echoed him: she loved being called AE *a la* Madison Avenue. They were GP and AE. Despite the growing frisson, it is doubtful GP fully understood AE's lack of pilot experience.

Fortunately for her, the flight was a disaster unwitnessed by the public. In August 1928 she left. She upended upon landing at Pittsburgh. Only upon landing at Fort Worth, Texas, did she realize it was Forth Worth, Texas. Then in a series of clumsy mishaps in her cockpit she lost her map. She followed a highway which eventually ended, and then she was able to land on the main street of Hobbs, New Mexico. Locals gave her directions to Pecos, Texas. She *eventually* found a railroad track and ended up continuing south to Pecos. Several mishaps followed trying to get to El Paso, including a blown tire when landing on a highway. On one occasion, the Avian had to be towed back to Pecos. In New Mexico she landed in a plowed field and nosed over again. She finally made California. Glowing publicity in Los Angeles followed wherever she went, including being covered watching the National Air Races.

AE started back home to New York with great fanfare. Another engine failure caused her to dead stick land in Utah and nose over in a plowed field again. Eventually, she made it back to New York, to cheering crowds and much news coverage.

Soon she was firmly in place at *Cosmo*. She was now both the first woman to fly (over) the Atlantic and the first to solo pilot across the USA back and forth. She was in a perfect position to become a motivational guiding light to her readers. She answered questions and made recommendations. Her articles appeared starting in November 1928, and needless to say they were highly anticipated.

A snapshot of her at this time is found in O.O. McIntyre's introduction of her to their *Cosmo* readers. He called her a "wistful slip of a girl" (she was actually 31) and a "highly moral reaction" to the "inflamed appetites" of the modern era wherein women were "gin guzzling and calculated harlotry." AE would "become a symbol of a new womanhood—a symbol, I predict, that will be emulously patterned after by thousands of young girls in their quest of the Ideal." Such praise truly reflected Amelia Earhart's charismatic character.

However, it is the conduit via which this potential archetype had come to prominence that had little substance. She was not, once again, the premiere aviatrix. . .but she obviously was very courageous. This last fact really could not be fully embraced by the public because they didn't know she fearlessly engaged in flights that were truly beyond her current level of proficiency.

AE knew she had to improve exponentially. She sold the obsolete Avian, and in spring of 1929 she made the leap up to a beefy Lockheed Vega. She bought it in time for a highly publicized event— the First Women's Air Derby also called "The Powder Puff Derby." Although she came in third, she soon set a couple of firsts. In June 1930, she set a speed record (for women) for the 100 kilometer run. In July she set another speed record at 181.18 mph.

As an editor on a major magazine, she remained in the public eye as the First Lady of Aviation or as Lady Lindy. To the adoring public she was the "famous aviatrix," the "premiere" or "foremost" aviatrix. To her new crowd of Big Apple friends she was AE.

This was an ideal time in her career. She dabbled with starting and promoting airlines and her speeches encouraged the public on the future of progress. She considered what she did to still be an adjunct to social work— only now she could help the nation and not just a single house in Boston. She truly considered this her career. However, her distaste for being in the public eye may have blindsided her to what awaited if she lost her momentum. Then it happened. A series of setbacks over 1930 rocked her independence. Transcontinental Air Transport, an airline she was involved in, had one too many disasters (air crashes) and she also lost the *Cosmo* gig. Without new aviation firsts, she would soon lose her promotional value (via paid speeches)— i.e. she would soon be without any income. Her big problem was no doubt finding a "first" she was qualified to pull off. Flying the Atlantic solo, a vow she had long made, was beyond her ability at present.

From the very beginning she was aware of GP's ardor. Even before she had been invited to stay at the Putnam house in Rye to write her book, Hilton Railey had slipped her a piece of paper with the word "brushfire" on it. Should she need help keeping Putnam at bay, she was to use it as code and Railey would come rushing to her aid. According to Briand, "Amelia grinned, took the paper, folded it, and put it in her purse."

For a couple of years, AE had kept the Madison Avenue rover at idle. He had long dumped Dorothy and proposed to her, but she had politely demurred due to her career. Yet by early 1931 the man she had spurned at least 6 times was becoming more appealing, ostensibly because of his promoter abilities. The early Hollywood episode in her life had proved how fame didn't last. She knew the same could be said for this stint of publicity. She had felt the lean years. She could no doubt foresee them again.

She wrote GP a cautionary letter, stating she felt marriage right now was "as foolish as anything I could do." Nevertheless, she consented, but with this codicil: "I must extract a cruel promise and that is you will let me go in a year if we find no happiness together." GP must truly have been besotted by her to proceed to the altar with such an arbitrary codicil foisted on him last minute.

But he was smitten. On February 7, 1931, possibly with that note in his back pocket, they were married.

GP was far more aware of this juncture in Amelia's life and sputtering career. He knew she needed a "first." Under his guiding promotional light AE tried to make something of the autogiro, the precursor of the helicopter. The president of the company had received the award in aviation for that year, presented by President Herbert Hoover on the White House lawn. This was the prefect advertising fit. GP worked the deal to have Beech-Nuts give AE an autogiro. She soon took it up to 18,415 feet for an altitude "first." Soon thereafter in May 1931 she would fly around the country, advertising Beech-Nuts at preplanned engagements and carnivals. AE would write a glamourous article in *Cosmo* (freelance) for the autogiro, envisioning one in most everybody's garage one day, a means by which to go fishing, golfing, etc.

The autogiro was a nightmare. AE believed she was making the pioneering coast to coast flight in one when she took off from Newark, New Jersey, on May 29, 1931, with mechanic Eddie Gorski burdened with loads of spares. The autogiro was so uneconomical that Earhart had to land every 2 hours to get fuel. Its speed was poor. Cars sometimes passed her below, and one motorist even clocked her overheard and almost beat her. They eventually arrived at Oakland only to discover that she had been beaten by another pilot only the week before.

This rather carnival interlude with the autogiro, however, appears to have been George's only influence on her choice of flights, and she never let that happen again.

But in terms of publicity, GP was his usual true to form efficient spinmeister. He was always careful in how he spun her actions. She simply could not be piloting an advertising vehicle. He ennobled the stunts. Ostensibly, the money Earhart was making on these advertising trips was to pay for her own attempt to fly the Atlantic. She was building up money to make the ultimate "first" flight, the one she had vowed when she stepped off the Fokker. Toward this end the autogiro episode was wise in one substantive manner: she was increasing her navigational experience.

On the ground AE's life was far more dynamic than her flying career. Fame and influence and meeting interesting, adventurous people were the norm for her now. She had received medals, been invited to the White House, had been made an honorary Major in the US Army Air Corps, was meeting all the who's who of New York City and the International scene, always with GP on her arm. GP and AE were truly "social royalty."

Despite GP's promotion, AE really had not made much progress toward the Atlantic goal. It cost money, of course. But already in 1929 she had enough money to buy a muscular Vega, a plane that could do the job. But this is a utensil. It is acquired by cash and not by skill. She hadn't spent the time to acquire the expertise to fly the Atlantic solo. Long range navigation via the autogiro flights was essentially it.

Yet the Atlantic had to soon be crossed by a woman. The feeling it was coming was palpable. In June 1931, Ruth Nichols had tried to but cracked up upon landing at Saint John, New Brunswick. Nichols was 1931's top woman pilot, and her intent to follow in Lindbergh's footsteps had been highly promoted since spring.

Almost a year later in May 1932 word was that Elinor Smith was preparing. If anyone could earn the "Lady Lindy" title, it was Smith. Within aviation itself Smith had ratcheted up more prestige than AE. Licensed pilots were polled in October 1930, citing her as "best woman pilot in America." In March 1931 she had regained the altitude record (32,576 feet) in a Bellanca.

Still, no whisper came from Earhart's direction; no whisper from the one for whom triumphing the Atlantic had been a very public and personal vow. It was a terrible mistake to misjudge the silence. No one fully appreciated AE's daredevil nature. She had made her name. Now she was about to create her era.

Chapter 4

Goddess of the Sky

Despite secrecy surrounding aviation's golden age of competitiveness to set new records, in the spring of 1932 tremors of anticipation rippled toward the Atlantic.

The Atlantic was important. It was important because it was a powerful symbol. America had been the most significant discovery in history. Columbus discovered the New World via a voyage no one said he could achieve. Since then millions had braved it to the New World. It became the most significant ocean in the progress of civilization. The Blue Ribbon had been given to the fastest ocean liners. Every time a ship arrived in New York or Europe the schedule was checked to see if it set a new speed record. The fame that had gone with Charles Lindbergh reducing this crossing time to only 33 hours was the crescendo of centuries past and the harbinger of the future. What had taken months and then weeks, then a few days with the liners, was now only a day. Soon it would be hours.

The importance of the Atlantic is seen in Earhart's own fame. Just for crossing it as a passenger, AE had enormous press. Minimizing the status of being "just" a passenger has been done too much, and Earhart is largely responsible for it. Being a passenger was significant. She had inaugurated the very concept of routine travel back and forth, a symbol of progress replacing the luxurious ocean liners.

Of all "firsts," Earhart crucially needed the Atlantic. Her present fame rested on having crossed it. If and when another woman was first to pilot it, AE's status would diminish. She would remain a New York celebrity and a social locus due to her wit and marriage with über-George. But nationally it would be over. She would be a public personality but a *past* hero.

At the probability Elinor Smith was preparing, AE's planning began. She chartered her Vega to a friend of hers, Bernt Balchen. He was known to be planning an Antarctic expedition with Lincoln Ellsworth. This was an excellent bit of guile. If other women pilots caught wind (especially Smith) she was going to try, they could rush to ace her to the goal.

The intended flight was such a guarded secret that until favorable weather readouts came back AE was not committed to leave, even on the day intended. This day was May 20, the same day that Lindbergh had left in 1927. Imitating Lindbergh would seem to unjustifiably obscure the uniqueness of Earhart's endeavor, but at the same time it added the most famous name in aviation once again to the publicity if she succeeded.

That very day the weather for Saint John, New Brunswick, turned positive. There was a chance. She was driven to the Teterboro Airport with Bernt Balchen and Eddie Gorski. Bernt took the stick and flew them to Saint John; then next day to Harbour Grace, Newfoundland. From here they bid her farewell. The last image of her was through her cockpit window—her big smile crowded by her flight helmet and goggles. She left with the shirt on her back and a light snack.

It proved a harrowing flight. It was past 11:30 p.m. when her altimeter gave up and just spun around. Now in the inky void of the North Atlantic she would have no way to determine her altitude. But AE was able to cleverly guess her altitude by determining what speed the Vega would take. It had different capabilities at different altitudes.

Thunderstorms crackled and boomed about her. The moon snuck out once, casting tendrils of light through the ink and glinting off the treacherous sea swells. Icing was heavy and caused her wings to wobble. She had to drop to warmer temps. But then a wall of clouds and fog was before her. She had to pull up and fly over or through the clouds, without an altimeter, and hopefully low enough to avoid the deadly icing.

Dawn's light was evaporating to daylight, but things were not getting better. A gray bleakness had settled over the North Atlantic. Then the exhaust manifold began to vibrate loudly. Then gas started leaking into the cockpit, the fumes affecting her eyesight. The vibrating grew louder. She feared the engine wouldn't last long now. Ice was forming again. This alone made her give up Paris as her destination. She saw a dark silhouette on the horizon, rising slowly with each minute. She knew it was land. She turned her bright red Vega to a verdant green land behind the Atlantic's angry breakers.

As the coast drew nigh, it became obvious it had to be Ireland. She then followed a spine of mountains. She circled a city, looking for a field to land in. The best spot from her altitude was a lush green field dotted with cows. She came in and settled down, throttling back and coming to a stop at 11:45 a.m. It was now May 21, 1932. She had flown for 15 hours and 18 minutes. Success! Cows mooed.

Amelia Earhart was now the first woman and only the *second* pilot to fly solo over the tempestuous Atlantic Ocean. She now truly was Lady Lindy.

Cables of congratulations from the Lindberghs, and many other notables greeted her in London. She was feted in every way imaginable. She had met the Prince of Wales in private. After their meeting, he pinned a dark pink rose on her blue suit and escorted her back to her car. GP took the s.s. *Olympic* to Cherbourg, France, and met Amelia aboard the yacht of millionaire C.R. Fairley. Paris, Brussels, Rome— kings and queens were next on her itinerary. GP was by her side, and the newsreels were omnipresent. (She had actually flown to London from Londonderry in a Paramount Newsreel airplane— thanks to GP who was finalizing a deal to work for Paramount.)

Of this moment in time, Briand writes: "She was now ready to play the part of a true heroine. A smooth lyrical grace, the romantic quest of old, and the chivalric spirit of adventure had now combined in the boyishly slender figure of—this time—a woman. Like the lone eagle who preceded her, Amelia acted with ease, modest self-effacement, and exemplary good manners, becoming a good will ambassador for America."

After her grand ticker tape parade in New York, she spoke from the steps of City Hall. Behind a cluster of microphones, she declared:

> It is much easier to fly the Atlantic Ocean now than it was a few years ago. I expect to be able to do it in my lifetime again. Possibly not [pause for applause] as a solo expedition, but in regular transatlantic service, which is inevitable in our lifetime.

The nation cheered. She had inspired them with the prospects of an expanding near future.

Washington D.C. followed. An austere dinner adjourned to Constitution Hall where President Hoover presented her with the Gold Medal issued by the National Geographic Society. Congress would present to her the Distinguished Flying Cross — a military award that reflects her honorary appointment as a Major in the US Army Air Corps.

Earhart's fame was unparalleled after this point. It gave her a unique position as influencer more than ever before. Nevertheless, she didn't promote herself as a pioneer in the budding airline industry to which she referred in her speech on the steps of City Hall in New York. She again wrote a book, the title declaring her ultimate motive for her flights: *The Fun of It*. She also underwent an unusual metamorphosis.

Aside from Amelia Earhart, there was no one as popular at the time in aviation except Charles Lindbergh, upon whose likeness AE had dovetailed from the beginning, though it was not by her design. Humorist Will Rogers, however, was the most famous man in America. Rogers was a powerful promoter of all things in progress, of which aviation was the cornerstone. AE's transformation after this moment was to become a cross between both Lindbergh and Rogers. She was dressing in more masculine outfits — baggy pants that only accentuated her scrawny, androgynous figure (but hid her fat calves). Baggy plaid shirts did the same, and over the collar of these rustic shirts she tied a kerchief western-style. Her hair was short, cropped, tussled — not masculine but tomboyish. She was becoming a female Will Rogers.

This image is the AE entrenched in popular legend today: the cocky, self-assured pilot photographed strutting away from her plane in overalls, one hand clasping her other cuff— the body language of "it's a piece of cake."

With this new image, AE added to her Atlantic conquest with the conquest of speed. In late summer (August 24-25) she set the women's transcontinental speed record, flying solo nonstop from Los Angeles to Newark, New Jersey, landing at 19 hours, 5 minutes after takeoff. (The distance was 2,447.8 miles.) This arrival in Newark was the greatest she had ever seen. Reporters crowded around her.

"And what did you carry on the trip?"

"You mean to eat?"

"Yeah, to eat and drink."

"Wal, I carried some water, of course, because my cockpit is very warm, and I carried a sandwich in case; I didn't eat it though. I carried some hot chocolate and the old reliable tomato juice."

"What type of sandwich was it?"

Her grin broke into a girlish chuckle. "A chicken sandwich." She then laughed heartily.

A year later in July 1933 she beat this speed (though not non-stop). Over July 7th—8th she flew from Los Angeles to Newark again, setting the speed record for women at 17 hours, 17 minutes, 30 seconds.

To some extent these speed records were quite practical. Los Angeles was becoming a second home. GP had sold his interest in his publishing house to his cousin. After AE's Atlantic triumph he had taken a job for Paramount Pictures' editorial board in New York, weaving out new movie ideas. Though they remained based in New York, they had to journey to Hollywood occasionally and hobnob with the stars. GP pushed to get into the camera with her. He was condemned by photographers as the "lens louse." However, with GP's job she was guaranteed Paramount Newsreel footage of *anything* she did.

Starting in January 1933, AE also had another asset. The capital was becoming an inviting stopover for her now that Franklin Delano Roosevelt was the new president. She was feted at the

White House by FDR and First Lady Eleanor, and a true friend-ship would develop there.

Speed records and the Atlantic conquest had been the perfect strands to secure all her publicity to the nodal point of progress. It was the equation she preferred. She did these flights for fun. Progress simply came on the heels of her personal courage and zest for fun.

But in terms of flight Amelia wasn't expanding her résumé outside of the landlock of the US. The reason was fairly sim-ple— making money. AE had no regular income. She made money only by freelance articles, paid motivational speaking, or royalties from her books, and only a narrow window after each latest "first" to capitalize on them before the interest (and sales) died off. She wasn't a part of the Great Air Race (the Mac-Robertson) from London to Melbourne, Australia, in October 1934. She also might have been surprised to see Elinor Smith was now on the Wheaties Cereal box, the first woman so fea-tured. She was seen each breakfast by millions of Americans.

Her career momentum was dying out by the end of 1934, two and a half years after her Atlantic conquest. Since November 1934, GP and AE had lived in Toluca Lake in North Hollywood, California. Here she planned her new first.

In December of 1934, she and GP boarded ship and took her new Vega along. (After her Atlantic flight she had sold her old one to the Franklin Institute of Philadelphia.) This was a curi-ous way to travel the Pacific—a bulky high wing aircraft hanging over the stern of a cruise ship. Word reached Hawaii Amelia Earhart was coming with her plane.

When AE and GP arrived, they were instant celebrities. They were greeted by a photo shoot as they were presented with the welcoming laes. Earhart was cagey with the reporters. No, she wasn't up to anything significant, she declared. She brought the plane to do some flying about the islands perchance.

No one, of course, thought she had gone to the trouble of bringing a plane just to fly around the islands. In a way, she let the cat out of the bag herself. As the bright red Vega still dan-gled on the davits, a reporter asked her if Paul Mantz, an expert pilot and one of her new aviation friends in Hollywood, would fly with her to California. She shot back: "If I fly to the coast I will not take a cat along." Every reporter guessed: she was intending to fly to California.

For the first time Earhart faced public criticism before a flight. It got out that she had accepted $10,000 dollars from local businessmen to do the flight. Officially, the purpose was to promote closer ties and good will with the United States. However, the rumor spread that the backers were doing it to buy favorable tariffs for Hawaiian sugar.

Seeing the illogic of merely flying the Pacific for "the fun of it," the Honolulu *Star-Bulletin* was suspicious there was indeed an ulterior motive. "There is nothing intelligent about flying solo from Hawaii to the mainland in a single-engine land plane, which is very poor equipment for a long across-water flight." The article also claimed her radio had very short range.

To counter the criticism, Paul Mantz cruised the Vega about the islands and made radio contact with distant land bases, proving the radio had a 3,000 mile radius and was not inadequate as the article had said. He sent a note to GP who handed it to AE at the one speech she made in Hawaii— "Flying for Fun" at the University of Hawaii. She smiled and read it triumphantly, proving her flight was not foolhardy. The crowd cheered and applauded.

However, AE was different at the backers' meeting. They now wanted to pull out, but Amelia barged in on their meeting and declared boldly: "Gentlemen, there is an aroma of cowardice in the air. You know as well as I do that the rumor is trash, but if you can be intimidated, it might as well be true." AE won the day and they funded the flight.

January 11, 1935, was the day chosen to takeoff. That afternoon the clouds and storm were being blown westward, and a weather report confirmed to GP that there was nothing hazardous in the northeast between Hawaii and California. He dutifully woke her. A little after 4 p.m. they were at Wheeler Field. The mechanic, Ernie Tissot, was finalizing the plane while Amelia climbed in and inched down into the cockpit. She checked all her gauges. She was a little figure inside, studious and careful. She turned over the Vega and it spit and then purred perfectly. Finally at 4:45 p.m. she signaled Ernie to remove the chocks.

The bright red Vega lumbered onto the runway. It was heavy

with fuel for a trip no one had ever taken before. The Vega roared and then finally built to a loud purr. The 6,000 feet of runway shrunk quickly. She hit a bump and jumped into the air. Feeling the heavy bird coming back down, she gunned the engine and cleared the sugarcane. She had made it in 4,000 feet, and now she was angling out to the right over the city and Diamond Head. By 5 p.m. she had crossed Makapupu Point. Then Molokai came into view, clouds gathering around. She climbed above them to 6,000 feet. The sight was beautiful — cream puffs floating on a blue sea.

She cranked out her radio antenna and engaged her mic. "Everything OK."

She knew GP would relay the message to the press. She turned the dial on her radio to KGU Hawaii. She listened to the tropical music for a minute. Then the music stopped. The announcer intervened with excited gravitas. "We are interrupting our musical program with an important news flash. Amelia Earhart has just taken off on an attempted flight to Oakland, California." Of course, GP was in-studio. The announcer continued: "Mr. Putnam will try to communicate with his wife." Now all heard GP's voice. "AE," he said, "the noise of your motor interferes with your broadcast. Will you please try to speak louder so we can hear you?"

Gasps in the listening audience no doubt followed. She was the talk of Hawaii and California and thereafter the world. She was on her way, on another first.

Landing at Oakland was an incredible triumph. It gives us the image of Earhart waving at ecstatic crowds from the sunroof hatch of her gleaming Vega. Then the crowd rushed up and she was engulfed by her adoring public. The police quickly formed a cordon to protect her. At least 14,000 well-wishers had greeted her. President Roosevelt cabled her congratulations. The *New York Times* declared that she "holds the fair planet in her hands." After a short trip to Los Angeles, she returned for the celebratory dinner in San Francisco and was escorted to the landing field by 11 Navy aircraft. Every important person in the city was at the dinner including former president Herbert Hoover. Eleanor Roosevelt sent her open invite to the White House whenever she was in town, asking that she stay with them.

On January 31, AE visited Washington and took up the First Lady's offer. Then she had a private meeting with FDR.

More magazine article offers followed, with GP's guiding influence, and AE addressed several state houses, always ending her speeches with pleas for funding for more airports. Eleanor Roosevelt continued to invite her to come and stay at the White House.

The friendship between Amelia and Eleanor was so striking that GP came up with an idea. He thought it perfect for the two most influential women in the land— a joint radio broadcast weekly "touching on matters of basic interest to American women today."

Perhaps it was the glowing reception that set a new vigor in AE's and GP's plans. She had a major flight for spring already in the works. The Mexican government had seen the publicity that Earhart had achieved from her Pacific flight and they wanted to promote equal good will— i.e. the tourist trade. They invited her to fly to Mexico City. She thought it a brilliant idea.

Arrangements for reimbursing AE were a little more surreptitious this time. Mexico would issue a commemorative stamp of only 780 units. It would show the Aztec Emperor Cuauhtemoc contemplating the snowy volcano of Popocatépetl. Over this would be printed "Vuelo de Amelia Earhart, Mexico, 1935." Obviously, Mexico would pay for the trip. In addition to this, they would give AE 200 of the rare stamps which she could sell in the USA (the value was estimated at $100 dollars each).

On April 19, 1935, Amelia took off from Burbank Airport, California, and headed on her nonstop trip to Mexico City. However, hours into her flight when she should be nearing Mexico City she decided to land. She spotted a field and then set down. She was soon surrounded by curious peons. Since she didn't speak Spanish she pointed on a map where she wanted to go and inquired as to where she presently was. A "bright" boy understood her and pointed her position. She was at Nopala. When she landed at Mexico City, she expressed her lament that she didn't do as well as she had intended (it was to be nonstop).

She was, of course, feted throughout Mexico City.

On May 8, 1935, the day came for the return flight. George had already returned to New York and called in the weather report to her. It was fair, but the winds were not favorable. Still, she decided to go. She ordered the Vega topped to 470 gallons. Oil drums marked the makeshift runway on the dry lakebed. The headlights of cars parked behind them shined on them to make them visible.

With every gauge reading where she wanted it, she roared down the lakebed at 6:06 a.m. and zoomed into the air. It was a perfect takeoff yet again. She did it in one mile, though she had 3 miles at her disposal. At 10,000 feet she leveled off, the Vega purring perfectly. The forest green mountains passed beneath, and before her was a sky daubed by bubbling clouds.

Between the angling shadows of the clouds and the rays of the rising sun, she saw the sea. Oil rigs were dark ugly things crowded together. She checked her map. It must be Tampico. She pulled her stick to the right, heading northeast. In 700 miles she should be overflying New Orleans.

The Gulf flight went safely enough. She had settled in and flew it easily. At New Orleans she was finally back in the radio communication network. She contacted Mobile, Alabama, and reported in. Everything was set in motion. America knew she was on her way. Montgomery was next, then Atlanta, then Charlotte, then Richmond. She would later liken herself to an operator on a party line—there were so many conversations. When at 9:05 p.m. she passed over Washington D.C., she reported her position and was then surprised when Gene Vidal's voice came over the headset. "You've' done enough," he crooned. "You'd better land at Hoover Airport." He was head of the Bureau of Air Commerce. Like so many others he had been marking her progress. (He had his own radio in his office.)

"No thanks," came back her cheery voice. "Going through to New York. Cheerio!"

She knew that Gene merely wanted to see her. She had known him since 1930 when he was manager of a budding airline. He was part joking about her landing, part serious. They were close, and no doubt a Washington D.C. landing would have been significant— a flight between two capitals. But she knew GP had arranged triumph ahead in Newark. If a plane could get to New York (via Newark's airport) from Mexico City, one could get to Washington D.C. as well. She had paved the way for air commerce and the airlines again.

She took a sip from her thermos of hot chocolate. Anticipation was as sweet as the hot cocoa.

The Consul General for Mexico awaited her, watching the red and green navigation lights as she maneuvered the growling Vega in line with the runway. The diplomatic coup which Mexico had paid for was thus represented. But airline people were there too. Paul Collins was there, a veteran of more than a million air miles. Aviation weather expert "Doc" Kimball too was there, proud to call her one of his fliers. "Such people are good for us all," he declared as she touched down.

But for the people, it was because Amelia Earhart was coming. As the Vega stopped at the parking area, the crowds, straining at the ropes, broke free and rushed the Vega. Amidst the adoring throng, AE looked the part of the returning heroine. Her goggles removed, her face was drawn by grime. Yet her eyes sparkled. She was a tiny thing bundled in her flying leather. But her exuberant smile and wave signaled appreciation to all.

For the businessmen at hand, it was proof that Mexico City-New York flight route was soon to be routine for passenger service. For the crowd, it was proof this skinny tomboy was irrepressible. She was a true pioneer.

Had another pilot done this—a man of utilitarian skill but no charisma— there would have been few to mark it except those itching to build the airline business. AE's popularity was indeed good for the entire business of flight.

A dichotomy was to enter her public image. She was becoming so inspiring, a university would soon come calling. With it would come a gift for the "advancement of science."

Silver Plate Adventure

Chapter 5

A very interesting door had begun to open for Amelia, and the publicity from the Mexico City-Newark flight opened it wider. AE had already been in talks with Purdue University's president, Dr. Edward C. Elliot, to take up a counseling position there as "visiting faculty." He had felt that out of the 6,000 student body, the 800 female students were missing many opportunities. Purdue was also the only major university in the country with its own airfield. A position there for Earhart would be perfect, he felt. After her triumphant return it was finalized.

On June 2, 1935, the appointment was made. She would spend a month of the school year counseling the female students and encouraging them to take hold of their future.

Of the appointment, Dr. Elliot declared: "Miss Earhart represents better than any other young woman of this generation the spirit and courageous skill of what may be called the new pioneering. At no point in our educational system is there greater need for women. The university believes Amelia Earhart will help us to see and to attack successfully many unsolved problems."

Until fall semester Amelia did not need to take up residence. When she arrived at Purdue (November 1935), she gave a speech on why she came to the University. In this speech is Earhart's entire mentality expressed. She made no secret of the fact that she learned by doing, and in a pioneering age there was no other way to learn. She also wanted to have fun doing it. Her approach to the future of education was to reeducate youth in the new opportunities. Then bring those who had pioneered the new ways to the schools so they can teach those who truly want to follow in their pioneering footsteps; basically, what Purdue had done with her.

A logical pragmatism, however, was mixed with the unrealism of an idealist. "It is a fundamental problem, and I can imagine that reform may involve the entire reconstruction of our educational system." The motive for choosing one's profession had to be personal enjoyment. "We have watched our colleges produce countless graduates who could only demand jobs for which, notwithstanding the adequacy of their formal education, they might be totally unprepared or unfitted, and in which they were often even just plain uninterested. . .Because Johnnie liked to play with tin soldiers, his mother has jumped to the conclusion, since the year one, that he wanted to be a soldier! So she packed him off to military school—which he hated . . ."

Throughout her month stay, she gathered the coeds and addressed them in large groups. "After all, times are changing and women need the critical stimulus of competition outside the home. A girl must nowadays believe completely in herself as an individual. She must realize at the outset that a woman must do the same job better than a man to get as much credit for it. She must be aware of the various discriminations, both legal and traditional, against women in the business world."

In addition: "I cannot tell you that you will be able to bounce right out of college into your life work. I believe, under existing conditions, that it is almost impossible to do. But I believe also that it doesn't greatly matter, for the business world will draw out one's aptitudes." She forewarned her charges that they would still enter the workforce and this would continue to direct them into their true aptitudes for what they really want to do in life. In other words, what they really want to *enjoy* doing in life.

If anything truly gives us insight into Earhart herself, it was such statements. The road was tough. Graduation and finding a job in your major, for both men and women, wasn't necessarily the way. Get out in the world and hone your aptitudes until you find the right thing for you. And "right" meant something you enjoyed.

This is what AE had done in her own life. She believed this worked for all others—work and fun should be combined if you had the intelligence to adapt. It was the essence of fulfillment.

The above quotations impress up the reader what they did upon the powers that be at Purdue. There was a way to combine fun with progress. And securing Amelia had been a great way to advertise this was their *weltanschauung*.

But her speeches there, as peppy as they were, had occurred within a dark shadow. Only days after the competitive and much prized Bendix Race (Labor Day 1935), Laura Ingalls had shattered AE's nonstop coast-to-coast speed record by 5 and a half hours (13 hours, 34 minutes and 5 seconds). Naturally, there were those who chalked this up to the advantage of her new Lockheed Orion.

AE had always complained about the restraints of money. "I'd like to find the tree on which new airplanes grow. I'd certainly shake myself down a good one." When she was heard to say the above, GP told Dean Elliot. It probably seemed an easy 2 plus 2 that if Amelia had a new, sleek airplane the sky was no longer the limit. And this, too, would look great for Purdue.

The Purdue Research Foundation set up the Amelia Earhart Fund. In early 1936 the funds were there to buy a sleek twin en-gine Lockheed Electra—the type of plane she had wanted for a long time. It was hers with certain restrictions. It was to be used for research for the advancement of the science of aeronautics.[1] The experimental way she would use the plane, she said, would be to test the effects of long distance flying.

It is probably more than coincidence that AE jumped on the endurance bandwagon after Ingalls aced her record on speed. Laura Ingalls *also* held the endurance record. She had flown from New York and around South America and back to New

---

[1] Its registration number carried "R" for this reason— NR16020.

York, holding the solo endurance record of 17,000 miles. AE had *never* had an endurance flight.

It was now that she told GP the world was her goal. Such a flight would cost lots of money and need a backer. GP went to work. He got $10,000 dollars for envelopes and flyers that AE would carry aboard. They came from Elmer Dimity of the Philatelic Society. He was a huge fan. Putnam got another $25,000 from Gimbals for letter covers which they had sold to cover expenses. AE had also agreed with GP to write a book *World Flight* which she would write from jotting notes while on her journey. Thus they could publish it quickly after she returned.

Although she dubbed her plane the "Flying Laboratory," nothing about the proposed flight, of course, appeared remotely scientific. The upcoming junket smacked of personal excitement and publicity rather than anything academic. GP had to figure ways to combine the two. Since she had decided to leave California for Hawaii and from there go to Tokyo, GP approached the Navy about Amelia being the first to inaugurate midair refueling for the Navy. This would make it possible for her to reach Tokyo from Hawaii.

Amelia spelled out the problems in a letter to FDR on November 10, 1936, writing in part:

> The chief problem is the jump westward from Honolulu. The distance thence to Tokio is 3900 miles. I want to reduce as much as possible the hazard of the take-off at Honolulu with the excessive over-load. With that in view, I am discussing with the Navy a possible refueling in the air over Midway Island. If this can be arranged, I need to take much less gas from Honolulu, and with the Midway refueling will have ample gasoline to reach Tokio. As mine is a land plane, the seaplane facilities at Wake, Guam, etc., are useless.

Despite FDR personally writing on the letter "See what we can do and contact Mr. Putnam" nothing came of it. Perhaps FDR's advisors didn't want a spotlight placed on the whole idea that a midair refueling was possible over the Pacific, especially considering the geopolitics of the Pacific at the time between America, Britain, Russia, and Japan. (Concealing the fact that a B-25 could fit on a carrier made the Doolittle Tokyo Raid possible during WWII). They might also have thought that a Navy pilot would be more appropriate to do this first.[2]

In any case, nothing came of it. However, Earhart's ardent admirer Gene Vidal played a hand. He proposed they enlarged an airstrip already scaped-out on tiny Howland Island southwest of Hawaii. This would make it possible for her to fly to Australia. This won the day.

Howland was an insignificant island upon which the US Department of the Interior had settled a few Hawaiians in order to lay claim to it. Yet for Earhart's Electra, it had a perfect and economical position. It was 1,897 miles from Honolulu and just a little over the same distance to northern Australia as it is from Midway to Tokyo (2,500 miles), her original respective mid-air refueling location and destination.

During this preparation time, Earhart stayed often with the Odlums on their California ranch. Floyd Odlum owned a large stake in RKO Studios, and was the heavy hitter at Atlas Corp. His wife was the top woman pilot Jackie Cochran. In her own autobiography *The Stars at Noon* Cochran gives us a snapshot of Earhart at this time. ". . .We were close friends and she spent most of the last few months before her last flight at my ranch, resting, building up strength in the swimming pool and on horseback and making preparations for her flight.

Another pastime was psychic. Jackie was a strong believer in her own remote viewing. When she had discovered that Amelia was interested in the psychic studies at Duke University, she confided in Amelia her own abilities. Over several experiments, AE had come to believe that Cochran was a natural. "A few weeks later," Cochran writes, "Amelia called me from Los Angeles with the news that a transport airliner en route to Los Angeles had gone down somewhere on the last leg of the flight. Would I try to give her the location? Within an hour I had called her back, told her exactly where the plane was, which way it was pointing down the mountainside and the condition of the occupants as between the dead, the injured and the safe. The plane was located promptly just where I said it would be; all my

---

[2] The Army had already proven spectacularly the feasibility of midair refueling in 1923, but as yet the Navy had not engaged in it.

information proved correct."

At one point, Amelia had even asked that Jackie psychically follow one of her flights in the Electra to New York and send her telegrams as to stops, incidents, etc. The results were impressive. "By this time, Amelia was convinced that if we practiced together, I could locate her should she be forced down on her proposed round-the-world flight."

On a more concrete approach, AE had enlisted her Hollywood friend Paul Mantz as her technical advisor. Captain Harry Manning also joined her crew. He had shipped her home in 1928 on the *Roosevelt* and both had hit it off. They had decided that someday they would do something together. Manning would take leave of the Navy for a short time in order to act as her navigator across the major portion of the daunting Pacific.

There was really no reason to be secretive about it anymore. Nobody could pull off such a flight without enormous government help, and only AE had those contacts. GP arranged for a Paramount Newsreel exclusive.

"Miss Earhart set to fly 'round the world," grandly declared the announcer.

Headlines: Los Angeles—In exclusive Paramount News interview, famous aviatrix outlines 27,000 mile journey.

Earhart sat at a desk and addressed the camera. "The contemplated course covers about 27,000 miles. It will be the first flight [blushes] if successful which approximates the equator. The plane I'm using on the proposed flight is a transport plane. It is for Lockheed Electra, normally carrying ten passengers and two pilots."

Amelia spun the globe before her, pointing with a pencil: "I hope to fly from Oakland to Honolulu, then Howland Island, then to the northern tip of Australia, up through Singapore . . ." and she continued to name stops around the world.

Continuing news releases added to the proposed venture. Earhart's flight would test long endurance flying, the news blurbs proclaimed, and she declared herself the first guinea pig.

In Oakland a few days before the flight, AE and GP played her role for fun in another Paramount Newsreel. Staged as it was at the time, in which subjects are often wooden and unrehearsed before the camera, GP and AE sat next to each other:

GP: AE just why are you making this flight?

AE: Wal, GP you know it's because *I want to.*

GP: (chuckles) To a husband that has a fairly familiar sound. But aside from that you expect to accomplish something for aviation, do you not?

AE: Wal, yes, I do. . . and if the flight's successful I hope it will increase women's interest in flying. If so it will be worthwhile as far as I am concerned.

GP: Well, how about taking me along?

AE: Wal, of course, I think a great deal of you, but 180 pounds of gasoline on a flight . . . perhaps might be a little more valuable.

GP: You mean you prefer 180 pounds of gasoline to 180 pounds of husband.

AE: (blushes) Think you guessed right (chuckles).

Then called "Major Earhart" by the narrator, she posed in front of her Electra with her 3 main team players. Paul Mantz was declared "technical advisor," Harry Manning was "navigator to Australia," and Fred Noonan "familiar with Pacific airways."

Specifically, Fred Noonan would navigate the way to Howland Island, there to remain and return with a Coast Guard cutter to Hawaii while Earhart and Manning continued on to Australia. There he would remain and Earhart would continue around the world solo.

On March 17, 1937, they took off and Paul Mantz landed them at Honolulu 15 hours 47 minutes later. Nothing much was made of his hard landing until the next day, March 18, when Amelia took off. The Electra almost looped and she ended up crashing it on the runway. The beaming silver aircraft was a wreck, with bent props, broken wings, dislocated engines, and a chewed up undercarriage.

Paramount covered it quickly. Over pictures of the wreck sitting on the field:

Here is ended for the time being Amelia Earhart Putnam's hopes for a flight around the world. Her plane is rather a complete wreck.

By June 24, they were at Bandoeng for repairs. Afterward, they had only
began their most perilous leg of the world flight— 2,556 miles to tiny

But America's ace woman flyer is safe and so is her crew. Their
skill saved them when a tire burst on the takeoff from Honolulu
airport.

Instead of calling off the world flight, which was essentially
impossible due to the accumulated debt to the backers, it was
time to scrounge. A tremendous $50,000 dollars was needed to
repair the plane.

By May, just two months after her devastating Hawaii crash,
the Electra was almost ready, thanks in part to friends, especially
the Odlums (at whose ranch she continued to relax).

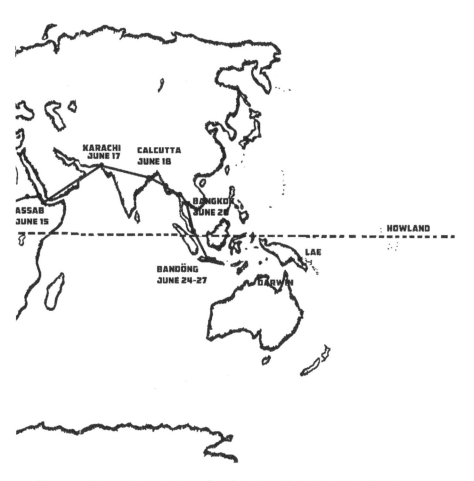

Koepang, Timor, Darwin, Australia, then Lae, New Guinea, before they Howland Island.

Changes had to be made. Harry Manning could no longer take more time off, so he went back to his Navy duties. Fred Noonan would be the sole navigator, and he would remain for the entire flight. Paul Mantz remained as the technical advisor.

What changed the most was the route—it would ostensibly begin at Oakland and go eastward cross-country to Miami. The publicity also changed. There was essentially to be none of it. No grand farewell, no bands, no MovieTone or newsreel fellows cranking their cameras.

Earhart flew her team from Burbank to Oakland to pick up Elmer Dimity's philatelic covers; then back to Burbank. From there she left with Bo McKneely, her mechanic, GP, and Fred Noonan. They were making just short hops across the country to Miami. The flight had been so tentative that until she was sure the Electra was fit she was prepared to turn back to Burbank for more fine-tuning.

After they arrived, Miami was jumping with the news that Amelia Earhart was beginning her much (previously) advertised flight. The papers closely covered her final preparations.

With GP watching from the airfield, at 5:56 a.m. June 1, 1937, Amelia took off in her bright silver Electra. One thousand miles away they made their first landing— San Juan, Puerto Rico. Here she reclined at the plantation of a friend, Clara Livingston. From there they made it over the sapphire Caribbean and then thick green jungle carpet of Venezuela to Paramaribo, then from there over more dense jungles—the green sea—to Caripito, where they stayed at the house of Henry Linam, the general manager for Standard Oil in Venezuela. From Natal they cut across the South Atlantic at its narrowest point headed to Dakar in Africa. Here there was a major mistake. AE came into the coast far north of her destination, the result of disagreeing with Noonan over the navigation. Overriding his advice and taking her own way, they passed Dakar far enough not to see it and landed at St. Louis, Gambia.

From here the dauntless duo cut across Africa, made their prescheduled fuel stops in isolated desert oases, and then across Arabia, Persia, India, and fought monsoons over southeast Asia. Finally, after weather delays, they proceeded to Singapore and then Bandoeng, Java. It was now late June 1937. They had been at this for near to a month. They were coming closer to the critical legs of the flight. The world press and the US Coast Guard started to prepare.

Early Amelia Earhart— As she looked just prior to flight of the Friendship *and world fame, June 1928.* Wide World Photos

Earhart, early in her public career; self-conscious of a gap in her front teeth, she usually only gave a "winsome half smile." Library of Congress

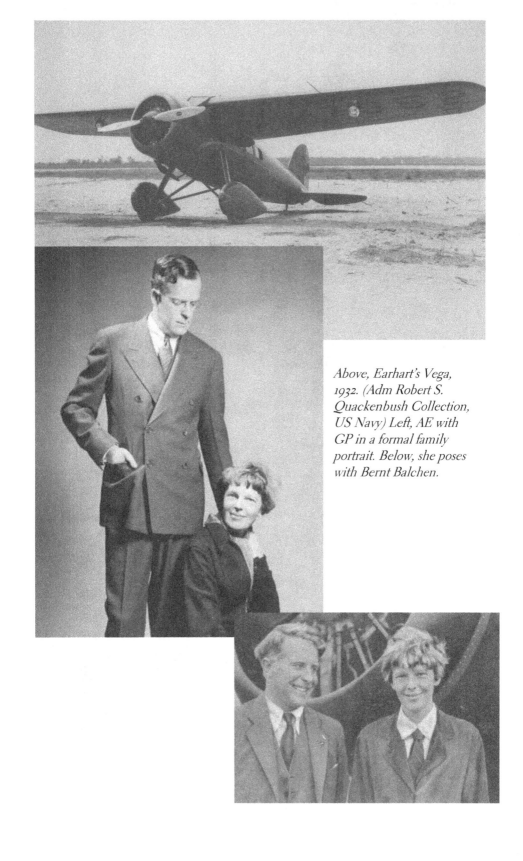

Above, Earhart's Vega, 1932. (Adm Robert S. Quackenbush Collection, US Navy) Left, AE with GP in a formal family portrait. Below, she poses with Bernt Balchen.

Earhart at the height of her image and fame— tussled locks, half smile, scarf, unflattering masculine outfit—March 1937 (National Portrait Gallery/Smithsonian Institution); Below, with Electra behind her. (Smithsonian Institution/NASA)

AE in the cockpit of her "flying laboratory," 1937 (Library of Congress). *With Dean Elliot of Purdue, below. He made Earhart's exponential leap possible.* (Wide World Photos)

Chapter 6

Eye of a Needle

The captain of the Coast Guard cutter *Itasca*, Warner Thompson, had no idea that his orders to proceed to Honolulu from San Francisco were for anything other than a routine cruise of the Line Islands. However, on June 9 while en route he got the first message indicating there was something special involved. Then on June 11, he had to assume he was being sent to Howland in connection with the much publicized Earhart flight.

When his mission was confirmed, he deduced the primary duty of the *Itasca* was to act as a radio beacon upon which Earhart could home-in in order to find the tiny island. Naturally, he asked Coast Guard Division HQ in San Francisco just what radio schedules he was to be working in regards to her flight. The response from two sources was not reassuring.

San Francisco didn't have anything definite. They sent back that on the previous attempt the plane was equipped with a 50 watt transmitter for working on 500, 3105, and 6210 kilocycles. Her direction finder covered from 200 to 1500 kilocycles. Coast

Guard Miami, of course, would have the most recent information. They now said she wasn't going to be contacting any radio station in particular. Rather she would broadcast her position every 15 and 45 minutes after the hour on 6210 and she will
also use 3105 kilocycles. "She stated that her receiver will be
used most of the time taking radio bearings." Secondhand information at best, and nothing official, but Thompson figured it
would get clarified when he reached Honolulu.

There he was surprised, to say the least. Instead of clarification, there was confusion. Accompanied by Lt. Daniel Cooper of
the Army, Richard Black, identifying himself as a field representative for the Department of Interior, came aboard and informed him that he had arranged with the Navy Department to
bring aboard special radiomen. Black also wanted to ship aboard
a high frequency direction finder. Thompson declined. He had
three radiomen aboard already and there was no need for the ex-
tras. As for the direction finder, Thompson didn't think it was
worth the trouble. From what he understood from his own officers it wouldn't give enough accuracy over their own equipment.
Nevertheless, as a precautionary measure, it was packed aboard.
It would be set up on Howland Island. But the radio experts
were still left ashore.

The secondhand information Thompson had from San Francisco and Miami was still the closest official information he had
concerning radio use. If accurate, Earhart wasn't going to initi-
ate communication much. Given this, "It was the decision of
the Coast Guard officers in conference," Thompson would
write, "that the procedure to be followed in connection with the
radio navigational assistance of the Earhart plane in coming into
Howland Island would be governed by the apparent desire of the
plane to use its radio direction finder on signals sent by the
Itasca in the hope that in case of difficulty approximate bearings
might be obtained which would be of some value."

Thompson had reasons to see the duties of his ship as being
very narrow. They were to send a radio beacon signal and she
would home-in and follow it. This, Thompson discovered, was
also the limited duty of the other sentinel ships stationed along
her Pacific course.

Aside from taking the avgas to Howland for refueling the

Electra, the *Itasca* was merely one of a few guard ships being placed on duty. The U.S.S. *Ontario* was stationing itself about midway between Lae, New Guinea, and Howland Island, in order to act as a radio beacon for the flight to stay on course over the perilous Pacific. Thompson's *Itasca* would be the next link in the homing beacon chain. Between Howland and Honolulu, the U.S.S. *Swan* was stationed to do the same as the *Ontario*; after Earhart took off from Howland the ship was to act as a radio beacon to keep her on course to Hawaii.

Thus three official US warships were in place as guards to help Earhart detect their radio signals and use them to maintain course. So to speak, she was to use these to thread the eye of a needle, and this eye was miniscule Howland Island. Due to Earhart's political influence, her 'round-the-world flight for *Fun!* was being made possible by a dutiful if not indulgent government. The political influence around the flight was obvious.

Thompson's radiomen made full checks on their transmitters. Using the frequencies they *believed* AE was going to use, they made good contact with Palo Alto, California (over 2,000 miles away), and nearby Navy Radio Wailupe (Hawaii). Given what they knew, this seemed more than adequate range.

The *Itasca* left Honolulu on June 18, heading south for Howland. It wasn't long after this they received a radio update from San Francisco Coast Guard Division. Earhart had just left Calcutta for Bangkok, Siam (Burma).

Things aboard ship, it seems, were not running entirely smoothly. Insofar as Thompson could figure, the setup was becoming haphazard. Black was hogging the radio. He was sending messages to Putnam, informing him what duties the *Itasca* will perform, which would include frequent weather reports. But Thompson didn't even have a meteorologist aboard. It remained confusing as to who called the shots. Richard Black was designated by GP Putnam as Earhart's representative aboard, though he was an employee of the government. Cooper was involved in the special direction finder, and took orders from Black. Yet Earhart was supposed to be homing-in on *Itasca*. Only the purpose of the two newsmen aboard was obvious.

GP confirmed to Black that AE will send messages at a quarter to and quarter after the hour on 6210 kcs during the day and

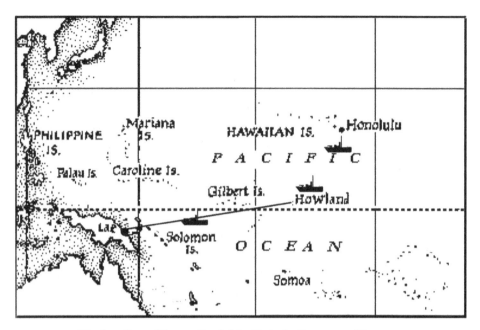

The location of the sentinel ships Ontario, Itasca, *and* Swan.

3105 kcs at night. Still, this was secondhand information. Thompson wanted direct communication. Obligingly, Black sent back to GP that Earhart was requested to contact *Itasca* direct to determine just what frequency she wanted to use for homing.

As far as Thompson was concerned, the relay system between Black and Putnam was only confusing things more. As the *Itasca* bore down on Howland, Thompson sent direct to Earhart at Port Darwin, Australia, or Lae, New Guinea (whichever port she was currently at), via Naval Radio Tutuila (Samoa):

> "Request you advise this vessel twelve hours prior to your departure from New Guinea full information regarding your desires in matters of radio frequencies and communication schedule. We will conform to any frequencies desired. Important anticipate your departure as communication via Port Darwin very slow. Itasca on station Howland Island at 2200 this evening."

And true to his word, Thompson had the anchor dropped that evening, June 23, 1937. They had arrived.

The first tasks were to unload the high frequency radio direction finder, avgas, and get ashore the equipment to help length-
en the airfield (it was cut only into the coral).

He sent a message to Coast Guard Division HQ: "Ship will
give smoke by day and searchlight by night. Have her give us
flight progress and make final arrangements before takeoff via
Samoa Tutuila radio."

Still there was no direct answer from Earhart.

GP was now at Oakland, California, and had a message sent
to *Itasca* saying that Earhart was now at Bandoeng, Java, for motor and other repairs. "Departure indefinite." However, he said
that when she reaches Port Darwin she will cable her communication arrangements direct to San Francisco, and immediately
Itasca will be given "all information." Putnam also sent the following, echoing his earlier transmission. "All communication
from plane will be on 500, 3105, or 6210 kilocycles by voice, posi-
tions being given at fifteen and forty-five past the hour." This
was secondhand again and then GP added: "Itasca adjust transmitter for possible use 3105 kilocycles for voice." GP then informed them that the direction finder on Earhart's plane covered the band of 200 to 1400 kilocycles.

"Possible use" didn't work with Thompson. He waited for
everything to come direct from Earhart, including the homing
frequency to be used, which so far had not even been implied.

Fortunately, Earhart personally sent a message to *Itasca*
through Honolulu (not Tutuila). She suggested that the U.S.S.
Ontario transmit the letter **N** (on 400 kcs) for 5 minutes on request, with its call letters repeated twice end of every minute.
She suggested the *Swan* transmit by voice on 9 megs or "if I unable receive" to be ready on 800 kilocycles. "Itasca transmit letter **A**, position and own call letters as above on half hour 7.5
megacycles." She asked they position the ships and "our leaving
will determine broadcast times specifically." She appended: "if
frequencies mentioned unsuitable night work inform me Lae."
She clarified: "I will give long call by voice three one naught
five (3105) kcs quarter after hour possible quarter to. Earhart."

Too many radio frequencies were being mentioned, plus the
last cable said Earhart's homing device had a band of 200 to 1500
and 2400 to 4800. Above she asked for homing signals **A** sent on

7.5 megs, which was way outside her homing loop's bandwidth. She also said she will voice on quarter hour and "possible" on quarter to hour. "Possible" again.

Thompson sent to San Francisco Division that "*Itasca* communication unsatisfactory and possibly dangerous to Earhart contacts and other vital schedules." He requested complete communication independence. In other words, Earhart was to contact him direct, and then he would respond through the Naval network of communications (Naval Radio Tutuila) and Hawaii sector. He also requested the discontinuance of all *Itasca*-San Francisco radio schedules until Earhart is in Hawaii. Permission was granted. *Itasca* and Earhart would start over.

On June 27, Earhart re-sent her previous cablegram to *Itasca*, this time directed to Richard Black. This reiterated the same radio frequencies. This was now taken as gospel.

Itasca soon sent to Earhart (via Naval Radio Tutuila) that their transmitters were calibrated now on 7500 (7.5 megs), 6210, 3105, 500, 425 kilocycles. Their direction finder frequency range was 550 to 270 kcs. "Request we be informed as to time of departure and zone time to be used on radio schedules. *Itasca* at Howland Island during flight."

Amazingly, the first word *Itasca* had that Earhart was on the move came via Mr. Carey, one of the newsmen aboard, when on June 29 press San Francisco sent to him: "Earhart enroute Port Darwin to Lae. Begin cover anything available movements."

Soon thereafter *Itasca* was copied in a message from San Francisco. It contained a message from Putnam to his wife. "Request approximate time your takeoff from Lae." They got a copy *only* because San Francisco's division requested that the answer be copied to *Ontario* and *Itasca*.

Through Tutuila Radio, Earhart finally responded directly to *Itasca*. "Plan midday take off here please have meteorologist send forecast Lae Howland soon as possible if reaches me in time will try leave today otherwise July first report in English not code specially while flying. Will broadcast hourly quarter past hour GCT [Greenwich Civil Time]. Further information later."

Thompson's requests had finally been answered. They would use Greenwich Civil Time and use "English" by which *she* meant voice.

Then Earhart sent to Black that she planned to start on July 1 at 2330 GCT "if weather okeh." Then: "Now understood *Itasca* voicing three one nought five with long continuous signal on approach."

The brief moment of clarity was over. This was contrary to her instructions from Port Darwin. Thompson would later write: "The Itasca had thus far given no indication of intention to broadcast on this frequency [3105], although preparations have been made." Nevertheless, Thompson acquiesced to her assumption. He reported that they would transmit "**A** on 7.5 megacycles and voice on 3105 kcs on request or when in range."

Things were coalescing, or so it seemed. Then Earhart sent another message to Black. She asked that *Ontario* be told to send **N** "for five minutes ten minutes after hour GMT on 400 kcs with call letters repeated twice end every minute. Plan to leave 10 this morning New Guinea time. Earhart."

This was now a different time standard than previously stated and a different requirement for *Ontario* which previously was to transmit **N** upon request. The last message Black received: "Due to local conditions takeoff delayed until 2130 GMT July second."

So far as records are concerned, both sides were left with assumptions.

Thompson and the entire crew braced themselves. Finally, at 6:30 p.m. local time *Itasca* was informed by San Francisco Coast Guard Division that "United Press reports Earhart plane took off at noon Lae time." This was 2:30 p.m. *Itasca* time (though a day before due to the International Date Line). Then at 7:55 p.m. local time an urgent message came in for Black. It was from Lae via Tutuila Radio. "Amelia Earhart left Lae 10 am local time July 2nd due Howland Island 18 hours time." This now meant she had taken off at 12:30 p.m. *Itasca* time, July 1, 1937.

With 18 hours estimated in flight, *Itasca* placed her ETA at Howland Island at 6 30 a.m. to 7 a.m. the next morning, July 2, 1937—she was now flying into yesterday.

U.S. Coast Guard cutter Itasca *(or sister ship) on maneuvers.*

Chapter 7

Flying into Yesterday

The *Itasca* sat silent between dark sea and sparkling night. Streamers of starlight wiggled back and forth on the shimmering sea. The breakers against nearby Howland Island issued only a tired sigh to disturb the suspended solitude. To be at sea in the middle of nowhere is to always be on the top of a polished dome. Come daybreak, rising up over the southwest of this dome would be Amelia Earhart's bright silvery Electra; the goddess of the sky for whom the US government set all this preparation in motion. Until the men crowded at the cutter's rails would behold this dazzling sparkle, the *Itasca*'s only perspective would be the same as it had been: a keyhole glimpse provided through the radio messages pecking in key or the voice messages whining over the receiver from distant ports.

Earhart had been overheard only twice so far, and neither time by *Itasca*. The first time was at 6:18 p.m. Lae time. She had made her first position report: "Position four point thirty-three south, one five nine point six east— height eight thousand feet over cumulus clouds; wind twenty-three knots." This placed her 795 miles out from Lae.

The next time was at 10:30 p.m. Nauru Island radio heard her report "a ship in sight ahead" as she passed south of the island. *Itasca* had not heard her, but they heard Nauru Island Radio calling her back.

Midnight had struck. It was now seven hours until AE's silver sparkle of success would streak over the horizon and purr in for a carefully filmed landing. *Itasca* commenced sending voice and signal checks with San Francisco. Howland Island also sent a check with San Francisco. Coast Guard Division HQ told them to slow their code transmissions (they had been sending 15 words per minute) to 10 words per minute. This was the only *inference* that both Noonan and Earhart were very poor with Morse code. Other than this a long silent routine ensued.

With officers and two reporters in the radio room, the radioman listened closely between 12:15 a.m. and 12:18 a.m. to hear Earhart's first message. They expected it to be just a casual position report. Nothing was heard.

At 12:25 a.m. the first of *Itasca's* transmissions on the half hour commenced. By key on 7500 kilocycles (7.5 megs) and voice on her night frequency of 3105 kcs., they sent:

> Itasca to Earhart, Itasca to Earhart, Itasca at Howland to Earhart—
> Weather wind direction east wind direction east force 11 miles
> wind force 11 miles partly cloudy, partly cloudy barometer twenty
> nine point nine two cloudy barometer twenty nine point nine two
> visibility 20 miles visibility twenty miles air temperature 82 air
> temperature 82 calm calm swell direction east swell direction east.

At 12:30 a.m. **A** was sent for 4 minutes.

Soon afterward *Itasca* asked Radio Tutuila if *Ontario* had heard Earhart. Tutuila responded negative.

At 12:55 to 12:58 a.m. the routine repeated— the weather report was resent. At 1 a.m. the homing signal **A** was sent again. AE was asked to use key in "observing schedules."

No response.

At 1:12 a.m. *Itasca* informed San Francisco that Earhart had so far not been heard at the scheduled times. However, Thompson saw no alarm in this as the plane was still 1,000 miles away. He had 2 men listening in the radio room and one on Howland, so he would let San Francisco know immediately when first signal was received.

This routine repeated at 2 a.m. Near to 15 minutes after the hour, *Itasca* listened carefully. Nearing the half hour they sent the weather by voice on 3105 kcs and then by key on 7.5 megs, adding: "have not heard your signals yet please observe schedules with key, go ahead, am listening now on 3105." It went unanswered.

This records the first incident of confusion. This frequency was solely voice for Earhart. She could not respond by key, and she had plainly told them "use English and not code." She could hear code on 400 and 500 kcs and, she believed, on 7.5 megacycles. Her limit in code was understanding **N** and **A** (because they were commonly used for homing in America), call letters, alphabet, and tapping out S.O.S.

There was every reason for the radioman, Chief Leo Bellarts, to want a reply. Presently at 2:30 a.m. *Itasca* time she must have been about 600 miles away and well within radio range of the *Itasca*. She should be sending some position report to *Itasca* soon . . . it should be assumed.

This assumption proved correct at 2:45 a.m. On 3105 "cloudy and overcast" came through the loudspeaker in a "very low monotone." Carey and Hanzlik (the men of the press) had heard her voice before. "There was no question as to hearing Earhart."

Captain Thompson and Richard Black were informed. A very terse message was drafted and sent via San Francisco to Putnam. It had to be done quickly to maintain the listening schedule at a quarter after.

Between 3 and 3:06 a.m. *Itasca* sent weather by key and voice. In response (at 3:15 to 18) *Itasca* heard nothing.

Again, weather was sent at 3:30 a.m. with the addition of "What is your position? When do you expect to reach Howland? *Itasca* has heard your phone. Go ahead on key. Acknowledge this broadcast next schedule."

As 3:45 a.m. approached they awaited her signals or voice. "Itasca from Earhart, Itasca from Earhart, Overcast—Will listen on hour and half hour on three one naught five [3105] - - - - -

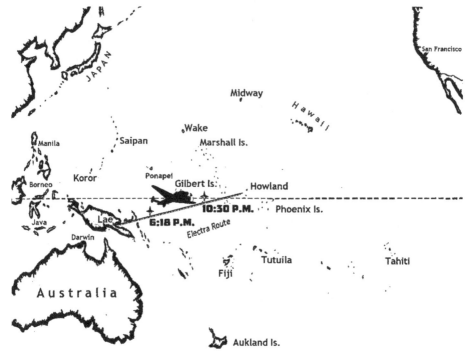

At 6:18 p.m. Lae picked up Earhart's first position report, which placed her 800 miles out. At 10:30 p.m. Earhart had said "a ship in sight ahead." Nauru Island radio had overheard and called her back (it is their message Itasca had heard). Plotting these reports indicates she was on course. When she sent her 2:45 a.m. message she must have been approaching the Gilbert Islands.

Will listen on hour and half hour on 3105."

This response sent joy though the radio room. It seemed as if two-way communication had been established. But she was so briefly on the radio—only a few seconds— and she hadn't given her position as requested.

Then at 4 a.m. there was reason to question she had responded specifically to *Itasca* 15 minutes before. Bellarts sent the weather, and added once again: "What is your position? When do you expect to reach Howland? We are receiving your signals. Please acknowledge this message on your next schedule."

Listening carefully over 4:15 to 4:18 a.m. Bellarts heard nothing yet again.

This was frustrating. At 4:26 a.m. Bellarts started sending the weather by key and voice on 3105 until 4:35 a.m.

He then asked Howland and San Francisco if they had

picked up Earhart. Negative. Nothing again at 4:45 a.m., but a few minutes later Bellarts repeated the weather. At 4:53 he heard her repeat "partly cloudy, partly cloudy." The reception was poor (S-1 or Signal Strength 1).

Poor reception should have been regarded as strange. Her ETA at *Itasca* was 6:30 a.m., about an hour and a half away. She should be within 200 miles of the island.

At 4:55 a.m., just a few minutes later, her voice broke over again, but she was unreadable.

This seemed to reflect an abandonment of the scheduled call and listen times. But Bellarts listened carefully at 5:15 a.m. anyway. Nothing was heard yet again.

Again, at 5:30 a.m. he sent weather on 3105 kilocycles by key and voice, continuing for 5 minutes.

Frustratingly yet again there was no message heard from her at her next scheduled call-in time of 5:45 a.m.

Earhart was apparently sticking to what Miami had sent Warner Thompson early-on. She wasn't going to contact much, just listen for the radio signals to home-in on. Despite Bellarts specifically asking that she send routine reports, she wasn't going to do that.[3]

Again, Bellarts sent weather by key at 6 a.m. to 6:05 a.m.

Finally, at 6:14 a.m. they heard her at a scheduled call time. She wanted a bearing on 3105 kcs on the hour. She will whistle into the mic for them.[4]

There was some confusion about her takeoff time. Was it 12 noon Lae time, which is 2:30 p.m. their time, or was it 10:00 a.m. Lae time and 12:30 p.m. their time? Time in flight was estimated at 18 hours, which if she had taken off at 12:30 p.m. their time this would put her ETA, once again, between 6:30 a.m. and 7 a.m. She should be close by. But the radio reception of her message was still Signal Strength 1 — in other words, poor.

Then, just a minute later (6:15 a.m.), her voice came over. As

---

[3] We are walking through this chronologically from the point of view of the *Itasca* as events unfold. Discussions about whether her receiver was working or why key was often used verses voice are for later.

[4] Did this mean 6 a.m.? Earhart may not have compensated for a half hour time zone change. Her clock may have said 5:45 a.m.

recorded tersely by the log: "About two hundred miles out// appx//whistling//NW." The Signal Strength was 3 or Weak.[5]

She was getting closer but clearly was delayed (or had taken off later than understood).

Sunrise's pink splatter daubed the eastern sky. To the west it was a watercolor of bluish-indigo. Plumes of black smoke started burping from the *Itasca*'s smokestack. Captain Thompson had ordered the engine room to start making smoke, so the plume would rise up and she could see it as her Electra arced over the indigo horizon.

At 6:30 a.m. *Itasca* sent **A** for homing (on 7.5 megs). Bellarts asked her position again and listened on 3105 until 6:36 a.m. Then he called her again. No acknowledgment. *Itasca* sent **A** at 6:41 a.m. and asked for acknowledgment.

At 6:42 a.m. Earhart's voice was again heard calling *Itasca*. The signal strength was "fairly clear."

At 6:45 a.m. Earhart elaborated: "Please take bearing on us and report in half hour-- I will make noise in microphone— about 100 miles out." Signal strength was 4 or fair to good.

Previously, she had asked they take a bearing on her at 7 a.m. or, specifically, "on the hour." A minute later she whistled into the microphone. Now she repeated her request. Now she also asked that they report back on her call time of 7:15 a.m. instead of the top of the hour (7 a.m.). This only makes sense if she hadn't adjusted her clock properly. She had probably said "on the half hour" which if her clock read 6:15 a.m. she meant 6:30 a.m. only 15 minutes away for her.

Not understanding this, Bellarts was justifiably bewildered. Logistically, what she asked for didn't make sense. They could only take a bearing on her if she talked into the microphone for a while. She had whistled in the mic, "but on air so briefly bearings impossible." But why would she ask them to wait to report it to her in 30 minutes? What good would it be then?

This was frustrating for Bellarts. Earhart was not acknowledging *Itasca* even when asked to do so. Was she hearing them and these were her responses? Position reports were being asked, but

---

[5] She had probably not adjusted her clock properly. She is now whistling only a minute later, expecting *Itasca* to wait 15 minutes to reply with the bearing.

"about 100 miles out" was the sum total of what had come back from Earhart. Was this in response to requests or just a general, gratuitous update?

Between 7:05 a.m. and 7:16 a.m. *Itasca* sent **A** on 7.5 megs and 3105 kcs. As requested, Bellarts intentionally stepped on her 7:15 a.m. call time by sending the homing signals between 7:14 and 7:16 because she had (at 6:45 a.m.) asked the "bearing" be sent "in half hour."

Finished at 7:18 a.m., he spoke concisely into the mic: "Cannot take bearing on 3105 very good. Please send on 500 or do you wish to take bearing on us. Go ahead please."

No answer.

From 7:19 a.m. to 7:29 a.m. Bellarts asked her to contact them on 3105 kcs. No response. He intermittently sent out **A**. At 7:30 he explicitly asked her to acknowledge their signals by key. No response. Both on 7.5 megs and 3105 kcs, *Itasca* sent **A** until 7:41 a.m.

At 7:42 a.m. Earhart's voice finally broke over the radio speaker again. "KHAQQ (Earhart) calling Itasca, We must be on you but cannot see you but gas is running low been unable to reach you by radio. We are flying at altitude 1,000 feet."

The log was amended by what others in the radio room believed they heard: (Other log: "Earhart now says running out of gas only half hour left ((verified as heard by other witnesses))/can't hear us at all/we hear her and are sending on 3105 and 500 same time constantly and listening in for her frequently.")

Earhart's Signal Strength was S-5 or Good. She must have been nearby. But her short statement "been unable to reach you by radio" confirmed what was already feared aboard: her radio receiver was not working.

Over 7:43 to 7:46 a.m. *Itasca* sent "Received your signal strength 5." They sent **A** on 500 and 3105. "Go ahead."

No reply.

Over 7:47-48 a.m., Bellarts repeated "KHAQQ received your signal strength 5." He sent **A** on 3105.

Over 7:49-51 a.m., and again at 7:57 a.m. *Itasca* sent: "KHAQQ from Itasca Your message Okay. Please acknowledge with Phone on 3105" (then he sent **A** by key).

At 7:58 a.m. her voice crackled over: "KHAQQ calling Itasca

We are circling but cannot hear you. Go ahead on 7500 either now or on the schedule time on the half hour."[6]

From the good signal strength (S-5), Earhart must indeed have been close. Collectively (as Thompson would later write) they believed her receiver wasn't working. However, her direction finder antenna, separate from her radio receiving antenna, should still have been receiving their signals, and it was not yet understood why Earhart hadn't homed-in on them.

For the next minute *Itasca* sent **A** on 7500, then asked her to go ahead on 3105.

Then finally, though confusingly, between 8 a.m. and 8:03 a.m. the following is logged. "KHAQQ calling Itasca-- We received your signals but unable to get a minimum. Please take bearing on us and answer 3105 with voice."

She then sent long dashes (Dah, Dah, Dah, by voice) on 3105 for only 5 seconds.

Again, it wasn't long enough! The tension in the radio room was palpable.

Bellarts quickly called Howland. Radioman 2nd class Frank Cipriani, manning the special radio direction finder, confirmed that he couldn't get a minimum either.

At 8:05 a.m.: "KHAQQ from Itasca-- Your signals received Okay. We are unable to hear you to take a bearing. It is impractical to take a bearing on 3105 on your voice. How do you read that? Go ahead."

Bellarts sent this on 7.5 megs believing she had been referring to that frequency when she said she heard their signals. But it appears he was sending this by key, and Earhart couldn't read a sentence in Morse quickly.

And from the sounds of her voice, she was growing frantic. It wasn't just the brevity of her communication. When last heard, she spoke so quickly it was sometimes hard to determine what she had said.

Since 6 a.m. the direction finder on Howland had been listening in but couldn't get a cut on Earhart because she used only voice and was so brief. "Earhart's maximum transmission time

[6] If she had not adjusted her clock, she may have thought it 7:28 a.m. and meant in a couple of minutes.

probably never exceeded 7 or 8 seconds."

At 8:07 a.m. *Itasca* sent on all channels (500, 3015, 7500 kcs.) to "Go Ahead."

Her signal strength had been consistently good in the last couple of communications, indicating she was remaining close by. But there was reason to worry. Some had heard her say "half an hour fuel left" about half an hour ago. Thompson was growing desperate to get a bearing on her to help in any search and rescue operation if they couldn't bring her in.

So far nothing had been working. Even the *Itasca*'s smoke screen wasn't pluming high overhead, but was clutching the sea and "remained concentrated and did not thin out greatly."

At 8:11 a.m. Bellarts repeated: "Did you get transmission on 7500 kcs (7.5 megs)? Go ahead on 500 kcs so that we may take a bearing on you. It is impossible to take a bearing on 3105 kilocycles. Please acknowledge." This transmission was repeated on 7.5 megs since that was the only frequency she had acknowledged (but the log is not clear if it was sent in key or voice).

Again at 8:15 a.m. she was asked if she had heard them on either 7500 or 3105 kcs. She was asked to acknowledge and "go ahead."

Yet again no response.

Over the next 25 minutes *Itasca* kept telling her "Go Ahead" on 7500 or 3105.

"Three receivers, loudspeaker, Howland loop, and ship's direction finder covering Earhart's frequencies throughout this entire period—no answers." They told her they were constantly sending on 7.5 megs. "Please answer on 3105."

Finally, at 8:43 a.m. they heard Earhart's voice. "We are on a line of position 157-337. (Others present heard "We are running north and south.") Will repeat this message. Will repeat this message on 6210 kilocycles. Wait. Listening on 6210 kilocycles."

Bellarts turned to 6210 kilocycles and waited. Her message did not repeat on that frequency. No message ever came over again— not even a Mayday or a final word they were going down.

After an hour of calling her without answer, Bellarts thought that it was because of 6210 kcs. The daytime frequency had a range limitation compared to the nighttime frequency. He called again at 9:45 a.m. telling Earhart they had heard her fine on 3105. "Go ahead on 3105." This was repeated on all channels they had been using.

Nothing was ever heard from Amelia Earhart.

Going over her radio reports quickly, Captain Thompson carefully assessed the few clues they had. Early-on, a brief wisp of her voice had said "cloudy." It was cloudy to the northwest. Thompson put it together and deduced that she passed the island to the northwest and didn't see it because of the glare of the rising sun to the east. Her signal strength had remained good to very good in the last hour because she had been circling or running that line 337-157, remaining fairly close by. He up-anchored at 10 a.m., believing she had already ditched at sea.

Thompson's calculated hunch drove the *Itasca* northward at flank speed. Radio messages alerted civilian traffic to scour the area. British steamer *Moorby* was in the vicinity. The cruise liners *Mariposa* and *Monterey* were approaching. *Swan* headed south from its holding position.

Thompson informed San Francisco and Hawaii of the probability Earhart was down.

At 7:23 p.m. (Hawaii Time) Honolulu sent a PBY designated Plane 62. Its mission was to reach Howland and refuel with the avgas intended for Earhart's plane. It would then conduct an extensive grid search centered on Howland Island. However, it turned back about 500 miles from Howland due to increasingly bad weather.

This became the first SNAFU of the search mission. *Itasca* had diverted from searching what, on the face of it, was the most probable area where Earhart had gone down in order to rendezvous back at Howland with the incoming PBY. When it turned back, Thompson had to up-anchor again and return to search the northern area. Valuable search time had been lost.

The *Itasca* crew collectively believed that the Electra, if ditched properly, would float because so much of the fuselage was nothing but empty gas tanks now. Thus it had been quite frustrating to divert from the probable ditching area on a wild goose chase back to Howland to await a plane that turned around halfway there.

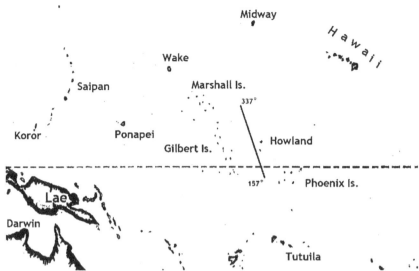

Fred Noonan had the ability to take a sunline with celestial navigation, and this is apparently what Earhart referred to when she said they were "on a line of position 157-337." The line of position marked on a map—ostensibly they believed it ran through Howland Island.

Thompson and his crew also believed that Earhart could transmit from an emergency radio while her Electra floated. Although she was very brisk on the air while flying, now down on the sea one would expect her to be speaking for more extended periods, trying to direct rescuers to her. Therefore the current radio silence was very disturbing. It indicated she had cracked up on ditching and sunk quickly.

Without being able to get a PBY there quickly, the closest thing the Navy had was the battleship *Colorado* on an ROTC cruise with cadets and three university presidents as observers. The battleship had three reconnaissance float planes. With the *Itasca* covering the northern area, it was determined that it was best to send the *Colorado* to the Phoenix Island Group area, which was at the south end of the 157-337 line of position Earhart had mentioned.

The newsmen aboard *Itasca* were preparing to file detailed stories as soon as the radio was free to transmit anything but urgent search information. When that time came, headlines around the world proclaimed in bold print:

EARHART PLANE LOST AT SEA
NAVY HUNTS AMELIA LOST IN PACIFIC OCEAN

In addition, the carrier USS *Lexington* and its escort destroyers were dispatched from San Diego. Its 60 or more planes would be crucial for searching the ocean.

Despite the initial radio silence which so disturbed the *Itasca*'s crewmen, things changed and it seemed for the positive. A woman's voice careened through the United States over shortwave frequencies, the next day, Saturday July 3.

Greatest Air Rescue Force Heads South

Honolulu, July 4.— (AP)— The greatest rescue expedition in flying history sped tonight to aid Amelia Earhart in the remote South Seas while radio lanes buzzed with recurring reports of a tiny voice— perhaps Amelia's—trying to break the silence veiling her fate.

The news first covered Dana Randolph, a 15 year old boy with a high powered shortwave antenna at his house in Rock Springs, Wyoming. He heard this woman's voice say she was on a sandbank south of the equator.

Another report came in from Los Angeles amateur shortwave radio enthusiasts giving location 179 by 1.6 yet without specifying east or west, north or south. Coast Guard San Francisco thought this was credible.

Based on these coordinates, *Colorado*'s officers did calculations. Winslow Reef was charted about 200 miles southeast of Howland Island. At low tide, the bare wiggle of sand was 6 feet above the surface. At high tide, it was just below, shining brightly as a turquoise patch of sea.

While *Colorado* steamed there at full speed, the biggest event so far in the search happened. Three radio operators in Hawaii picked up a very poorly keyed transmission in Morse Code. It came in between 11:30 p.m. July 4 and 12:30 a.m. (GCT) July 5.

281 North Howland. . .Call KHAQQ. . .Beyond North. . . Don't hold with us much longer. . .above water. . .shut off. . .

What the message meant, which wasn't entirely clear, wasn't as important as that it was poorly keyed and took a while to finally finish. By this time the searchers knew that both Earhart and Noonan were poor with Morse. The poor nature of the keying, including the lack of coherent grammar or sense, meant it could indeed be from the Electra.

Warner Thompson took this ambiguous message to mean 281 miles north of Howland Island. It fit with his calculations about Earhart having gone down north of the island. The *Itasca* steamed toward the area, slashing searchlight beams through the inky sky and skimming them over the heavy, dark swells.

In the darkness of July 5, Thompson's confidence seemed confirmed. Scouting the horizon from the guardrails, crewmen saw a streak of light. The radio room quickly broadcast: "Earhart from Itasca, did you send up a flare? If you did, send up another. Please go ahead." Two minutes later another streak arced across the starry ink. "Earhart plane from Itasca, we see second flare; we are coming for you. We are starting toward you." The radioman continued to assure Earhart they were coming. Then Howland confirmed the streaks were falling stars (meteors).

News then came that dampened their hopes Earhart ever could have broadcast that Morse code message. Lockheed confirmed that the Electra could not transmit while on water. One of its engines had to be turning for its generator to work.

Lockheed's clarification meant that if the 281 North Howland message was from the Electra, it had to be on land. The problem, naturally, there was no land anywhere near 281 miles north of Howland. The only messages so far picked up that said she was on land were those July 3 messages. The "tiny" woman's voice had stated they were on a sandbank *south* of the equator. Is "south" what the poorly keyed Morse message actually intended to say? Winslow Reef, on the northern fringes of the Phoenix Island Group, approximated this position *south* of Howland.

The Phoenix Group had presented itself rather early as a very likely spot for Earhart's ditching. It was at the end of the 157 direction of the line of position. Moreover, on July 4, radio bearings had come in to Wake Island, Midway Island, Mokapu Point, Hawaii, and at Howland Island. They all had homed-in on a

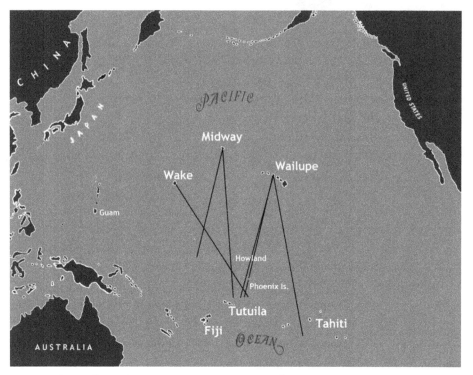

*Lines indicate bearings on a carrier wave which three major Pan Ameri-
can high frequency stations had picked up. They triangulate over the
Phoenix group of islands.*

carrier wave, nothing more, indicating some form of radio message was being attempted from the Phoenix Islands area.

Analysis of these bearings at Coast Guard headquarters San
Francisco further strengthened this interpretation. George Putnam urged them to search. On July 6, he sent *Itasca* and the Navy ships the following cable, summing up the consensus.

Quote Please note all radio bearings thus far obtained on Earhart
Plane approximately intersect in Phoenix island region southeast of
Howland Island. Further line of position given by Noonan if based
on Howland which apparently reasonable assumption also passes
through islands. Believe navigator after obtaining such line naturally would follow it to nearest indicated land. Additionally if message
stating position 281 miles north of Howland actually was quote
south unquote instead of north also indicates same region. Weather
analysis indicates likelihood headwinds aloft much stronger than

Noonan reconed [sic] with probability never got 100 miles from Howland as they thought. Lockheed engineers state positively plane could not operate its radio unless on shore and no islands apparently exist north of Howland therefore suggested that planes from Colorado investigate Phoenix area as practicable. Unquote

Colorado was bearing down on the area of Winslow Reef, anxiously anticipating finding Earhart. Amazingly, over the entire day of July 7 none of *Colorado*'s search planes could find the reef. Captain Wilhelm Friedell and his officers weren't even sure now if the reef actually existed. Maps were out of date and imprecise. They began searching their maps for any other potential sandbanks, hoping these were accurately charted.

This revealed another option: Carondelet Reef. It was in the Phoenix Group where they were ultimately headed. They set sail for that location.

As the *Colorado* approached the islands, more messages from a woman's voice came into Australia and the United States. The one in Australia said "Plane between Howland Samoa Group ten hours west" (implying Phoenix Islands). The other, late that day, was the most significant. Mrs. Freitas of Yreka in northern California reported receiving a message via shortwave. The woman's voice said: "Plane on reef 200 miles directly south of Howland, both okay, one wing broken."

This message echoed the earlier messages of July 3, wherein the woman's voice had said they were on a sandbank to the south of Howland. This message now almost pinpointed the location of the "mythical" Winslow Reef.

. . .Yet *Colorado* hadn't found it the very day before.

Those enticing radio bearings on mere carrier waves, however, triangulated over the Phoenix Group, hundreds of miles south of the supposed area of Winslow Reef. Put together, everything still pointed to the south and that the *Colorado*'s search planes would soon overfly the stranded, broken Electra.

Chapter 8

Voices from Nowhere

Riding the high seas, the captains and crews of the ships scouring the Pacific were completely unaware of the excitement back in the United States. That "tiny" voice, in staccato bursts, had captured the hopes of the nation that its beloved Amelia Earhart was safe on a sandbank.

The gist of what the searchers actually knew was summed up by Wilhelm Friedell, captain of the *Colorado*. He wrote: "that on July 3 on 3105 kcs a woman's voice had made four distress signal calls followed by KHAQQ, followed by '225 garble, off Howland, battery very weak, can't last long, garble indicated sandbank'. . ." He added: "considerable credulance" by headquarters "was given to the possibility of the report having been actually received" from Earhart. Friedell concludes with what seems a quip: "This began the whole lost on sandbank theory."

The *Colorado*, of course, headed south. The point here is to introduce the "voice."

This voice came from nowhere. It first had been picked up in the continental United States on Saturday, July 3, the day after Earhart vanished. It was 7 a.m. in Los Angeles. Amateur shortwavers Carl Pierson and Walter McMenamy heard "S.O.S" thrice and then about 20 minutes later "KHAQQ," her call letters. Pieces of other signals required interpretation. McMenamy heard "lat" which he took to mean "latitude." Also, "179 by 1.6" was overheard. McMenamy and Pierson came to believe Earhart was between the Gilbert Islands and Howland Island, apparently drifting. "I recognized Miss Earhart's voice from conversations I have had with her, although I never heard her on the air before," Pierson told the newspapers. "Walter recognized her because he had maintained radio contact with her plane on her flight from Oakland to Hawaii this spring."

In the case of Dana Randolph in Rock Springs, Wyoming, it was Sunday, July 4, at 8 a.m. He heard this woman's voice say: "This is Amelia Earhart. Ship is on a reef south of the equator. Station KH9QQ." Over the next 25 minutes, the voice would repeat but fade away quickly. She tried once to give coordinates.

Paul Mantz believed this mysterious reef was in the Phoenix Group. "The Pan American station in Hawaii," he conveyed to the news mongers, "sent out instructions to her including one to send out three long dashes if on land. George Palmer Putnam, her husband, telephoned me a short time ago he was advised that three dashes were heard almost immediately after the instructions were sent out." The papers added that Putnam declared this to be the most hopeful news yet.

Supporting Mantz's deduction was the HMS *Achilles*. Sailing near Samoa, the British warship had also heard the dashes. *Achilles* logged them as "good signal strength." Then a station started sending "KHAQQ," Earhart's call letters.[7] *Achilles* then realized the initial question had been sent to KHAQQ as well. The 3 dashes therefore could have been Earhart responding. The British warship was south of the Phoenix Group at this time, so a "good signal strength" meant the person who sent the 3 dashes must have been close by.

No one really knew where that voice was coming from, but it was only being picked up in the continental United States. On

---

[7] The unknown station was the *Itasca* calling for Earhart to respond.

the other hand, these three dashes had been picked up locally. As of July 5, this fact along with the carrier wave bearings from 3 points triangulating over the Phoenix Group indicated a location south of Howland.

Altogether this aggregate of clues changed matters. The Coast Guard/Navy Intelligence now believed these dashes and the woman's voice had credibility. Thus starting on July 7 Captain Friedell was justified in his extended effort to find Winslow Reef and then to devote careful examination to Carondelet Reef in the Phoenix Group. Carondelet was visible to the search pilots from 10 miles away, making Friedell sure that Winslow Reef had been grossly mischarted. (He also noted that some of the Phoenix Islands had been mischarted and were miles from where his map placed them.) The truth of the matter, once again, is that Winslow Reef was never found.

Long after the search was concluded, this would become a sore point. It allowed this voice from nowhere to haunt history. Belief in this voice's authenticity or in its inauthenticity is the result of individual rationalization.

Friedell was the first. Initially not finding Winslow Reef had troubled him. However, more messages were relayed to him that this woman's voice was still being picked up in the continental United States, most recently on July 8, 1937, by Mrs. Freitas. "Plane on reef 200 miles directly south of Howland, both okay, one wing broken." This was just a day after *Colorado*'s scout planes scoured the ocean trying to find the reef. He became suspicious. If AE was on what seemed that mythical reef nearby, they should have picked up the same message loud and clear. But they hadn't.

As the *Colorado* continued to search the Phoenix Group, it became obvious Earhart wasn't stranded on and broadcasting from any of the islands. Lt. John Lambrecht and his squadron of search planes overflew the islands. Buzzing low overhead, no one ever came rushing out onto the beaches except at Hull Island. Lambrecht landed and spoke with the European supervisor of a group of guano harvesters. They knew nothing nor had they heard a plane fly nearby or crash.

By far the most significant witness to this voice from nowhere was Nina Paxton of Ashland, Kentucky. She picked up radio messages, crystal clear, on July 3 from a station identifying itself as KHABQ (Earhart's previous call letters in her Vega). The first record of her account was local on July 9, 1937, in the Ashland *Daily Independent.*

"The message came in on my short wave set very plain," Mrs. Paxton said, "and Miss Earhart talked for some time. I turned the radio down one time to talk to my little child and then turned it back up to catch the last part of the message.

"I didn't understand everything Miss Earhart had said," Mrs. Paxton told the *Independent,* "because there was some noise."

She gave the following message as she understood it:

"Down in ocean." Then Miss Earhart either said 'on,' 'or' near little island at a point near. . . ." After that Mrs. Paxton understood her to say something about "directly northeast," although she was not sure about that part. "Our plane about out of gas. Water all around very dark." Then she said something about a storm and that the wind was blowing. "Will have to get out of here," she said. "We can't stay here long."

In remarkably more detail, she elaborated in a letter to Walter Winchell on July 30, 1937.

Saturday, It was July 3, 1937, about 2 p.m.

'art this is an SOS. K.H.A.B.Q calling, KHABQ calling, we are down here on the ocean in a little island—perhaps a coral reef at a point near the Marshall Islands. Directly north-east of a part of the Marshall Islands, 90 ****** 173 Longitude and 5 latitude [she said these coordinates were heard later]. We missed our course yesterday and came up here. This is a bleak place. We can see part of the Marshall Islands in daytime. There isn't any habitation or life here, but some vegetation. There are no trees here, but we can see a few trees on the Marshall Islands in daylight. It is storming now and getting very dark. The wind is blowing. The ocean is very rough. We came down here yesterday at 2:20 ~~or it~~ is now 2:20. Our plane is out of gas. The plane was badly damaged in landing here near a part of the Marshall Islands. (Damage to plane described). We have everything. The Captain is with me; the Captain isn't right here with me;

he is over near the plane. We landed near the water's edge and our plane is drifting. The Captain doesn't walk very well. He bruised his legs badly when landing yesterday. The Captain was shaken severely in landing.

The water is all around us, and it is warm. We are very comfortable right now but we will have to get away from here soon.

Howland Island is-- -- - miles (south west).

The Gilbert Islands are - - - miles south (east)

(Mulgrave or Musgrave Island is very near.) (The name of Smith was used in some manner). Our food supply is good but the water supply is not so good. It has become contaminated. We are alright now, but we can't stay here many days.

Miss Earhart gave a description of the above islands as she mentioned then. Words in parentheses are as I understood them.

The above message came in with as much volume as local broadcasts. The last time I heard Miss Earhart speak her name was 10 p.m. E.S.T. August 10th, 1937.

Captain Friedell was eventually joined by many officers and men in a joint suspicion of this voice from nowhere. It may have come from nowhere but it remained only in the USA. It also seemed to be originating from the east coast. Mrs. Paxton heard it as clear as local traffic. Randolph in Wyoming picked it up much better than any amateur station in California. McMenamy and Pierson (in Los Angeles) barely heard the voice enough to piece together a workable latitude and longitude. The newspapers couldn't help but report that the Coast Guard in San Francisco had heard nothing, "though reception was unusually good." Hawaii reported "not a wisp."

The lot of suspicion finally fell on a radio drama. Messages were sent to the search ships warning them that (by July 8 anyway) those amateur radio operators had probably been picking up the *March of Time* broadcast. It was dramatizing the events of Earhart being stuck on a desert island and an actress was imitating Earhart calling out to her searchers. This now explained why none of the search ships had heard the "voice."

The search continued until July 18, when it was finally called off. Seven Navy ships, 63 aircraft, and "several thousand men" had scoured a section of ocean the size of Texas and had found nothing. The next day newspapers declared Amelia Earhart and Fred Noonan dead at sea.

Head of the search, Admiral Orrin Murfin, concluded:

> We used all the information that was available and some of which we believed to be accurate. For the most part, however, our search was based on conjecture.
>
> If we had secured information that would have given us the position of the plane within 200 miles perhaps we could have found it.
>
> The case, as it was, left us looking for a needle in a haystack.
>
> We feel that we've done everything possible now.

Newspapers followed Murfin's quote with reports of how the officers of the fleet had always been suspicious that the Electra could have floated even with a perfect ditching. Ultimately, all the news articles concluded it was likely the Electra went down quickly with Earhart and Noonan sealed inside. *All* the radio messages were categorized as false.

However, Murfin's summary is not the most reassuring. It is an honest admittance that they had very little to go on from the beginning. Finding nothing, they basically fell back on Warner Thompson's original estimate that she ditched northwest of Howland and sank quickly. Every conclusion had to pivot on Thompson's input because he had been there. His conjecture explained why nothing was found, and since nothing was found that justified his conjecture.

But as time would have it, eyes would eventually behold Thompson's once-restricted report. He only lists without comment events that didn't fit his crash and sink theory. For instance, he admits that Navy Radio Wailupe picked up one of these voice messages from nowhere. Obviously the voice wasn't limited solely to the continental USA. Also, Thompson admits that Howland also picked up a bearing on the 281 North Howland message, but with what seems only anticlimactic reluctance writes that it "conformed" to that location, but then doesn't qualify if he meant directly north from Howland indicating Hawaii and a prankster. There was an alternate interpretation.

Although doubtful of the message, Captain J.S. Dowell (overall destroyer squadron commander) and Captain Leigh

Noyes, captain of carrier U.S.S. *Lexington*, wondered if "281 North" didn't mean miles but *degrees* from Howland Island, which could place AE on a reef in the Gilbert Islands. It is really quite an important point, especially in light of a significant radio reception.

Starting at 9:31 p.m. on the first night of the search (Friday, July 2), Nauru Island Radio reported more than once hearing a woman's voice making a call. The operator couldn't understand what she was saying, but he asserted it was the same voice that had made the observation "a ship in sight ahead" when passing near Nauru at 10:30 p.m. the night before. That had been Amelia Earhart. The difference now, clarified the operator, was that there was no background sound of engines. At times the voice came in Sig Strength 3, which is Weak reception.

It is unlikely that Nauru would hear AE's voice again at Signal Strength 3 if she was further east than the Gilbert Islands. Her radio, including any attempt to rig Morse, could not be working unless she was on land, and the Gilberts are the only land bearing 281 degrees from Howland.

Thompson never reinterpreted the "281 North Howland" Morse message as indicating degrees rather than miles north of the island. Essentially, there seems to be only one reason why. By the time he had written his report, the *Itasca* had cruised the major islands of the Gilberts. They had landed at main inhabited areas. They circled uninhabited islands. No one came running onto the beaches, hollering for rescue. A reinterpretation of the bearing was probably a moot point for him.

Thompson wrote in his report that the 281 North Howland message was "probably faked" by a prankster in Hawaii, thus explaining why only Hawaii operators picked it up. (*Itasca, Swan, Moorby* were in the actual area and didn't pick it up.) Again, it was only in the vein of an afterthought that he admitted that Howland also "apparently" picked up a bearing on it.

His repeated caution about Howland picking up a direction on the "281 North" message seems to reflect his discovery that radioman Frank Cipriani had actually been using a pocket compass to take bearings. Having sailed the Gilberts, it was obvious Earhart wasn't there. Therefore he must have cautiously accepted Cipriani's makeshift deductions had been reliable enough in pointing to the north. Yet all we can really be sure is that the message was local enough for Howland to detect it.

The Nauru messages never registered with Thompson, but the significance of local, unreadable messages the very first night cannot be minimized. Nor have they ever been explained.

Back in San Francisco, analysis was forming a very different theory. From a variety of source information (to be discussed later), the Navy's captain T.K. Johnson, George Putnam, and Gene Vidal believed that AE and Noonan had been on land for their first 2 nights and then drifted free. Thompson never considered this as an explanation for how a message could have come from the Gilberts and yet why the *Itasca* didn't find the adventurous duo later while cruising the same islands.

Admiral Murfin was right. All they had was conjecture. And at the center of it was Thompson's conjecture made possible by his gloss of major clues that pointed to the Electra being on land (briefly) in the Gilberts.

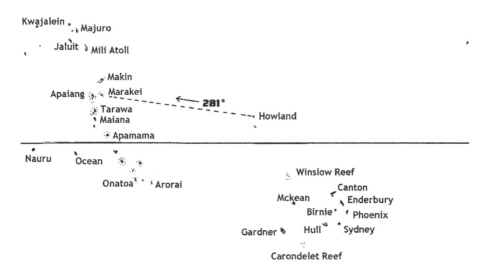

If 281 North Howland meant degrees instead of miles.

It was not just Thompson's redacted logic that swayed the Coast Guard and Navy to agree with him. It was that voice, that voice from nowhere. It never said it was in the Gilbert Islands. It said it was south of Howland. To Thompson's and the brass's satisfaction, Captain Friedell's cruise proved it could not be. Thompson's cruise of the Gilberts proved to him it hadn't been there either. Earhart didn't have the fuel to reach the Marshall Islands. Therefore what else could they conclude?: the "voices from nowhere" were hoaxers based in the continental USA.

However, taking the full dossier of radio communications, one has to classify the contents. Those Nauru messages heard the first night and heard locally in the Pacific were not readable, and the Morse message made no sense. These Nauru messages were picked up too soon and too locally to be something as un-likely as dramatic radio reenactments originating in the USA. This is the first class of messages. Contrariwise, those that came to direct and misdirect the search for Amelia Earhart were quite readable sometimes and became quite elaborate. These came a day after the disappearance. These were the ones heard throughout the USA. These are the second class of messages. It would be the worst and most negligent conjecture to lump them all together as from the same source.

It is therefore necessary to sum up some of the things these voices from nowhere had said. If genuine, they shed light on Amelia Earhart's fate and help lead us to her final resting place. If hoaxes, exposing them helps expose theories based on or con-tingent on them.

It is evident that if Pierson's and McMenamy's interpretation of what they heard (regarding latitude and longitude) is correct then they and Randolph/Freitas could not possibly have heard the same voice whether that voice was a radio program, prank-ster, or really Earhart. However, since there is so much interpre-tation in what Pierson/McMenamy reported, it remains prob-lematic whether they heard the same voice as the others. The Los Angeles radio duo had her drifting between the Gilberts and Howland whereas Randolph's contact distinctly said: "This is Amelia Earhart. Ship is on a reef south of the equator. Station KH9QQ." Mrs. Freitas' voice echoed same: "Plane on reef 200 miles directly south of Howland, both okay, one wing broken."

On the other hand, Nina Paxton's case stands distinctly on its own. Her account came to overshadow the others because it con-tains far more details of what this voice from nowhere said; and she wrote so many letters her account remains concise and influential to this day. Copies of letters she wrote to *Time* Magazine, Walter Winchell, GP Putnam, and Mary Bea Noonan, still exist, and in one case a copy of a second letter to Winchell is in the F.B.I. files.

To put her account in context, one has to know that Nina Paxton had put together piecemeal the gist of what she inattentively had heard. In her earliest letter (extant) to the editor of *Time* magazine (July 14, 1937), she wrote (disagreeing with the article's statement that Earhart's voice was weak): "Thinking Miss Earhart an amateur on a small island off the coast trying out a set I did not pay any attention after hearing the call letters, and first sentence. Turning the volume lower while I talked with someone in the room I could still hear Miss Earhart's voice distinctly." Not paying better attention Mrs. Paxton considered an "inexcusable blunder," but she clarified she hadn't known Amelia Earhart was down and being sought. In her letter to GP Putnam, she apologized: "Sadly regretting not listening more closely, because I could have heard each word distinctly."

As well-intentioned as she may have been, Mrs. Paxton only heard the first sentence clearly, and only after-the-fact she tried to reorganize the bits and pieces she had heard in the background into something that looked cohesive. But she was certainly convinced or had convinced herself this voice was really Amelia Earhart. She had tried to reach GP in San Francisco by cable in early July, and continued until finally getting a written reply from him on August 5.

Quite frankly, Mrs. Paxton had heard a talkative prankster. The first news reports of July 2 called Fred Noonan "Captain Noonan" by mistake. Statements from Walter McMenamy reinforced the idea, widely reported, that AE carried a hand-crank portable radio aboard when, in fact, she did not. Mrs. Paxton hears "Earhart" say "The Captain is with me; the Captain isn't right here with me; he is over near the plane." In calling him "Captain" and in stating he was by the plane and not with her, the voice from nowhere was inspired by inaccurate news reports and was implying it was speaking from a hand-crank radio. Both statements prove the voice is from a hoaxer.

Along with Paxton's account another account stands out suspiciously. Oakland based Charles McGill (also called Charles

Miguel) of station W6CHI had picked up a series of messages. Starting on Saturday the 3rd "the voice" placed AE floating 225 miles "northwestward" of Howland. Then July 6, the day he got major news coverage, he claims he heard the now-famous 281 North Howland message, adding Earhart saying: "Cannot hold out much longer. Drifting slowly northwest. We above water. Motor sinking in water. Very wet." Possibly next day he received another message indicating she was now on a coral reef southwest of an unknown island.

Summing up the main accounts thus:

McMenamy's and Pierson's voice from nowhere on July 3 was drifting between the Gilbert Islands and Howland Island (by interpretation).

McGill's voice from nowhere on the same Saturday July 3 had them drifting toward the Marshall Islands (by effect) and days later on a coral reef.

Mrs. Paxton's voice from nowhere already had them in the Marshall Islands on day one (July 3), on a reef near Mili Atoll (Mulgrave), 1,000 miles north of the equator.

Dana Randolph's voice from nowhere on July 4 was on a reef south of the equator, as was Mrs. Frank (Philomena) Freitas' voice from nowhere on July 8.

McGill's voice from nowhere was the most malleable. It comingled with the others, having her drifting and then finding a coral reef.

The only logical deduction is there was more than one voice from nowhere. Mrs. Paxton heard a loquacious East Coast crank, who said impossible things. A few cranks had AE drifting at sea. Another woman, heard vaguely in the western states, the one who was but a brief interrupted garble, spoke of a sandbank south of Howland Island— the fabled Winslow Reef which was never found.

Because information swung back and forth like a pendulum, each commanding officer had to swing with it, scouring wide locations of sea to then steam flank for islands to chase yet another message. The pendulum never came back to rest in equilibrium— meaning that some reports might have been authentic, some false. All officers came to believe *all* the messages were false. Thompson put an edge in his report: "Amateurs reported several messages, all probably criminally false transmissions."

Thompson's conclusion was basic deduction, and he essentially spoke for all. "If Earhart was down and sending messages, the guards maintained by Itasca, Swan, Samoa, Howland, Colorado, Baker, plane 62C, Wailupe, Pan American, San Francisco Radio, Honolulu Coast Guard Radio, and British stations in Gilbert Islands should have intercepted legitimate Earhart traffic, whereas the only interceptions were by amateurs, with the exception of one Wailupe interception."

In essence, the baby went out with the bathwater because of a very narrow view. Basing Earhart's ultimate fate on the existence of post-loss radio signals or *lack thereof* is a fatal presumption. The fine captains of the Navy and Coast Guard made this presumption, and many have followed in their wake. The truth is Amelia Earhart and Fred Noonan could have survived and yet were unable to send *any* post-loss radio messages.

Unaware of the Nauru radio reception that very first night, there was little reason for the Navy to challenge Thompson's summation. He concluded that it was very doubtful Earhart sent any signals after 8:46 a.m. local time July 2, 1937. He believed she went down apparently without even sending a Mayday. The Electra sank with a rush from the flooding of the empty gas tanks, with both Fred and Amelia still inside.

This is what was reported in the newspapers to the world on July 19, 1937, when the search was terminated. So this has become the accepted canon today.

Chapter 9

The Endless Horizon

The first step of any trek is always the easiest step. In the search for Amelia Earhart, it is to stand upon the beach at Howland Island and contemplate the endless horizon of the whispering sea. Gulls mew. Breakers rumble. Now as then one accepts what seems easiest— the meaning of an empty ocean.

"Crash and Sink" was begun by Commander Warner K. Thompson and essentially accepted to be the official conclusion by default. Yet Crash and Sink actually has the least evidence of any of the theories that have since been put forward to explain Amelia Earhart's fate. This is not because the sea wipes out all evidence. The theory relies on only a few radio messages Earhart sent and the rest is interpretation based on an empty ocean. Not even the content of the messages is presented as important. It is only that their signal strength was stronger. Thus she was close to Howland Island. The search found nothing. The empty ocean has spoken.

Those who follow in Thompson's path did not know that he

had another, and very unstable, reason for believing Earhart could not have survived. He believed she had cracked-up in the cockpit. By implication, he didn't believe that in such an hysteric state Earhart could pull off a ditching properly. "Toward the end Earhart spoke so rapidly as to be almost incoherent." Also, "Earhart's last message was hurried, frantic and apparently not complete."

Like all other contemporaries, Thompson believed in the public image of Amelia Earhart as the world's foremost aviatrix. Therefore something else had to explain what appeared to be outright incompetence on her part. Hysteria seemed to fit. Throughout his written report Thompson never outright says Earhart cracked-up, but the implication is always there that everything was her fault.

From the very beginning Thompson was expecting a lot of heat from his superiors, and for this reason the reader of his report must view it with caution. It is a shallow and sometimes contradictory account in which he is remarkably passive as to his involvement. He glosses that he is the one who refused to take aboard the expert radio technicians. He merely asserts his own radiomen were good enough. Yet Frank Cipriani apparently used a pocket compass to obtain bearings— something that belies the concept of expertise. Experts would also have questioned why 7.5 megs was being used for a homing frequency, and it seems if he had bothered to consult his own radiomen they would have questioned it as well. Aside from being blatantly outside of her bandwidth, it was not a viable frequency for homing anyway. It is clear from Bellarts urging AE to use 500 kcs that he knew 7.5 megacycles was unreliable for the task at hand.

Despite what others had told Thompson of her homing bandwidth spectrum (200 to 1500 and 2400 to 4800 kcs) he had acquiesced to Earhart's request of 7.5 megs for the homing frequency. He never questioned it, and if he had consulted his radiomen his attitude must have been a mere bagatelle. But now in his report he dogmatically asserts it was outside her bandwidth. "The signals which Earhart acknowledged were transmitted on 7500. Her direction finder loop could not handle this frequency. It is possible she was referring to other signals." He implies she should have switched to 500 kcs to home-in on their beacon on that frequency. Then he exaggerates: "Earhart knew that *Itasca* could give her accurate bearings on 500 and yet never transmitted on 500 in order for *Itasca* to assist her. *Itasca* had continuous direction finder watch on 500 from 7:25 a.m. on."

Earhart knew no such thing. Many frequencies for *calibration* had been mentioned within the various cablegrams going back and forth. At last Thompson and Earhart had agreed to the simple and ostensibly foolproof plan of sending homing signal **A** on 7.5 megs and voice on 3105 kcs, the standard nighttime frequency. In his report, he had already expressed his suspicion Earhart had radio receiver trouble. Therefore how could she possibly respond to Bellarts telling her to switch to 500 kcs?

Thompson's verbal report had stunned his boss, Henry Morgenthau. He had squarely blamed Earhart for disregarding every instruction given her. But in his written report, from which the above quotes are taken, he constrained himself and somewhat graciously wrote that they didn't know Earhart's side of the story, so that to an extent judgment had to be reserved.

Much has been uncovered since Thompson's report. To an extent it does give Earhart's side of the story. At the time he was venting himself, Thompson didn't know that Earhart couldn't transmit on 500 kcs. She had dumped the necessary equipment to do so at Miami because it was essentially useless weight to her. There was no way for her to send a signal to the *Itasca* for them to take a bearing. Earhart wasn't being incompetent by not getting a minimum on their signal. She had no way of knowing that her Bendix radio could not receive on 7.5 megs. The frequency was indeed stenciled thereon as one of 5 channels, but that particular channel had not been set up on her radio. Harry Manning had been the one schooled in the use of the Bendix. Yet he apparently never told her about it. When he dropped out, Earhart had no way of knowing it was a useless frequency.

As for Thompson's suspicion Earhart's receiver wasn't working, an explanation can be found in footage of Earhart's takeoff from Lae, New Guinea. Burdened with an 1100 gallon fuel load, the Electra twisted and turned as she brought it around in line with the runway. On the bottom of the plane's fuselage was the radio receiving antenna. Examining the footage anew in July 1995, Jeff Glickman of PHOTEK noticed the sudden burst of smoke or dust under the fuselage as the Electra bounced down the grass runway. An enhancement of a still-frame does not show the receiving antenna and its bases. Most likely the antenna, strung taut, had snapped and whipped the ground with deadly force, striking up that cloud of dust. This finally explains why Earhart could never hear the *Itasca* on 3105 kilocycles.

The above, of course, conjures images of malevolent Fate as the hunter. Homing signals were no good on her main channel of 7.5 megs. It was impossible for her and *Itasca* to establish two-way voice communication so as to be able to rectify the current dilemma. As for picking up *Itasca's* signal just once, on whatever channel this was, this remains a tantalizing mystery.

As for Earhart being hysterical, there is also mitigating information. Leo Bellarts was certain that Earhart was over-modulated. Interestingly enough, Harry Barnes, the operator at Nauru Radio, would also state that the voice issuing those intriguing post-loss messages was also over-modulated. Shortly, this will be reintroduced as a vital clue that leads us onward.

Put together the above clues do make Earhart look less inept and/or hysterical. There is little reason to believe she could not pull off a ditching successfully.

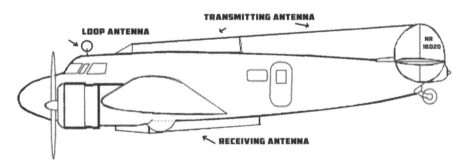

The Electra in profile. Homing signals would have been received up forward on the loop antenna. The transmitting antenna was also on top. Her lack of being able to receive supports the theory her receiving antenna, the only one on the bottom, snapped off on takeoff from Lae.

Internationally acclaimed pilot Elgen Long would become a lifelong champion of the Crash and Sink theory. His unwavering stance rated him a segment on the popular TV series *In Search of* in 1976 dealing with respective theories on Amelia Earhart's fate. His theory finally found written form in 1999 with his own book *Amelia Earhart: Mystery Solved.*

He has, of course, the exact same conclusion as Warner Thompson. However, he augments this simple fact with layers of false statements and erred exposition about the radio setup. To the uninformed reader it is not apparent he has no other evidence for Crash and Sink than Thompson had. Thompson's evidence was, of course, merely the stronger signal strength of her last few radio messages, indicating she was close to Howland Island when she vanished.

To explain the lack of two-way communication, Long's laborious presentation has the sole purpose of blaming the *Itasca.* Radio mishandling is a necessary accusation because he does not even touch upon the likelihood the Electra's receiving antenna had snapped off at Lae. Therefore he looks for explanations elsewhere to account for the lack of two-way communication on 3105 kilocycles. To do so he must invent radio error that simply did not exist.

One of his examples surrounds *Itasca*'s powerful 200 watt radio transmitter. Long reminds his readers that they put a Tare Ten Transmitter on 3105 kilocycles, so they could use it for voice. According to Long, a Tare-10 worked between 2000 and 3000 kilocycles, so the *Itasca* was stretching its capabilities a bit by putting it on 3105. This greatly reduced the ship's 200 watt transmitter's power to less than 100 watts and its daytime range on that frequency to *under* 300 miles.

Asserting this limited radio range as fact, he states erroneously that the *Itasca* only once sent a voice message on 3105 kcs "during the entire two and a half hours that Earhart was in range. . ." He says this was at 7:30 a.m. and that Bellarts remained on air for only one minute. This assertion completely overlooks that Bellarts was also sending the **A** on 3105 during the entire morning, switching back and forth from 7.5 megs to 3105 kcs and sending the homing signals on both frequencies for a few minutes at a time. Even by Long's estimations, we must conclude Earhart was in range for a couple of hours and should have heard the **A** on 3105 if she was receiving on it at all.

Long's explanation is to claim Earhart was too busy to listen except at the proscribed times. Yet the log shows that Bellarts was faithful to transmit at the hour and half hour. However, Long blames him for sending too much in code rather than voice. This is a spurious argument. Earhart could not read code well, but she could have heard it beeping over 3105. She never acknowledged any signal except toward the end, and *Itasca* wasn't sure on what frequency.

Long also asserts that Earhart failed to compensate for a half hour time change when crossing zones (probably true). This meant that when Earhart said "on the hour" it was really *Itasca's* half hour. Because this half hour confusion is reflected in some messages, Long writes: "If Earhart had listened on the hour GCT for the *Itasca* to send her a radio bearing on 3105, she would have heard nothing." This is an incredibly vacuous statement. So what if her clock read on the hour and *Itasca's* clock read on the half hour? Half hour and hour transmissions were identical. She would have heard the homing transmission on 3105 kcs *if* her receiver was working.

At 6:45 a.m. (6:15 a.m. by her clock) she had asked for a bearing in half an hour. Long believes she had meant "on the half hour"— *i.e.* only 15 minutes away. "Again, the radiomen interpreted that Earhart wanted a call in a half hour instead of 'on the half hour.'" Long uses this to propose that Bellarts stepped on her 7:15 a.m. call time by sending her the message he believed she had requested at 6:45 a.m. This was preventing her from communicating to him on her call time while now definitely in range.

This argument is really immaterial, since *Itasca* was transmitting on 3105 kcs continuously between 7:05 a.m. and 7:16 a.m. At any time during that period she should have been able to pick up their **AAA**s on 3105, *if* her antenna was intact. At 7:18 a.m. Bellarts tells her that they cannot take a bearing on 3105 "very good." He then asks her to send on 500 kcs. He asks her if she wished to take a bearing on them. Long writes that he called her at precisely 7:15 a.m. and stepped on her time to call in. This is not true.

Long is blatantly false about other radio reports. He says as soon as the *Itasca's* radiomen knew she was in flight they "started sending the weather reports by CW (code) on 7500 kilocycles [7.5 megs] at 25 and 55 minutes after the hour." This is not true.

Itasca also sent the messages via 3105 kilocycles since the early morning (at least by 2 .a.m.) His constant omission of the extent 3105 kcs was used seems his attempt to put more blame on *Itasca* for radio mishandling than the possibility Earhart's antenna had blown off at Lae and she was incapable of receiving messages.

Long's summation is grossly in error: "It was indeed tragic that the *Itasca* radiomen did not know that neither Earhart nor Noonan could understand Morse code. That simple misunderstanding negated over 90 percent of the *Itasca*'s efforts to establish two-way radio communications. In addition, because the *Itasca* was using code exclusively when transmitting on 500 and 7500 kilocycles, over 90 percent of the ship's total transmission time was of no value to Earhart."

This is stunningly wrong. Since the earliest morning hours, *Itasca* was using 3105 kcs. for "phone" and continuing to do so up to the end. The radio log plainly enters that each time the code **A** was sent on 7.5 megs it was sent by key as well on 3105. She could read **A** in Morse, so it would not have been spurious code to her. And there were a number of attempts to contact her by phone on 3105. She simply was not receiving either voice or key on 3105.

And as for the Morse messages being of no use on 500 kcs, this is not true either. True, she could not read a long message quickly enough, but she supposedly could home-in on the Morse bleeps on her loop antenna (direction finder). She could not transmit on 500 but she could receive on it. As we know, some signal *did* come in, at least once, on her homing loop antenna, channel unknown.

Long then enters the cockpit with her: "Earhart was busy running the engines, managing the fuel, flying the airplane, looking for the island, conferring with Noonan, and making decisions. She put on the headphones to listen only a few minutes out of each hour. Though it had been repeated in message after message that Earhart transmitted at one time and received at another, this was never understood by the men of the *Itasca*."

This is so false it naturally raises cynicism. Cynicism before the fact is blindsiding; after the fact it is called experience. My experience with some authors has shown me how their publishers at times ask an author to pad their book with information that is far outside their expertise because otherwise their thesis simply is not long enough. Long's approach to the Earhart subject was very narrow. One has to note that no one can devote their life to staring at a blank square of ocean. This is essentially all those who believe in Crash and Sink have. I must assume the publisher asked Long to bulk up a thin thesis with dramatic information on the flight, and it was only at this time that he studied actual historical documents related to the case.

For, in truth, Earhart would not have been excessively busy in the cockpit. In her own notes (mailed back to GP), there is preserved this entrance, written while flying over the Bahamas. "I certainly have a sissy trip. The Sperry Gyro Pilot does much of the flying and Noonan navigates."

Moreover, the men of the *Itasca* knew perfectly well her call-in and receiving times. Every page of the log underscores that.

Long's knowledge of the radio transcript is very poor and his logic at interpreting what he asserts is contradictory.

With equal and questionable minutiae, Long laboriously details fuel consumption and evaporation, but unlike with his dissertation on the radio setup it cannot be verified.[8] As known "facts" *Lexington*'s air group calculated the Electra's fuel endurance. "With optimum carburetor adjustment" in still air, its range was 3,120 nautical miles "or an endurance of 24 hours at 45.8 gallons per hour." From Burbank (through AE's secretary Margot DeCarie), Paul Mantz said the Electra ate 42 gallons per hour and could adjust to 30 gallons per hour. Obviously, no one knows what Earhart's exact fuel adjustment was. The idea she had said "half an hour gas remaining" is ludicrous. One and a half hours later she is still flying and communicating. She probably had said "gas running low" as Bellarts initially recorded. Burning 45 gallons an hour, what constituted gas running low to her gauge? With (for argument's sake) 150 gallons remaining, gas was indeed running low, but it still gave her a 400 mile radius.

During her Pacific flight in January 1935, she had said over her radio "I am getting tired of this fog;" only "I am getting

---

[8] All we really know is that San Francisco Coast Guard Division informed the searchers: "Lae verifies Earhart took off Lae with 1100 gallons gas. Estimated flight time 24 to 30 hours." A headwind was believed to be stronger than estimated.

tired" was heard, and Oakland had a medical team standing by for when she arrived. How much did *Itasca* actually hear of her gas estimate? Four and a half hours? Two and a half hours?

With both his fuel and radio expositions, Long's ultimate goal is to place Earhart close to Howland Island when she switched to 6210 kilocycles. He believes silence followed because she was overwhelmed, ran out of fuel, crashed and sank quickly. Same, just the same, as Thompson and the canon.

Despite Long's intent, ironically he cannot see that he actually made a case for Earhart *not* being close to Howland. All of his computations are based on the Electra's receiving antenna still being in place. If he is correct about this, and Jeff Glickman of PHOTEK is wrong, then *Itasca*'s inability to reach Earhart means she was much further away. The Tare Ten did not affect *Itasca*'s ability to receive Earhart's messages on 3105 kilocycles. Yet in reception these too were only "fairly good" in the last hour of contact. To sum it up: it means that Earhart's lack of receiving *Itasca*'s voice messages, reduced in range as they were by the Tare-10, indicate she was still a few hundred miles from Howland when she finally broke off and switched to 6210 kcs. Coincidently, it is only after she switched to the shorter range frequency that she is never heard from again.

"It could have been they were too damn far away to be heard," Paul Mantz had once said. "And 6210 doesn't have a fraction of the range of 3105. Signals on 3105 at night can skip thousands of miles across the ocean, but 6210 is usually good for just a couple of hundred miles."

To this context can be added another tidbit of evidence — the time zone discrepancy. USCGC *Itasca* was on the 11+30 hour GMT zone. Earhart apparently never compensated for the 30 minutes as she advanced through the changing time zones. Thus her clock always read 30 minutes less than *Itasca*'s. When at 6:15 a.m. (by their clock) she asked for the bearing on the hour, her clock had read 5:45 a.m. and she meant in 15 minutes at 6 a.m. When at 7:58 a.m. (by *Itasca*'s clock) she asked for the bearing on the half hour, her clock read 7:28 a.m. and she meant in 2 minutes at 7:30 a.m. Therefore at 7:42 a.m. (by *Itasca*'s clock) when she had said "We must be on you but cannot see you" her clock read 7:12 a.m. With an 18 hour flight time projected at

Lae, she clearly believed she was essentially on time. Yet with the updated weather studies revealing stronger headwinds, we know today it is impossible she could have been on time at Howland Island. She, in fact, must have been a couple of hundred miles short of the island at this time.

Signal Strength 5 is good to very good, but if she was on them they should have been hearing her better than that, and they should have been picking her up far more clearly than they had been for quite a while. Radio signal strength reception, the 30 minute time zone error, and stronger headwinds, support the theory that Earhart was much further west of Howland. In short (for here anyway), she was in fuel range to break off and head back to the Gilbert Islands.

There is every reason to consider Earhart abandoned trying to find Howland. She had not been getting any response from the *Itasca*. She only once had heard them, and how clearly we do not know. She may have come to believe she was hell and gone from Howland and barely within radio range. She was receiving no homing signals worth anything. In such circumstances, from her perspective, it was reasonable to abandon Howland. If Fred objected, she wouldn't be put off. She had overruled him before.

The lack of *Itasca* hearing a radio Mayday, plus the window of error on how much gas was truly left, would open a door that many have walked through in their search for Amelia Earhart. It remains open to this day. We too must now walk through it. In doing so, we must confront what the first biographers immediately encountered.

Chapter 10

Silence and Conspiracy of Silence

Two lasting epilogues were placed on Amelia Earhart's life. One of the moneymaking facets of the flight was a book. With AE having dutifully mailed off most of her jottings and ruminations, George Putnam had in-hand the ability to finish writing and editing *Last Flight*, which he published posthumously in 1937 in her name. In addition, he wrote the sentimental story of her life, *Soaring Wings*, which came out in 1939. This was the year that saw AE archived, to put it coldly but not inaccurately. GP had her declared legally dead in January, long before the statutory time of 7 years. A few months later he remarried.

After *Soaring Wings* there was silence. With the fate of having drowned, Amelia Earhart faded from the public mind.

The earth-shattering events of World War II consumed society. In the bleak reality of the postwar atomic world there was no rebirth for such a tomboy image and zest for *The Fun of It*. We had entered an era of jet pilots and rockets into orbit and the potential of sudden atomic destruction. She, Charles Lindbergh, Wiley Post, Will Rogers, Admiral Byrd, belonged to a dated period in which we fancied safaris might encounter Tarzan, or that dinosaurs might still exist on an isolated escarpment in South America. It was the adventurous and exotic world of Rice Boroughs novelettes, and these dauntless luminaries were its real-life incarnation. Their entire age— the age of "firsts"— seemed archaic. It was their world that was blown away, not their reputations. The stunning exponential progress in response to the war was a hard tonic that by comparison had made Earhart's far more elegant and adventurous era look like fizzy lemonade.

To brutally sum it up, the cachet of "firsts," in which she had carved her name, has no memorial value. But mystery does. . . and mystery lingers and curiosity therewith endures.

It is the mystery of her disappearance rather than a recital of past glory that resurrected her name. During the war it was very brief and inspired by the 1943 movie *Flight For Freedom* starring Rosalind Russell as "Tonie Carter," famed aviatrix— a very thinly disguised Amelia Earhart.

According to the movie plot, on her world flight Carter is asked to intentionally ditch in the restricted Pacific island area held by Japan. The purpose: feign she has vanished. Her world fame would demand that the US Navy be allowed to search the area, even the mandated Japanese islands. The Navy could then assess any war fortifications the Japanese were building. The future of the country may depend on the success of the mission.

But— there is always a *but* in such a Hollywood scheme— but the Japanese discover the guile at Lae, New Guinea. They intend to thwart it by picking her up and rescuing her immediately. Thus they look like heroes and the US Navy can't come and do its critical reconnaissance of their mandated islands. Yet— there is always such a trope conjunction in a Hollywood scheme— yet Carter discovers that the Japanese have learned the real reason for this leg of her world flight. So in true Hollywood heroine style she sacrifices her life by crashing headlong into the sea in the designated area, thus vanishing at sea and preventing the Japanese from finding her and thwarting the Navy plan to search for her in the Japanese mandated islands.

Two days before the film premiered, promotional publicity

implied a real life version of this cinematic drama. Marion Brittain, President of the Georgia School of Technology, had been one of the guests aboard the battleship *Colorado* when it was diverted from its ROTC cruise to search for Earhart. In a San Francisco *Chronicle* article on April 13, 1943, he was quoted as saying: "We discussed the Japanese Mandated Islands and the rumors that the U.S. Government had sent person after person to take a look-see, trying to discover whether or not the Japs were illegally fortifying their possessions. We got a very definite feeling that Amelia Earhart had some sort of understanding with officials of the government that the last part of her flight around-the-world would be over those Japanese islands."

A year later in March 1944 a brief story was posted from the Marshall Islands by Associated Press stringer Gene Burns. It spoke of the rumors that an American woman flier had come down in the Marshall Islands before the war and subsequently had been taken to Japan. It seemed there was some thin justification to Marion Brittain's theorizing of the year before despite its obvious use to promote the fiction plot of a Hollywood film.

One would imagine such reports should cause much anticipation after the war's end. Yet they really didn't take hold with a public bereaved by the atrocities of the war. There were no published stories confirming Earhart had been in Japan or had ever been in a Japanese POW camp.

Partially inspired by Burns' news report, Amy Otis Earhart pled with the US Government through an AP dispatch on July 25, 1949. She asked the government to do something with Japan to determine the fate of her daughter. "Amelia told me many things. But there were some things she couldn't tell me. I am convinced she was on some sort of government mission, probably on verbal orders." Again, it didn't seem to capture the interest of the public.

Then there's the 20-year-turnaround. It is a pattern that perhaps antique and collectible dealers are more familiar with, though publicists and marketing people also uncovered the pattern. It seems every 20 years we humans wax nostalgic for the period 20 years ago. It is especially powerful at 30 years of age, when one awakens to the fact childhood was 20 years ago— a huge span of time at that age. Every 20 years fashions seem reborn in a diluted way— the 1970s' yearning for the "idyllic" 1950s, the 1980s' fashion trends reflecting to some extent the 1960s, the 1990s' obsession with the 1970s, making everything collectible from Star Wars toys to Disco memorabilia.

There are many more examples, but of importance here is one of the most obvious: the 1960s' nostalgia for World War II. Aside from inspiring dozens of movies, there was an interest in all things about this glorious period of American victory.

Nostalgia about the 1930/1940s had placed Amelia Earhart's era toward the front of the collective mind. It was partly this fact that had set Captain Paul Briand, a US Air Force Academy English teacher, to write the first independent biography of her life. Ironically, however, Briand had felt he was not always welcomed by those who had been AE's closest friends and associates. They were polite, but reticent. Except for reinforcing her public image, none were very keen to talk about her life.

The result of Briand's effort was *Daughter of the Sky*. It was published in 1960, and the nostalgic times and seasons caused his work to be well-received. It was also a glorifying look at Earhart. Briand wrote of her as would an enamored schoolboy. Personally, however, he was bothered by the strange reticence that had greeted him in the days of his research. There was some "conspiracy of silence" within Earhart's closest surviving friends and family. He made no reference to it in his book. Rather, he would stun his readers with a smash ending.

Not long before the book's national release, the nation heard the shocking story. On May 27, 1960, the *San Mateo Times* broke the news.

SAN MATEAN SAYS JAPANESE
EXECUTED AMELIA EARHART

The witness was Josephine Blanco Akiyama. As an 11 year old girl on the island of Saipan she had been a witness to a sudden and tragic event: a plane had crash-landed in the harbor near Garapan, the island's capital. She was pedaling down on her bike that day to take lunch to her brother-in-law José Matsumoto when she saw Japanese soldiers gathered around the two survivors. She was told they were American pilots and one was a woman. From a distance she was able to get a glimpse of them. They looked tired and thin. Then they were marched off into the surrounding jungle. Then she heard the volley gunfire of a firing squad. She was sure this was before the war.

Akiyama had moved to America with her husband, Maximo Akiyama, and now lived in San Mateo in the San Francisco Bay Area. Her story had gotten around locally and finally the *Times* did the article on it.

It swept the nation.

It wasn't long before San Francisco CBS radio journalist Fred Goerner visited her to do a follow-up story. In interviewing her, he discovered that she had first told the story in 1945. She was then a dental assistant on Saipan helping an American Navy dentist named Sheft. Goerner also discovered that Captain Briand had been to talk to her already, even before the publication of her story. He had asked her not to talk about it publically. But her attorney, a locally respected barrister, William Penaluna by name, had told her to talk about it anyway.

When Briand's *Daughter of the Sky* came out, the glorifying biography's end seemed hastily set in place. Its crescendo was Earhart and Noonan being executed by the Japanese on Saipan. "When they survived the crash landing in Tanapag Harbor only to be taken as spies, their joy must have turned to inexplicable bitterness: they had been saved not for life, but for death before a Japanese firing squad. . . Yet as she had so often before, Amelia Earhart must have met this challenge with stubborn self-control and resolute courage. For here at last was her unmistakable, but irrefutable, fate." He declared them the first victims of World War II.

While the idea that Earhart had been on a secret spy mission escalated throughout America, Goerner was in action verifying Akiyama's story. He discovered Dr. Casimir Sheft in Passaic, New Jersey. He remembered Akiyama telling the same story in 1945. Goerner soon spoke to Paul Mantz. Here he uncovered inferences that Earhart had been up to more than just an 'round-the-world stunt flight. Mantz declared that he had put more fuel tanks aboard and her Electra really had well over a 4,000 mile range, far more than the 2,556 miles from Lae to Howland.

Mantz initially whetted Goerner's curiosity with the possibility that Noonan could have gotten lost and they accidently flew to Saipan, but the CBS reporter continued to dig. Simply getting lost seemed unlikely, for he too had uncovered the same "conspiracy of silence" that Briand had uncovered. It was only logical now to assume the "conspiracy of silence" had something to do with a secret and still potentially controversial mission.

Meanwhile the nation's newspapers were trying to find more Earhart stories of a similar vein. It wasn't long before they reported on the existence of "Operation Earhart," an unofficial Air Force project composed of Majors Joe Gervais and Bob Dinger, both stationed nearby to Saipan on Okinawa.

Fred Goerner felt CBS was going to be aced to any investigation on Saipan since military men like Gervais and Dinger could far more easily get to the restricted island. (Saipan was under US military jurisdiction.) But Goerner discovered he had little to worry about. His KCBS radio segments (from his initial investigation) had been a huge success. He was surprised at how easy it was to get CBS to fund an investigative trip to Saipan. As a journalist he was able to get past the red tape that protected the island from outside visitors. He would go with Maximo Akiyama, Josephine's husband, as his interpreter. This began his 6 year investigation. The culmination would be his runaway bestseller in 1966: *The Search for Amelia Earhart.* Her penciled image on the cover would be surrounded by a huge question mark. The evidence he uncovered and the questions he asked led America to believe Earhart had been on a secret spy mission and that she had indeed been captured by the Japanese but *not* executed.

Paul Briand also continued to pick up clues Earhart had survived as a Japanese prisoner. In 1967, during the glut of national interest in Goerner's bestseller, Briand wrote to Joe Gervais:

> Let me say this about all my research for *Daughter of the Sky* and my conversations since. The closer you get to friends and family of Amelia Earhart, the more you feel a conspiracy of silence. Do they all have something to hide, something so big or embarrassing to the Earhart name and fame that they are reluctant to tell the truth? They are and were: Muriel Morrissey and her mother, Paul Mantz, Clyde Holly, the attorney, and Jacqueline Cochran. Is the truth so fantastic that the courts readily declared Amelia Earhart

and Fred Noonan legally dead long before the mandatory seven years?

In writing *Daughter of the Sky,* I proceeded from the understanding that Amelia Earhart was one of America's greatest heroines; indeed my heroine had no feet of clay. Could I be wrong? What did Amelia Earhart know of Tokyo Rose? There is evidence to indicate she was in Tokyo during the war, hearsay to be sure, but evidence nonetheless. Why did Jackie Cochran rush into Tokyo right after the war and before the occupation forces? Was it to find her old friend and bring her back to the States as quickly and quietly as possible? What did Major George Putnam of Intelligence overhear in monitoring Tokyo Rose programs in the CBI [China-Burma-Indonesia]theater? His own wife's voice? What is Holly afraid of if you think AE is still alive? And Fred Noonan?

Here, my friend, is where I'd like to dig.

Briand, now a Lt. Colonel, had written the above as a way of confiding in and encouraging a fellow Air Force officer to continue on with his own research. Briand's *Stars & Stripes* article in 1960, designed as a promo for his upcoming book, had basically set Gervais and Dinger in motion. Much had happened since then, and it is obvious Briand no longer believed the Akiyama story. Nor did Gervais. After Dinger had dropped out, he continued on his own quest to find the truth of Earhart's fate. The result was the explosive but very short-lived 1970 bestseller *Amelia Earhart Lives*; short-lived because it was taken off the shelves in 7 weeks under threat of lawsuit.

Newspaper zest to find stories about Earhart's fate in 1960 was such that a *San Diego Tribune* reporter uncovered Floyd Kilts. As a Coast Guardsman stationed on Gardner Island in 1946, he had been told that skeletal remains of a woman had been found on the island before the war. They were subsequently shipped off to the British Colonial head office on Suva, Fiji. He asserted these were believed to have been the remains of Amelia Earhart. The story didn't catch on and was quickly forgotten. It was too dull compared to the nation's new obsession with Earhart as a secret spy and then victim of the Japanese.

Close to 30 years later Kilts' story was uncovered again by Ric Gillespie, head of TIGHAR (The International Group For Historical Aircraft Recovery). It proved the starting point of

TIGHAR's continuing and much publicized search for Earhart's remains and the wreckage of her Electra on Gardner (Nikuma-roro) Island in the Phoenix Group.

The conspiracy of silence was not relevant to TIGHAR's approach, but it is necessary here for the reader to understand that insofar as the public is concerned all modern theories for Earhart's fate stem from 1960. The Josephine Akiyama story activated and influenced Briand, Goerner, and Gervais. It sired indirectly all the elaborate Spy and Die on Saipan theories, all of which assumed the "conspiracy of silence" was to protect compromising political events that still weighed on the scales of national interest.

We now enter the world of the most controversial theories. They are islands in the sky. They hover like a mirage over the ocean, never approachable but they nevertheless remain visible and alluring. In the chapters that follow we must tackle these theories and uncover the origins of the conspiracy of silence if we are ever to put reason back in place in the search for Amelia Earhart.

Part II

Islands in the Sky

Chapter 11

Bestselling Question Mark

Admitting he had a bad case of Earhart fever, Fred Goerner landed on Guam with Max Akiyama (as interpreter) in late June 1960 in preparation to get cleared to Saipan. The KCBS journalist was relieved to discover Majors Gervais and Dinger hadn't been cleared to enter Saipan. (Despite being military men, they were personnel without a need to be on the highly restricted island.) This left the field open for him and Max to be the first to question Saipanese natives. For Goerner this meant everything. Based on what Paul Mantz had told him, at this stage of his research he truly believed Earhart could have flown to Saipan.

According to Goerner, Mantz stated to him explicitly: "With the extra gas tanks I put aboard her plane, she had a range of well over 4,000 miles. She could have flown a good part of the way to Howland and still would have had enough fuel to make Saipan." Mantz had impressed Goerner, both by the fact he was a part of the famous flight's preparations and by his own daredevil confidence in flying. This would overwhelmingly influence Goerner's first visit to the island.

Both he and Max were led aboard a C-54 and flown the 115 miles north to Saipan. There the liaison officer, Commander Paul Bridwell, seemed skeptical. He admitted in the last couple of weeks they had heard of Akiyama's story from the news furor in America. He arranged for Goerner to have a meeting with several of the natives who had worked for the Japanese and were still alive. If anybody would know, they would.

On the surface, this seemed very gratuitous behavior on Bridwell and the Navy's part, but Goerner instinctively had suspicions of cover-up, an antiestablishment attitude so popular at the time in American culture.

Nevertheless, he went with Bridwell to talk to 6 Saipanese. Of the first two, he writes: "Their nervousness was apparent as Bridwell questioned them." Answers were short and simple in their heavy accents. Elias Sablan: "I do not know of such a thing." Vincente Galvan stuttered "No. . . no. . . wh-wh-white lady and man." A more formal response came from Juan Ada, who had been some sort of judge under Japanese rule. "To my knowledge, that did not happen." Another: "No American. No white lady on island." Another: "Sorry, I do not know of this."

Bridwell felt certain the CBS investigation should be over, but Goerner was only getting started. Over Bridwell's objection, he declined to stay with the Navy and wanted to stay in the town, with Maximo's relative José Matsumoto.

The best support Goerner received was from the Catholic priests. They would assist him in speaking to their parishioners. There would be no leading questions about a white woman or fliers. They would speak only about times before the war and ask if any white people had been on the island. "After talking with more than two hundred Saipanese, we found that the testimony of thirteen could be pieced together into a story that apparently supported the contention of Josephine Akiyama."

Goerner summarized these key witnesses: "A white woman and a man, Americans, and fliers according to what the Japanese had said, either came ashore or had been brought ashore at Tanapag Harbor sometime in 1937. The woman resembled a man, at least she was dressed as a man and had short hair. The man was injured; his head was bandaged. Under guard, they had been held at the dock area until a Japanese military car arrived from Garapan and took them away. . .The pair were next seen being taken into the Japanese military police headquarters . . . ostensibly for questioning. A Gregorio Sablan had been summoned to serve as interpreter. The interrogation had lasted several hours, and then the woman was taken to Garapan prison, the man to the Muchot Point military police barracks. The woman was held in the prison for only a few hours, then transferred back to the city and placed in a hotel the military police had taken over in 1934 to house political prisoners. None of the witnesses knew what had finally happened to the mysterious white people, although several felt that either one or both of them had been executed."

Questioning native divers Goerner learned that there were two twin-motor aircraft wrecks in the harbor. Along with the natives he dived and with their help retrieved some wreckage. He chipped off the coral from what looked like a generator, revealing the serial number NK 17999. Goerner quickly telegrammed Paul Mantz to see if this number had relevance to AE's plane.

Meanwhile a Navy technician was allowed to examine the artifact. He said it wasn't from a Japanese plane. Moreover, it was wired together—something done in the early days of flight because in those fledgling days strong vibrations would loosen the nuts and screws. It was indeed a generator. It could have been used in a Lockheed and was possibly a Leese-Nevil or a Bendix. Earhart had carried a Bendix. Witness stories were now coupled with tangible evidence from a non-Japanese plane wreck that shouldn't be in the harbor.

In a nutshell, this is the beginning of the entire Earhart Spy and Die on Saipan Theory. Fred Goerner was sufficiently impressed to send a message to CBS headquarters. The message sent CBS and eventually America into a frenzy. "Everything but a band was at San Francisco Airport to meet Max and me."

An excited press conference followed on July 1, 1960, almost to the day Earhart and Noonan had vanished 23 years before. At this conference Paul Mantz, true to Goerner's appraisal as a man with a keen "sense for publicity," turned up unexpected. He strutted through the crowd of reporters. "Hi, Fred, my boy. Got your cablegram about that generator number. Sorry I couldn't

get back to you while you were still on the island, but I've got fil-
ing cabinets full of records about AE's plane, and I haven't been
able to find the exact numbers yet."

It had the expected effect. He and the generator became the
focus. The press clamored for more pictures. They asked
Goerner to get in close with Mantz and examine the generator
for a photo shoot. Mantz straightened and turned. He faced the
throng of press. "Well, it looks exactly like the generator I put
aboard AE's plane."

Goerner admits he had dreaded this would happen. As the
flashbulbs burst their stark light, preserving forever a triumphant
Paul Mantz holding up the generator, Goerner realized that the
truly impressive part of their research—the 13 witness stories—
would be ignored. Newspaper headlines proclaimed the generator was believed to be Earhart's.

The nation went swooning.

But Bendix HQ soon came back with disappointing news.
The generator wasn't exactly like the one Mantz supposedly had
installed aboard the Electra. Minor parts were definitely Japanese made. It was a knock off! The press groaned. Mantz countered. But "the damage was done," wrote Goerner. "All the evidence had become symbolized by the generator, and the testimony of the thirteen Saipanese was discarded along with the
'wreckage'."

Joe Gervais and Bob Dinger's "Operation Earhart" was also
dealt a severe blow at this time. They had gotten huge news coverage when they had announced they had photographic evidence, plus the eyewitness accounts of *72 people* to the impris-
onment and execution of Amelia Earhart on Saipan. In addition,
they had found the gravesite. An Air Force Hearing in Japan had
uncovered that this claim had been grossly exaggerated. "Operation Earhart" only had a list of 72 Saipanese, attained from interviewing former Saipanese on Guam who could have information about a gravesite and execution.

The story of Earhart having been taken to Saipan, though
without any popularized evidence now, was still attractive to
CBS. Clues continued to come in. "When a story breaks as
widely as the one of July 1, 1960," wrote Goerner, "it touches the
lives of millions of people. Memories awaken; the attic of the

past is sorted; bits of information, ideas, attitudes, long endured feelings of guilt, all emerge and are sometimes drawn to a central point. I became such a point."

Principle among these witnesses was Tom Devine. He had been a technical sergeant with the 244th Army Postal Unit on Saipan in 1945. His letter to Goerner reached him on August 15, 1960.

Devine and his information would prove both interesting and frustrating for Goerner. Devine had claimed that a native woman had shown him and his mates a grave where two white people were buried who "came from the sky a long time ago." The graves were on the outside (unconsecrated ground) of a small cemetery. He had taken pictures of the general area back then, and gave them to Goerner.

Finding the gravesite would clinch the matter on a number of controversies. For example, the Japanese were offended by the claim Earhart and Noonan had been executed on Saipan. Zenshiro Hoshina, a retired Imperial Navy Captain, had been in charge of executions at the Naval Affairs Bureau. No such execution had ever happened on Saipan, he declared. Things had gotten so hot politically that the US State Department politely asked the Japanese to search their records. No records were found, they said. Robert M. Stanley, president of the Stanley Aviation Corp., had made a big stink in the newspapers. He had been on the *Lexington* as a junior officer in 1937 and partook in the search. He could show from the Navy reports that the signal strength of Earhart's last messages proved she was near Howland. There was no way she had flown to Saipan. Then "Francisco Galvan" came forward. He had been a feared local police sergeant on Saipan working for the Kempeitai—the Japanese secret police—both before and during the war. *Guam Daily* broke the story on November 14, 1960. Galvan had told them that a woman spy had indeed been executed. The woman executed was half Japanese and American, from Los Angeles.

None of this fazed Goerner. As far as he was concerned, Galvan was merely covering his own culpability by throwing a red herring out there. And Stanley's argument was the weakest of them all. The CBS journalist had already seen a deeper problem in AE's messages to the *Itasca*. Estimated flight time allowed

Earhart another 3 to 4 hours in flight after her last message. For Goerner, this left the door open to believe that she had the fuel to make a landfall somewhere. By leaving radio range this explained why the *Itasca* heard no more messages from her.

Based on the thirteen Saipanese witnesses' testimony, Goerner knew somehow Earhart had gotten to Saipan. He felt she and Noonan had been found by the Japanese and *taken* to Saipan. He now had a two-pronged approach. First, he had to probe into the whole idea there was a secret mission. This meant talking to people from long ago and going to Washington DC to pound on some very old memories. Second: dig up the bones and see who these mysterious fliers really were.

After a long battle between CBS and the Navy, Goerner was finally cleared for Saipan in late August 1961. Tom Devine was not cleared due to the fact he was not an accredited journalist. This critically hindered the mission, as a large part of Goerner's purpose was to locate the gravesite. In lieu of going, Devine sent him many pictures that showed the area as it was back in 1944.

With the padres' help again, Goerner spoke to a couple more Saipanese who had information. One was Matilda San Nicholas. She was just a kid in 1937, but she lived next door to the hotel that the Kempeitai used for their headquarters. For many months in 1937 and into 1938 she had seen a white woman at the hotel. The Japanese called her the "flier and spy." At Father Sylvan's questioning, she gave this description: "She was tall and very thin and she had not much hair for a woman; it was very short. . . .When I first saw her she was wearing a man's clothes, but they later gave her a woman's dress." Although she was well guarded at the hotel, they let her walk out in the yard. Because this woman could not speak their language, her contact was limited to a gentle smile.

One day she came out into the yard and looked sadder than usual and very sick. Mrs. San Nicholas gave her a piece of fruit. The lady smiled in return and "put her hand on my head in friendship." Then: "The next day one of the police came and got a black cloth from my father [town tailor] and had him make some paper flowers. The man said that the lady had died and they were going to bury her." Mrs. San Nicholas said the officer had said she had died of dysentery.

Goerner put 15 photos in front of her, all of different women. Only one was of Earhart. She picked Earhart's photo and said this was the woman at the Garapan hotel. He was convinced that Matilda San Nicholas had seen Earhart.

Another witness was Jose Pangelinan. His story was almost identical to Matilda San Nicholas' story, only that the man (Noonan) was held elsewhere. The woman had died of dysentery, he confirmed, but the Kempeitai had executed the man. The day after the woman died, the man had been beheaded by samurai sword. He didn't know the gravesite. Only the Japanese knew that location.

It was time to find the grave. Tom Devine's pictures clinched the location. The same cross and angel he photographed back in 1944 were still there. He also drew a map for Goerner based on his memory. Eventually, in company of Father Sylvan and various workers, they came across bones. These were carefully extracted from the earth and packaged into 7 cigar boxes.

Red tape required CBS and Goerner get the next of kin, in this case the next of supposed kin, to sign releases. He found Mary Bea Noonan was now a gracious and kind 60 year old woman, Mrs. Frederick Ireland. She stated there was an aura of mystery surrounding the last flight. Then afterward the official attitude in Washington had troubled her. "It was as if no one wanted ever again to hear the names Noonan and Earhart. No one was supposed to dispute the decision they were lost at sea."

Muriel Morrissey, Amelia's sister, was quite kind and friendly as well. After speaking with him in person, she too relented and signed the release. She was impressed by his level of investigation into the Saipan potential. "There have been so many stories, but for the first time, one sounds right." To his surprise, he also discovered that Amy Otis was still alive, 94 years old and upstairs in bed, beyond receiving guests. He asked what her opinions had been. "She feels there were things about the flight Amelia couldn't tell her. For many years she was sure my sister was a prisoner of the Japanese, but now she is resigned there will never be a final answer." . . . "Until this evening, Chief [her husband's nickname] and I believed Amelia and Noonan were lost at sea. That's what most people have accepted. Perhaps it was convenient and less painful to think so, but also there was some logic. The radio messages received at Howland from the plane seemed to indicate it had been close to the island at one point. A crash-landing on the ocean was more likely than capture by the Japanese." But in signing the release, Muriel made it plain to Goerner that she now had second thoughts. Saipan should be pursued.

When the bones landed at San Francisco on a Pan Am jet, thousands awaited. "These people came with the hope of witnessing a moment in history. Some wanted to see 'the bones' they had read and heard so much about. For them, titillation was the evening's order. Many there were there because Amelia had somehow been a symbol in their lives, and they wanted to pay their respects and feel once more the force of her personality. The scene was macabre, but dignity was present, too."

The day after the bones arrived to great news coverage, Goerner had a phone conversation with John Mahan. He had been a yeoman working with the senior US government officer at Majuro, the Marshall capital. "Amelia Earhart crash-landed somewhere between Majuro, Jaluit, and Ailinglapalap in the Marshalls." He told Goerner with certainty: "We knew that back in 1944."

The story originated with two brothers, Joe and Rudy Muller. "They told us the Japs picked up two American fliers, a man and woman, and brought them for a while into either Jaluit or Majuro, then took them to another island. They said it was 1937, and the Japs thought they were spies. According to Joe and Rudy, the Japs captured some of the equipment too."

From Mahan's tips, Goerner quickly found Lt. Eugene Bogan, Mahan's then-superior. He remembered the Muller brothers were interpreters, so they probably had heard the story, but Bogan said that all the information concerning Earhart he had heard came from an islander named Elieu. "He was the most trusted and respected of the Marshallese." About a week after setting up their administration, they were speaking about the Japanese administration and how secretive they had been. Elieu then asked Bogan if he had known about "the white woman flier who ran out of gas and landed between Jaluit and Ailinglapalap." Bogan declared to Goerner: "I nearly flipped."

Frustratingly, Elieu had not been an eyewitness. He had

heard the story from a local Japanese trader named Ajima with the trading company Nanyo Boeki Kaisha. She had been picked up by a fishing boat, Ajima had said. Bogan speculated she had probably been taken to Kwajalein or Saipan, since both were administrative headquarters.

The most surprising bit was that an AP stringer named Eugene Burns had been on the island and had heard them speaking about it. He filed a story which hit the news March 22, 1944, and Bogan still had a copy.[9]

Burns was now dead, but his widow lived across the SF Bay in Sausalito. Goerner spoke with her. She said he had spoken of Earhart many times and believed the Japanese had captured her.

Goerner was excited about the new Marshall Islands lead when Dr. Theodore McGown, the anthropologist examining the Saipan bones, delivered the bombshell. The bones represented a secondary interment of 4 islanders, mixed together. Although the Japanese government was delighted by the news, the US populace was crestfallen.

Goerner wrote: "The jibes and kidding tested my sense of humor and sometimes found it spent. I felt the fool many people thought me. For nearly two years, my personal hang up had been an old mystery, and as far as the public knew, I had twice tried and failed to solve it."

It would have ended here for Fred Goerner were it not for some intriguing information. One lead came from John Day, the recently retired VP of CBS News. While at the Democratic National Convention, he was approached by a man who told him a story. A man who did their audit had once worked on Earhart's plane. He said that more fuel tanks were installed along with belly cameras operated from the cockpit. If true, this underscored the basis of Goerner's spy theory for the flight. He quickly got in touch with the man. An air of concern was in this man's voice. He had sworn an oath. He was hesitant to divulge anything. Goerner was hooked again. He restarted his investigation.

Soon he met more people who had been involved in the last flight. He heard the same things as before—some aura of mys-

---

[9] Burns' story, referenced in the preceding chapter, obviously had little impact during the war. This was the first time Goerner had even heard such a story had been filed.

tery surrounded the flight's preparations.

One of the most significant contactees was AE's secretary, Margot DeCarie. She was certain more was afoot because Gene Vidal came to Burbank frequently and she used to pick him up and drive him around. "He made several trips during the period when the airplane was being rebuilt [after the crash in Hawaii]."

Goerner didn't think that was unusual, but she countered with direct questions; each ignited his latent suspicion about a government operation.

1. Do you really think Purdue bought that aircraft for vague experimentation?

2. If it was a publicity stunt, as it was written up, why did the government assign some of its top experts?

3. Why did Roosevelt build an airfield just for her?

4. Why did he spend 4 million dollars searching for "stunt fliers."

When asked, she believed absolutely that the Japanese captured Amelia. But as to where, her qualification is surprising. "All I can tell you is that it was within moderate range of Howland Island."

With the encouragement of Ross Game, editor of the Napa *Register*, Goerner believed it was time to head back to Saipan. They talked to more witnesses, trying to fill in the pieces of Goerner's growing thesis about a spy mission. Then on their return they stopped in the Marshalls. They were able to meet Elieu in person. Asking him only about two American fliers who disappeared around here prior to the war, he replied: "I know of only one flier, a woman."

From him they heard the same story Bogan had told. Elieu recalled the Japanese trader, Ajima, had said that an American woman flier came down near Jaluit and "that she was picked up by a Japanese ship." When asked about a man with this woman, Elieu said it was possible, but only a woman was mentioned. A woman flier was a big deal to the Japanese. All Ajima said was that she was a spy and taken by the Japanese. No one knew where. Ajima hadn't described the woman; just said "American woman."

One of the most positive effects of Goerner and Game's trip was that much of their film and recordings were used for a documentary on the Pacific War and what the battlefields look like 17 years later. As a result, John Pillsbury, Information Officer for the 12th Naval District, introduced Goerner to Chester W. Nimitz, former CINPAC himself—the commander of the Pacific Theater of the war.

Many people in Washington had mentioned Goerner's name, so at first introductions Nimitz knew who he was. Goerner asked him if there was anything he knew that could help in his search. Nimitz replied: "Not a great deal. I remember hearing during the war that some things that belonged to her had been found on one of the islands. I don't remember which one, and I didn't see the material." He believed that it had been sent through Joint Intelligence (G-2) at Pearl Harbor. When Goerner said that most people think he is crazy for not giving up, Nimitz responded with a smile and said: "You seem quite rational to me."

Goerner felt that Nimitz was encouraging him. When John Pillsbury retired, he approached Goerner at his retirement party. "I'm officially retired now, so I'm going to tell you a couple of things. You're on the right track with your Amelia Earhart investigation. Admiral Nimitz wants you to continue. And he says you're on to something that will stagger your imagination."

There's no way to play down such a comment, especially coming from the former CINCPAC. It clobbers the reader of Goerner's *The Search for Amelia Earhart* and helps set the tempo for the remainder of the book.

Nimitz's recollection that personal effects belonging to Earhart were found was corroborated in a sensational way by former Marine W.B. Jackson of Pampa, Texas. He told Goerner his story. Soon after landing in the Marshalls, three of his buddies found a suitcase in a room on Namur Island, Kwajalein Atoll. In the suitcase was a book entitled "10-year diary of Amelia Earhart." They turned it and the suitcase over to Intelligence (G-2).

By another stunning coincidence, Goerner was soon contacted by a Victor Maghokian, who had been a captain in the Marines at that time in the Marshalls. In February 1944, he had been ordered to find a Rudolph Miller (Muller) to act as an interpreter with the natives. They learned that in 1937 a man and woman flier had been on Kwajalein for a while and the Japanese took them to another island. He had heard that "a Marine" had found a diary and some belongings. (At re-questioning, Jackson vaguely remembered there was a Captain Maghokian, though Maghokian had never heard of Jackson).

In addition, there were Everett Henson and Billy Burks, ex-Marines who while serving in 1944 were seconded to dig up two graves on Saipan. Hensen told Goerner that their supervising officer, named Griswold from Intelligence, said the bodies were Earhart and Noonan. Burks confirmed that Hensen had indeed then told him.

This meant that for 20 years the Marine Corps or some office of the US Government had Earhart's remains and had not informed the next of kin. Why?

Was he finally on the path to discovering the thing that Nimitz said would blow his mind? Recalling these words, Goerner wrote: "There was something tremendous behind the disappearance of Amelia Earhart and Frederick Noonan in 1937."

The clincher, however, was a phone call from Chester Nimitz. "Now that you're going to Washington, Fred, I want to tell you Earhart and her navigator did go down in the Marshalls and were picked up by the Japanese." The source verification was General Harry Schmidt. He had commanded the Marines landing on Kwajalein in 1944. But even with Nimitz plaintive requests on the phone (while Goerner sat in), Schmidt said he just couldn't elaborate.

For Goerner, there could be only one explanation. Thus the I Spy and Die Theory on Saipan coalesced in his mind. Amelia Earhart and Fred Noonan were on a spy mission. The Electra had much more powerful engines than publicly reported, and a longer fuel range. They flew up from Lae to Truk and then over-flew the Marshall Islands, spying out new Japanese fortifications. She was approaching Howland from the northwest and thought she was close, but due to winds she was really a couple of hundred miles away. She flew along the sunline. Not finding Howland, she returned to the Gilberts. But being much further north, she actually ended up in the Marshall Islands. She ditched near Mili Atoll, where she was eventually picked up by the Japanese and taken to Kwajalein and thence to Saipan. Goerner concluded that the politics of the time, and the fact they were on a secret spy mission, prevented President Roosevelt

Fred Goerner's theory required the above flight track from Lae, New Guinea. The Japanese touted Truk as the "Gibraltar of the Pacific." As their main imperial naval base, it was essentially their Pearl Harbor.

from doing anything to recover them. The graveyard was probably impossible to find, and it didn't matter anymore. The Marines had dug up the bodies and they were probably hidden in an archive drawer in Washington D.C.

Now at the climax of his investigation, he and Ross Game filed a 12 foot long report on the newswires. Senator Ted Kuchel was ready to make a formal investigation. Admiral Nimitz had encouraged Goerner to go ahead with his book. "It will bring the justice that is deserved."

It had been a long search since 1960, and some of those who had helped and perhaps unintentionally hindered Goerner were gone, including Paul Mantz (who had died in a plane crash in 1965 while making *Flight of the Phoenix*). A few months later Nimitz suffered the stroke that took his life.

The Search for Amelia Earhart was a stunning bestseller over 1966-67. Fred Goerner became the first man of Earhart survival theories. His book laid the foundation for a cascade of Spy and Die on Saipan conspiracy theories that remain to this day. He remained in the pursuit until his death in 1994. He revised and altered some of his theory, but never gave up the basic premise. Bent on proving the crux of his theory, however, Goerner apparently minimized or omitted several facts that discredit some of his sources, and these facts will be introduced where they are most relevant.

First, we continue with the search of his one great rival: Joe Gervais. Their investigations paralleled each other, and yet despite their great rivalry one cannot stand independent of the other. Although Gervais came to a very different conclusion than Goerner, some of the facts he uncovered along the way shed considerable and sometimes unflattering light on the venerated CBS journalist's methodology.

Chapter 12

Hull and Gone

During his first visit to Saipan, Fred Goerner had breathed a sigh of relief when he was told that Joe Gervais and Bob Dinger—the "Operation Earhart" which had gleaned national news— hadn't been cleared to enter Saipan. What he didn't realize is that weeks before his arrival Gervais had been able to get to Guam, where he spoke to many native Saipanese who were now living there. In company of the police chief, Joe Quintanilla, he had the grand tour. Gervais had, in fact, been the first to interview natives and, unfortunately, plant seeds about Amelia Earhart having been captured by the Japanese.

Worse than that (in the sense of primary source integrity), we learn that Saipan was already aware of the Earhart story. Quintanilla had informed Gervais that the Naval Administration had commissioned a former mayor of Saipan, Elias Sablan, to conduct an investigation into the possibility Amelia Earhart had been on Saipan in 1937.

Obviously, Fred Goerner's interviews had not been the first, and any precautions he had taken with the priests cannot guarantee the witnesses were not leading their interrogators. Many, perhaps even most, knew who Amelia Earhart was by the time of Goerner's arrival in late June 1960.

This being the case, there is more integrity advantage in Gervais' interviews. Examining them may bear fruit for our present study. The eldest of the natives recalled a plane crash in the harbor and that the Japanese were upset by it, but none of the natives were allowed to get near it. Another, H. Tenario, admitted the Akiyama story was in the *Guam Daily* a month ago, but he remembered no such incident when he lived on Saipan in 1937. His wife vaguely recalled, but the crash supposedly happened off the Chico Naval Base, which was the most restricted area on Saipan. Natives would not have had details, and she didn't know if the incident truly had occurred. Akiyama's sister, Mrs. Bora, recalled Josephine talking about it, but she didn't pay too much attention to an 11 year old. Since it had to do with the military base, she didn't want her mentioning it. The Japanese were very suspicious of natives having military information.

Other natives had mentioned they had heard the plane clipped the treetops before it ditched in the harbor by the naval base, but Thomas Blas was a direct eyewitness. He recalled the air crash in detail, describing the plane as silver with no Japanese markings. The plane came to a rest on the beach, with only its left wing in the water at high tide. Both pilots wore khaki flying suits "like pilots wear."

Antonio Cepeda recalled the young woman who was billeted for a few months at the Hotel Kobayashi Royokan in the summer of 1937. She had short hair and wore a long khaki raincoat. He had heard she was arrested for spying. She took pictures with a hidden camera in a flying suit.

The natives gave the spy woman the nickname Tokyo Rosa. This had nothing to do with the wartime propaganda broadcaster. The natives referred to "American spy lady" as Tokyo Rosa already in 1937.

Another Saipan native was Carlos Palacious. He basically had the same story. He saw this American woman only twice over a few months period. She was staying at the hotel, had short hair which was reddish brown. He didn't know how she got there. He recalled she was referred to as Tokyo Rosa, and she had been arrested because she took secret pictures.

One native, Pedro Cepeda, recalled seeing the "American spy lady" being escorted by "Zuse" Guerrero and Japanese officers. Jesus de Leon Guerrero was the real name of the infamous "Francisco Galvan" of Goerner's book. He had not just been a head detective, as Goerner had written; he had essentially been chief of police of Saipan under the Japanese. Guerrero told Pedro that she was a spy who took pictures from the front of a suit.

Some of the accounts above underscored Josephine Akiyama's story of a plane crash. Up-close witnesses, however, describe only pilots in flight uniforms (Earhart was wearing normal slacks and a checkered shirt. Noonan wore dark shirt and pants).

The spy lady really isn't connected with the flight as a pilot, only as a woman referred to as Tokyo Rosa who took secret pictures. No one knew what happened to the spy lady. They thought she had been taken to Japan.

Of the few Saipanese natives on Guam who had been insular police under the Japanese, none had heard of the incident . . . or it seemed they didn't want to talk.

However, one of the former guards at the prison, Ramon Cabrera, remembers the two pilots in khaki outfits. One had "much whiskers." The other was soft, smooth, a "strange looking American man, who was "smaller in height, thin body." They didn't like their food and didn't eat for the first few days. Then they finally started eating. They were fed the equivalent of a meal a day. They were kept in their cells but allowed to walk in the yard. When Gervais asked if one was a woman, Cabrera didn't understand. He insisted they were two pilots. He didn't know what had happened to them. Maybe they were deported or executed. "They were taken away."

Only two men, Ben Salas and Joaquin Seman, believed the two Americans were executed and buried, but they believed that probably only Zuse Guerrero knows all about it. They could, however, take Gervais to the Liyang cemetery on Saipan where they had been buried.

Out of 41 people interviewed, Gervais believed that only 15 of them (from which the sampling above is also gleaned) had stories that had relevance to his quest for Amelia Earhart. From our vantage here, they paint a very different picture than that which Fred Goerner would develop, though there is some over-lapping. The pilots from the crash, whoever they were, could have been two men. These pilots were associated with the plane crash near the highly restrictive Chico Naval Base. Tokyo Rosa just seemed to appear one day and was billeted for several months in the hotel where the secret police made their headquarters. The most valuable clue gleaned from these first interviews is to what extent the Japanese were *not* involved. It was the insular police, all Saipanese, under Zuse Guerrero.

In mid-December 1960 Joe Gervais, Bob Dinger, along with Joe Quintanilla, finally were able to access Saipan. This was now 5 months since Fred Goerner had been there.

Things had, of course, changed. The islanders had been talking. From what the natives had been saying, Commander Bridwell was open with the trio about his belief that Amelia Earhart and Fred Noonan had indeed been on Saipan, but that they hadn't crashed here. Bridwell had talked to a number of them, and he felt there was no evidence of a crash. From what they had told him, the duo had been brought here. There was also no evidence they were executed here.

The trio also met with Manuel Sablan, the Navy appointed Sheriff of Saipan. Together they went on interviews. The first person "Operation Earhart" spoke to was J.Y. Matsumoto, Josephine Akiyama's brother-in-law. This is where contradictions come into the scene. At first he denied such a crash. Then when somewhat crudely prodded by Sablan, he admitted it happened and a man and woman were taken by the Japanese. This was at a contrast to the accounts on Guam before the story had gained such international attention over the summer. The Saipanese on Guam had said the two pilots were men in flying suits.

Mrs. Blanco, Josephine's mother, recalled her daughter telling her. But she told her to keep quiet or she could get in trouble with the Japanese.

From there they went to discover who owned the Kobayashi Royokan, where Earhart supposedly had stayed. The owner was Antonio Cabrerra. He had lived on the main floor of the hotel at the time. "An American woman and an American man lived in the hotel about that time, and they were under surveillance by the Japanese." When asked, he admitted that they had only stayed in the hotel for about a week. When shown pictures of Noonan and Earhart, he wasn't sure about the woman matching Earhart. However, he said that Noonan was definitely the man. (This answer was at a stark contrast to the Tokyo Rose spy lady story. She had stayed on the island for months.) When asked where they had come from, he replied: "Jose Camacho said they crashed in the Tanapag area."

They went to ask Joe. He got more specific, saying they crashed in the Sadog-Tasi area next to the Chico Naval Base. His wife told them the "two Americans" were taken away to Garapan. They estimated it was about 7 or 8 years before the liberation (thus about 1937).

Operation Earhart then spoke with Joaquina Cabrera, who in 1937 had been employed in the hotel. She used to take a list of the prisoners to the governor each day. While doing so one day, she saw two people in the backseat of a 3 wheeled car. One was an American woman. Both were blindfolded and had their hands tied behind their backs. She never saw them again.

Joe Pangelinan said that he saw a "white man and woman at Japanese military headquarters at Garapan. Someone told me they were fliers and spies. Later I heard that the woman had died and the man had been executed shortly thereafter."

Antonio Diaz was now a member of the Saipan legislature. He was a chauffeur for the Japanese back then. One day he had heard that a plane had crashed at Sadog-Tasi, and that "two pilots were apprehended. One was an American woman."

José Baza was stacking oil drums at the naval base at the time. He insisted he saw nothing. Sheriff Sablan was, however, overbearing yet again. When they returned with Antonio Diaz, he reassured Baza it was safe to talk. Baza then admitted: "I saw the airplane crash at Sadog-Tasi and the Japanese arrest the two American pilots, and one of them was a woman." Asked for more, he finally admitted they were taken off to Garapan.

Next they went to speak to Matilda San Nicholas. Sablan's patrolman had contacted him and said she wanted to talk to them about the matter. Matilda lived next door to the hotel in 1937. She said that the American woman only lived there 7 days and twice she visited her and her younger sister. "She was thin with short hair like a man's. She was dressed in a cloth trench coat. She was pale, as if sick. She ate very little of what they offered her, only some fruit. The second time they saw the woman, her left forearm was bandaged and bruised and the right side of her neck was scorched. She did not believe she was free to go on her own. "Two Chamorro [native Saipanese] detectives" watched "the hotel daily."

The busboy who lived there told her that the girl was found dead in bed, in a pool of blood. Over the days before she died she went to the toilet often. The busboy then asked that they make her two wreaths for her burial. Matilda didn't know where she was buried. She had not been a witness to it.

They laid out pictures of Amelia Earhart on the table and Matilda said they looked like the woman.

What is very significant here is that many of these witnesses were those that Goerner would finally talk to on his second visit to Saipan in September 1961. Some obviously told different stories. Matilda San Nicholas is a prime example. To Goerner she would say that the girl stayed for maybe months to a year. Goerner was also quite proud of the fact that when he laid out 15 pictures of American women, some from magazine layouts, with only one of Earhart included, Mrs. San Nicholas picked the one of Earhart. He hadn't known that Gervais and Dinger had already shown her pictures the December before.

With the San Nicholas interview we get the same picture Gervais's interviewees on Guam had painted—the insular police and not the Japanese were responsible. This is subtly reconfirmed in subsequent interviews. But what is also obvious is that more than one incident is being conflated. One revolves around a woman who was considered a spy and remained for months. Another was about a man and woman who remained for only a short time. The third is about two pilots in khaki flight gear who crashed near the base. One was boyish/feminine in appearance.

In the Operation Earhart interviews of December 1960 a subsection of witnesses associate a man and woman with the plane crash. As in Akiyama's version, the pilots are led off, but not to immediate execution. They may not be the same as the man and woman who stayed only a week at the hotel. From the interviews, Gervais summed up that as many people who claimed this woman died or was executed also claim she was taken away to Japan. But there was far more of a ring of truth in the statements this couple remained only 7 days as opposed to months.

On the 5th day of their visit, 7 witnesses were contacted and none of them would talk. Gervais sensed they were all afraid of something. In fact, a wall of fear had gone up. Quintanilla and Sablan went to find out what happened. They came back at night and shared their discovery. It was Kumoi.

"Kumoi" and "Zuse" were one and the same— Jesus de Leon Guerrero, Goerner's archenemy "Francisco Galvan;" (Goerner had given him the alias nickname "Kobei.") Quintanilla said that Kumoi had put "the fear of God" in the islanders and they refused to talk. He held great prestige through fear. Quintanilla explained: "For many years he was the 'jungkicho'— top investigator for the Japanese and number one Chamorro on the island of Saipan. The older people here still fear him." Sablan supported Quintanilla's assessment. "Kumoi was a cop—and a mean one at that—for many years." Sablan said he'd bring Kumoi to the courthouse for Gervais to question.

Kumoi gave them 4 hours of fruitless answers—"I remember nothing." But he promised to think about it (essentially) and return to talk tomorrow. He was far more talkative the next day. He insisted there was no military presence on Saipan until 1938, only the naval administration was here. Manuel Sablan refused to believe him, and tempers rose. After hours of denials, Kumoi said he'd return again tomorrow.

In the meantime, Dinger and Gervais went and spoke with Elias Sablan, who had headed the first investigation in May. He had 4 men waiting with him who had worked for the Japanese administration on Saipan in 1937. One was a guard at Garapan prison. The others had worked as construction workers at Chico Air Base. The gist of it is that two American spies, both men, had been picked up and brought here in 1937. The guard said there had been no woman.

The next morning they had their final meeting with Zuse. Prompted to speak of what he wanted (rather than answering questions) he said there was no American lady on the island. The spy was a Japanese-American woman who came from Tokyo. She was looking for work but dressed too nice. She spoke fluent English, and it was discovered she was born in Los Angeles. She was hanged as spy in 1938. "She is the one everybody thinks is Amelia Earhart."

Zuse admitted she was very beautiful, about 25 years old, and probably mixed race. She could pass for an American woman. She was kept in the jail for 2 months before being hanged. He used to feed her and she spoke only English. She nearly lost her mind at her confinement and cussed him out.

As for the spies crashing by plane, it was July, but 1942. Both were men. They were jailed for 18 months and then beheaded when the Americans started bombarding the island. They had been kept at the hotel. He was in charge of them. Both were buried in the Garapan cemetery. He didn't see the executions, but he was in a position to hear about it.

After he left, Dinger expressed his belief that Kumoi finally told the truth.

This, of course, fit with the thesis Gervais had already developed. He wanted to believe that Amelia Earhart was still alive. His theory crystalized into book form in 1970 when he finally achieved publication by collaboration with Joe Klaas, the account executive with KGO in San Francisco, KCBS and Goerner's local competition. *Amelia Earhart Lives* was highly and often pointlessly negative about Goerner's investigation.

This was an unfortunate tack to take, seeming even more petty and ill-conceived after Klaas' book would crash and burn in only 7 weeks when McGraw-Hill withdrew it under lawsuit from Irene Bolam. Gervais was the originator and chief proponent of the conspiracy theory that Earhart was repatriated to the United States after the war and given a type of "witness protection" treatment, which included a new name and identity. She was alive and well and living in New Jersey as this aforesaid Irene Bolam. This New Jersey housewife was vigorous, to say the least, in her denial at a press conference. "The fantastic story which makes me out to be some kind of mystery woman is *utter* nonsense. I am not a mysterious woman. I am not Amelia Earhart!"

Gervais had proven himself a loose-cannon theorist, essentially one who was pathetically self-deluding. Sadly, the destruction of his theory's credibility overshadowed the fact that he had discovered a lot of interesting data during his investigation that helps one to thrash out some modicum of truth on Saipan. Gervais' interviews reveal to what extent Goerner glossed over critical facts— the evidence the pilots were military men and then the whole affair of Tokyo Rosa. The original accounts had placed Zuse and the insular police at the center of these various affairs. It is only after investigation began on Saipan (first under Elias Sablan) that the involvement of the insular police is diminished and eventually over the years and more visits by Fred Goerner basically the Japanese are all over the story. If Earhart and Noonan had been on Saipan, it had only been brief and their stay clouded by being mixed with many other events.

Although Gervais' theory was ludicrous, a number of acolytes have taken up his quest to prove Irene Bolam was AE or, at least, that AE had survived and was repatriated to the USA as someone else. The theory, in its main, must be summarized here in order to remain faithful to the purpose of this book. Up to a point it is not that different from the Saipan Spy and Die Theory. It is just that there is no Die part of the theory anymore.

After the Electra's crash in Hawaii, Gervais believed AE had been approached to be a spy. Her plane had not been rebuilt. She had been given a much more powerful Electra, the 12 Model that had more powerful engines and a greater fuel range.

Her spy flight of the islands completed, Gervais proposed she then got lost for real in trying to find Howland. Believing that 337/157 were compass bearings, Gervais concluded that Earhart and Noonan most likely followed the 157 heading to Hull Island in the Phoenix Group. But the *Colorado*'s report was an obstacle. There was a European with native guano collectors on the island. Lt. Lambrecht, after all, landed and talked to them.

Gervais conceived an elaborate conspiracy theory, inspired by believing that the 1943 film *Flight for Freedom* was actually based on truth. RKO, the studio that made the picture, was owned at that time by Floyd Odlum and his wife was Jackie Cochran, both good friends of Amelia Earhart. The film's plot was their way of conveying the truth of Earhart's last flight.

The film's star/heroine "Tonie Carter" was engaging in a highly publicized "world flight," and in character she was obviously Amelia Earhart. The finale of her flight was not success. Rather she was to ditch at "Gull Island" and feign she had van-

ished. The Navy could then use their search as an excuse to re-
connoiter the nearby Japanese mandated islands. For Gervais
"Gull Island" was a subtle code that Hull Island was Earhart's
true landing spot. The guano collectors on the real Hull Island
meant it was a center of nesting gulls. So there it is.

But these selfsame guano collectors and their real European
supervisor were a problem for the theory. Gervais opted to believe the Japanese aircraft carrier *Akagi* was in the area. Its
planes intercepted and perhaps even shot down the Electra short
of the island. (This way the guano collectors would not have noticed it.) This part of the theory hinged on Earhart's word "Wait"
when trying to reach the *Itasca*. He thought this meant something dire. She might have seen the planes approaching. Then
there was no more communication because she was shot down.

Gervais's reasoning sizzled in a skillet to such an extent he
could pop onto a different theory without warning. Excited, he
called Bob Dinger and told him he had discovered that Winslow
Reef, only 170 miles southeast of Howland on 157 degrees, hadn't
been discovered back in 1937. He now believed that when Earhart said "Wait" she may have seen the reef and then ditched on
it. At high tide it is underwater. He was going to take a shallow
draft boat from Pago-Pago and dive on the reef for evidence.

Actually, this theory excited a lot more serious interest.
Those in Earhart's circle knew the reef had never been found at
the time and had been searched for as the actual ditching location. Word got back to the Odlums. Floyd Odlum might back
such an expedition, one of Odlums' chums had told Gervais.

This chum was William Van Dusen, Vice President of Eastern Airlines. Insofar as Gervais was concerned, Van Dusen was a
suspicious character. Van Dusen had inquired repeatedly about
any report Gervais might have written about Earhart while he
was in the Air Force. Gervais was so conspiracy bound that he
believed Noonan and Earhart had been given alias identities
when returned to the USA. He investigated Van Dusen, with the
object of proving or disproving he was the living alias of Fred
Noonan.

This plot device abruptly ends when Gervais gave up the venture and strobed back onto his Hull Island theory. He kept
watching the film the USS *Swan* had taken of the island at the

time of the search. He went over it frame-by-frame and in one frame he was sure he saw the Japanese flag flying near aircraft wreckage. He was back to his *Flight for Freedom* theory. He believed that Earhart crash landed on Hull Island and the Japanese had picked her up. They left their flag to mark their triumph. It was a subtle message they would be in touch. He believed they were going to use AE as a bargaining chip to blackmail Roosevelt into a better Pacific deal.

He was further strengthened in this belief, despite the natives and European manager on the island and Lambrecht's overflight, because he discovered a code. By playing anagrams with the names of the islands in the Phoenix Group he was able to spell the name "Guy Bolam," the husband of the "mysterious woman" in New Jersey, Irene Bolam, whom he believed was Earhart laying doggo.

Even before publication, everybody in Earhart's inner circle had lost interest in Gervais. Muriel Morrissey, Earhart's sister, didn't even want to see his information when he had visited her.

But Gervais thought he had done real, credible work; so much so he lamented that the Air Force had forced him against his will into early retirement when only 38 years old. Perhaps he thought by admitting this in his book, a book that would prove he was right, he was embarrassing the Air Force. On the contrary, after *Amelia Earhart Lives* was removed from the shelf in only 7 weeks the book had proved why the Air Force had essentially told him to get out back in 1962.

Like the others, Gervais had been set upon his quest by reading the account of Josephine Akiyama. Like the others, Gervais obviously forsook the basics of Akiyama's account (the execution). But before he lost credibility, his investigation proved a conduit for vital information, especially those first native accounts on Guam.

Altogether the combined information shows that a number of stories are conflated, and that most Saipanese accounts could hardly be termed uncontaminated. Any objective consideration of the Saipanese testimony underscores that the trail stops on Saipan. Goerner had the trail continue with bones in cans, dug up by Hensen and Burks while Griswold stood over. Gervais leapt from Saipan to Tokyo, to Tokyo Rose, to repatriation, to

Irene Bolam and a cascade of conspiracies involving dozens of people.

With the collapse of *Amelia Earhart Lives* and Gervais' theory, only Goerner's Spy and Die on Saipan Theory remained viable. Yet this eventually came to hinge on only a few Saipanese accounts. Too many subsequent discoveries would force him to modify his theory drastically.

It began when Paul Mantz's credibility waned. It became obvious the Electra did not have hidden fuel tanks. There were 1100 gallons of fuel aboard. Burning up to 49 gallons per hour for 18 hours = 828 gallons spent. This made the whole idea about overflying and scouting the Truk and Marshall Islands impossible. There was no such thing as nighttime photography back then. After she had taken off from Lae, flight time would have put her over these restricted Japanese islands at night, a time when it was impossible to see anything. So immersed in conspiracy, Goerner had also wanted to believe that the government had given her far more powerful engines that could propel her 200 mph and therefore place her over Truk in late afternoon. But he eventually had to accept that her position report, received at Lae at 6:18 p.m., placed her about 795 miles from Lae on course to Howland: "Position four point thirty-three south, one five nine point six east— height eight thousand feet over cumulus clouds; wind twenty-three knots." There goes the "Spy" from Spy and Die. Also, her remaining fuel would make it impossible for her to fly back to the Marshall Islands after having been near Howland.

Eventually, Fred Goerner had to accept this. Despite his rivalry with Gervais, he too had to look to the same Phoenix Group. It wasn't that evidence was pointing in this direction. Nothing else was left but that undiscovered Winslow Reef, which really did/does exist. Though not mentioning it by name, for the TV show *In Search of* (1976) he stated categorically:

It is my belief that Amelia landed on a small reef area between Howland Island and Canton in the northern Phoenix Group, was picked up after our search by the Japanese, taken to Saipan. She died in Japanese custody and the proof of her Japanese custody is contained in the records of the counter-intelligence corps captured from the Japanese at the end of World War II. Those records are today classified in Washington, records supposedly of Japanese interrogation of Earhart.

On the surface, his modification doesn't seem extreme. In substance, however, it is damning to his entire theory. Opting for Winslow Reef and the Phoenix Group caused him to over-write the Marshall Islands testimony of Earhart coming down there. It even required he ignore his beloved mentor Admiral Nimitz's certainty that she came down in the Marshall Islands. His location of Winslow Reef also can't explain why the Japanese would think Earhart a spy. The reef is located hundreds of miles beyond British mandated islands and 1,000 miles from Japanese mandated islands. The Japanese also knew well of her publicity flight.

For Goerner it came down to the Saipanese accounts. He came to rely on them. He really had nothing else. "The strongest evidence to me is the eyewitness reports on the island of Saipan," he declared in the same episode. "To me, it is inconceivable that these people were not telling the truth and it is inconceivable to me that anyone else answering those descriptions was on that island at that time."

Yet Gervais' and Dinger's interviews do undermine Goerner's use of the Saipan "eyewitness" accounts. And Goerner wasn't entirely faithful in recounting the context of his interviews. He makes Elias Sablan and his witnesses look like scared natives, when Sablan was actually the former mayor charged with the task of investigating Earhart's presence on Saipan in 1937, an investigation Goerner never mentions preceded him to Saipan. His interviewees were not unaware of whom he was inquiring, and almost all of them changed their stories to accommodate developing news stories coming from America. A case in point is the gaining popularity of the Marshall Islands Theory. After it gained ground, Goerner's "eyewitnesses" began telling stories about how Earhart's plane had gone down in the Marshalls and she had been brought to Saipan.

Neither Gervais nor Goerner altered their endings, only the beginning of how Earhart came down. But these changes underscore the inherent lack of evidence that existed upon which to base *any* theory. This basic instability, however, has not hindered those who followed in their footsteps. Motivated by various nuances in their theories, other authors have added to the corpus of Spy and Die.

Chief amongst them was Vincent V. Loomis. He published his research in 1985 (*Amelia Earhart: The Final Story*). He blithely summarizes (and often inaccurately) both Gervais' and Goerner's various theories before presenting his own search. Infatuated by the Marshall Islands Theory, he had made 3 investigative trips to them over the 1970s-'80s. Until Loomis there had only been one account from the Marshall Islands— the third hand account of Elieu via Goerner. When the CBS journalist had visited the Marshalls in 1962, Elieu even stated no one was around to remember anymore. Suspiciously, Loomis' witnesses grow more numerous, and yet their testimony only serves to prove they had been inspired by Fred Goerner's old book and (now retracted) theory of Mili Atoll.

For example, the first "eyewitness" on Majuro tells Loomis that she remembers a white man being beheaded on Jaluit before the war— a story lifted from an "eyewitness" on Saipan and transplanted to the Marshalls. Loomis also seems to fib a bit. He spoke with Elieu, he wrote, and Elieu now said Ajima "heard of a lady pilot who came down near Mili Atoll before the war . . ."

Crash landing at this desert atoll had been the weakest part of Goerner's original thesis. He either misread or believed a grossly inaccurate ONI report from 1960 wherein he says it was written by the investigative agent: "At 1030, the morning of the disappearance, Nauru Island radio station picked up Earhart on 6210 kcs saying, 'Land in sight ahead.'" The actual message was at 10:30 p.m. the night before and she was overheard to have said on 3105 kcs "a ship in sight ahead" as she passed south of the island. Yet for Goerner's tome in 1966 these were AE's last words as she approached the Marshall Islands. To give form to this land ahead, he had turned to Nina Paxton.

She never would let go of her story. Contemporarily, she had written to *Time* magazine, Congressman Fred Vinson, GP Putnam, Mary Bea Noonan, twice to Walter Winchell. After the rush of interest in 1943 from *Flight for Freedom*, she wrote to the Office of Naval Intelligence and even the Chief of Naval

Operations. After the Akiyama story made sensational news, and Fred Goerner got in the spotlight, she wrote to him. He bought into her information. She also wrote her own articles, such as "I Heard Amelia Earhart's SOS" in the *Courier-Journal Magazine*, 1962.

Her information is found in every book and seldom if ever qualified in the negative. Yet her own 1962 magazine article reveals not only the weakness of her information but to what an extent she herself was somewhat of a crank. The ham radio prankster she had been listening to clearly gave the wrong call letters— "KHABQ." But in a strange rigmarole, Paxton tries to justify it. "It must have been the work of the prince of darkness that, at the time of the crash, allowed the wrong letters (KHAQQ) instead of the correct call letters (KHABQ) to be given to the public in this area. Consequently, those who heard the correct ones and reported same were declared to be wrong." No, Paxton's crank had obsolete information from reading inaccurate reports that used Earhart's old call letters (from her Vega) instead of the current and correct KHAQQ. Newspapers alone called Noonan "Captain," the title Paxton still gave him in 1962, and newspapers stated erroneously that Earhart also had a portable radio, and Paxton's crank is speaking from a portable set. It is this crank that said "Mulgrave" Island was near, which is Mili Atoll.

Loomis, in fact, though inaccurately summarizing Goerner's work, and also apparently ignorant of Goerner's retraction of the Mili Atoll Theory, bases his entire search on it. Ironically, it can be said that it is off the thinnest plank in Goerner's (retracted) house that Loomis springboards to give credibility to his own investigation.

His Marshall Islands witnesses describe the Electra ditched on Barre Island in Mili Atoll. One wing is broken. According to Portuguese native Kurt Pinho, the Marshallese native Anibar Eini had been a witness to the crash. "After the Japanese picked up the aircraft, Anibar dived to a wing that had broken off. Apparently it had stayed in the water all these years." One cannot blame Paxton's shortwave crank for these errors. She didn't relay damage. It is the other "voice from nowhere" that talked about a broken wing upon ditching. This was the voice that young Dana

Randolph heard say (on July 4) they were south of the equator on a sandbank. Then Mrs. Frank Freitas heard the same voice on July 8 state: "Plane on reef 200 miles directly south of Howland, both okay, one wing broken." Mili Atoll is about 1,000 miles north of the equator and 600 miles northwest of Howland Island. But thanks to Nina Paxton, Fred Goerner and the massive publicity of his book, all the post-loss radio "voices from nowhere" got mixed together and then absorbed by Marshall islanders who could remember it all happening near Mili Atoll.

The cornerstone of Loomis' eyewitness accounts is Bilimon Amaran, a Japanese born islander. He claims that as an island medical assistant on Jaluit he was called aboard the Japanese ship (*Koshu*) in the harbor in order to treat a white man and woman flier. Disturbingly, the white man has injuries conforming to the news reports of the "voices from nowhere" and Goerner's book— i.e. "The wound on the right side of the head was not very serious, but the one around the knee area was kind of a four inch cut, inflamed, slightly bleeding while I was treating him."[10]

Amaran also recalls the plane. "It was on the backside of the ship, still in the canvas slings that got it out of the water. One of the. . .I think it was the right or left wing was broken. I wasn't really remember what wing it was, but one of the wings was broken."

Sadly, again, this has nothing to do with the Mili Atoll theory inspired by Paxton's talkative shortwave prankster. A broken wing is inspired by the voice from nowhere 200 miles south of Howland Island.

Loomis relates how his friend did some home plotting of her course and could prove that Earhart intentionally flew to Nauru Island rather than south of it. Instead of having Earhart say "ship in sight ahead," he has her say "lights in sight ahead" indicating the powerful mining lights the island had turned on for her. So this one line jumps around quite a bit. Goerner erroneously claims that the next morning she had said "land in sight ahead"

---

[10] Paxton's hoaxer had said: "He bruised his legs badly when landing yesterday. The Captain was shaken severely in landing. "

to indicate she was ditching at Mili Atoll. But Loomis erroneously asserts she said "lights in sight ahead" at the right time yet
cannot explain what the significance is of asserting Earhart
passed within sight of Nauru rather than south of it. Loomis' entire tangent is an academic McGuffin.

There are clues Loomis picked up that could be of help later
in our own quest, but as for trying to revive the Mili Atoll crash
theory he miserably failed. All witnesses but Elieu and the Muller brothers remain suspect.

Tom Devine would rise to be a trusted author in the Spy and
Die legend, even writing his own book in 1987. Unfortunately,
time and attention only caused him to convolute his own story, a
tendency Goerner had noted early on. He would admit that
Devine "was to play an interesting if frustrating role" in his own
investigation. His evolving claims actually became incoherent.
Originally, Devine didn't associate the native woman's story of
two fliers "from the sky long ago" as relating to Earhart and
Noonan. As Goerner's quest increased in popularity, Devine remembered events that blatantly contradict his original story.
Primarily, he came to assert that in 1944 he had heard Marines
arguing amongst themselves who would get credit for having
discovered Amelia Earhart's Electra at Aslito Field. Curious, he
went to the field the next day. The bright Electra was being
burned to erase the shocking discovery. This is immediately suspicious. How could he not associate the old native woman's story
with Earhart and Noonan given this experience? Why did he not
recall this in his first letter and many conversations with
Goerner thereafter? Instead it took over 3 years for him to tell
Goerner. This was just as they concluded their joint journey to
Saipan in December 1963. "Before leaving Saipan, Tom Devine
revealed additional information." And we are treated to the
elaborate conspiracy story above.

In addition, Devine said he heard the name of the Marine
who had made the discovery. It was Lt. Wally Greene. Goerner
ran with the story, apparently believing Devine was to be credit-
ed as reliable. He suspected this Marine was one and the same
as the current Commandant of the Marine Corps Wallace
Greene. As a result, his meeting with Greene on the matter became combative. One eyewitness told Linton Wells, director of

Storer Broadcasting: "The General categorically denied any knowledge about AE's plane, or the supposed digging up of her bones. Goerner wasn't convinced, and when the General offered to swear on a Bible, Goerner said he wouldn't believe him." Greene then gave Goerner a list of Marines who could substantiate the incidents in question never happened. Goerner refused to call them "because he knew the General would order them not to say anything." Greene then offered him his telephone on the spot, but Goerner declined. "I feel sure," continued Wells, "you can discount the Goerner Marine stories."

This account is somewhat in-keeping with what Goerner expressed in his bestseller, though his version is far less injurious to his own reputation. He conveys his meeting with Greene was tense, but that he did call the names given him. One was Tracey Griswold in Ohio. He had been a Major and matched the Intelligence Officer that Ev Hensen and Billy Burks had described. Griswold said he couldn't remember any such thing, but Goerner was already primed to doubt him. He wrote how he had spoken to several thousand people over the course of his long investigation. "Almost without exception it has taken several minutes to identify myself and properly introduce the subject. Such was not the case with Major Griswold. When I gave my name, he knew who I was." When Griswold couldn't remember ever exhuming any graves, by context Goerner implies he had been debriefed and ordered by Greene to lie.

Yet the Marine stories, as Linton Wells calls them, weren't Goerner's. They were Tom Devine's. And the events at Aslito field are utter rubbish, as is his entire conspiracy theory. If there is a shred of truth here, it is found only in his first letter. It may be the native woman was referring to the 2 Navy pilots who were beheaded when the island bombardment started. These may be the remains Hensen and Burks dug up.

The sum total of Goerner's and Gervais's research is not very positive. Nor is it very abundant. One must read between the lines of their Saipan witness accounts, but only those accounts taken in 1960. Thereafter witness accounts are tainted by the popularity of Goerner's bestseller, and before that, unfortunately, they were quickly tainted by Akiyama's story, as first published but widely reprinted, in May 1960. Thus the latter day investigator must beware from the beginning.

We must needs come back to Saipan, but in the interim we also must accept there was obviously room for another theory to emerge. It would be a long time. Goerner's and Gervais' works were long out of print by 1989. The current tomes that spun from them were only tardy rehashes. It was time for a less conspiratorial theory to capture the senses. It also began in the Phoenix Islands, but Ric Gillespie, its chief author, also had it end there.

Chapter 13

Gardner or Nikumaroro:
A Theory By Another Name

Of the major theories involving Amelia Earhart and Fred Noonan's mysterious fate, only one does not begin with or springboard from Josephine Akiyama's story. This is the theory that Earhart and Noonan were marooned on Gardner Island. It is in the same Phoenix Group as Joe Gervais' Hull Island. Today, the island is popularly called by its Kiribati name Nikumaroro. The group that has spearheaded the theory is, of course, TIGHAR (The International Group for Historic Aircraft Recovery), helmed by Ric Gillespie.

In like manner to those who engineered Saipan Spy and Die and its variants, TIGHAR was led to Gardner Island by a newspaper article printed in 1960. This one appeared in the *San Diego Tribune* on July 21, based on the memories of a former Coast Guardsman, Floyd Kilts. With all the excitement after Akiyama's account and the publication of Paul Briand's *Daughter of the Sky*, newspapers were looking for more stories. Kilts' story was one of them, but it was also one of those quickly forgotten. Ric Gillespie rediscovered it in 1989.

Temporarily serving on Gardner Island after World War II (working on building a Loran station in 1946), Kilts was told by islander-colonists of a surprising discovery. A skeleton had been found before the war, about summer of 1940. (Under a British magistrate, Polynesian men were planting coconut palms preparatory for settling a colony on the desert island.) Beside the skeleton was a cognac body, with water in it. Nearby was found a woman's shoe. It was found in the brush about 5 feet from the inner coastline (thus toward the lagoon). The shoe was really the most surprising part of the discovery. No islanders wear shoes, Kilts asserted, because their feet are too spread and this shoe looked like a Size 9 Narrow. "The island doctor said the skeleton was that of a woman. . .Farther down the beach he found a man's skull, but nothing else."

Floyd Kilts elaborates:

"The magistrate was a young Irishman who got excited when he saw the bones. He thought of Amelia Earhart right away. He put the bones in a gunnysack and with the native doctor and three other natives in a 22-foot, four-oared boat started for Suva, Fiji, 887 nautical miles away.

"The magistrate was anxious to get the news to the world. But on the way the Irishman came down with pneumonia. When only about 24 hours out of Suva he died.

"The natives are superstitious as the devil and the next night after the young fellow died they threw the gunnysack full of bones overboard, scared of the spirits. And that was that."

The story sounded too fictional and incapable of corroboration. For a world becoming fascinated by the ramifications of secret missions and Japanese executions, the story was also too dull. It was quickly ignored.

But in the main, the story did have a basis in fact. In the process of his investigation, Fred Goerner had looked into it and only touched upon it in *The Search for Amelia Earhart.* The Irish supervisor had actually died on Gardner of peritonitis. The bones had actually been sent to Tarawa where a British doctor examined them and declared them to be those of a Polynesian man. The rest of the story was bunkum.

But in 1989, Ric Gillespie pursued Kilts' story in more detail. He realized there were many fantastic embellishments, but the legend a body had been found on the island before the war obviously had a basis in fact. He wondered what happened to the bones. He dug into Gardner's background.

Gardner was an uninhabited island. The biggest incident to happen there was the wreck of the s.s. *Norwich City* in 1929 (the rusted hulk remains to this day). On December 20, 1938, the coconut planting expedition first came ashore. All were native males under Gerald B. Gallagher, a Cambridge educated Irishman.

Prior to this there had been few official visits. A significant one was in October 1937, only months after Earhart and Noonan had vanished. Eric Bevington had landed on the island, scouting to see if the island was indeed good for colonization. His report survived, and in it he noted he came across a campfire that looked as if someone had bivouacked overnight.

This report, of course, meant there had been some castaways on the island before the colonial period had begun with Gallagher and his planters in 1938.

Like Gervais and Goerner, Gillespie must speculate that Earhart followed the 157 direction along the 337/157 line of position. This brought her to Gardner, not Hull, he theorized. In addition, Gillespie believed that those radio bearings triangulating over the Phoenix Group were homing in on actual post-loss radio messages being sent by Earhart. He felt enough clues existed to warrant an expedition. He was finally able to get a trip financed in 1991.

Before TIGHAR landed on the island, their preliminary evidence really didn't amount to anything more than the few facts and standard interpretations that already existed in the first days of the search in 1937. (Even GP had sent a cable noting that the radio bearings from Midway, Wake, and Hawaii, indicated the Phoenix Group.) What TIGHAR's 1991 search added was some justification for Kilts' old convoluted story. Gillespie's team scouted the area of the island most probable for the campsite. Here they found the remnant of what they believe is the other

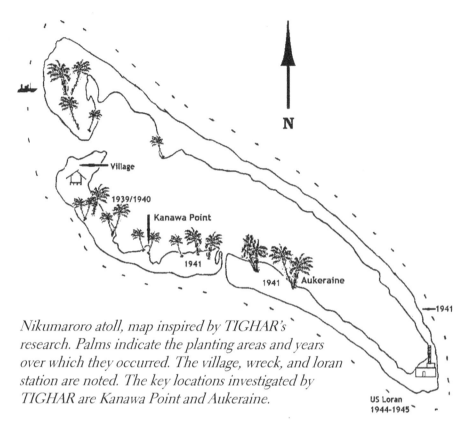

Nikumaroro atoll, map inspired by TIGHAR's research. Palms indicate the planting areas and years over which they occurred. The village, wreck, and loran station are noted. The key locations investigated by TIGHAR are Kanawa Point and Aukeraine.

shoe, the mate to the one Kilts had mentioned long ago. It's a woman's blucher-oxford with repaired heel. Gillespie asserted Earhart wore such shoes. This made world news.

Still, this wasn't proof it came from Earhart. However, in 1997 Gallagher's report was found. TIGHAR presented the details in "The Castaway on Gardner Island" published on July 22, 1997, Earhart Project Bulletin #1.

Then in June, World War II historian and author Peter McQuarrie (TIGHAR #1987) was doing research in the national archives of Kiribati in Tarawa when he stumbled upon a file labeled "Discovery of Human Remains on Gardner Island." The file contained a series of 16 official communications between Gerald B. Gallagher, the resident British administrator on Nikumaroro in 1940 and '41, and various senior British officials. These previously undiscovered documents confirm that a partial human skeleton, badly damaged by coconut crabs, was found on the island in 1940 lying under a tree, with the remains of dead birds, a turtle and a campfire nearby. With the bones were part of the sole of a woman's shoe, a Benedictine liqueur bottle, a box with numbers on it which had once contained a sextant, and a sextant component thought to be an "inverting eyepiece."

Gallagher suspected the remains of being those of Amelia Earhart and reported the discovery by radio to his superiors at the British Western Pacific High Commission in Fiji. He was ordered to ship the remains and artifacts to Fiji for analysis and to keep the entire matter "strictly secret." However, on the way to Fiji, the ship carrying the bones stopped at the colonial headquarters in Tarawa. There the senior medical officer caught wind of them, yet with no information about their possible significance. Feeling slighted that he had not been asked to evaluate what he later described as "wretched relics," he confiscated the bones and pronounced them to be those of an elderly Polynesian male who had been dead at least 20 years.

Present-day forensic anthropologists have expressed the opinion that the accuracy of such an identification by a colonial doctor in the early 1940s with access to only a partial and badly damaged skeleton is highly suspect. Nonetheless, based upon this colonial doctor's casual dismissal, British officials dropped the matter and the American authorities were apparently never notified. The file contains no attempt to explain away the woman's shoe, the Benedictine bottle, or the sextant box. Gallagher died a few months later and the mystery of the castaway of Gardner Island died with him, living on only as a murky island legend.

Now Gillespie was confident that the remains of the woman's oxford they found in 1991 "is almost certainly the mate to the one found by Gallagher and we know that shoe to be American in origin, dating from the mid-1930s and identical in style and size to Earhart's. Our campfire is, likewise, the one he noted at the site."

Despite the material TIGHAR discovered, they still only had *inferences* that a woman had occupied a campsite on the island, exact date unknown; and this was based merely from the shoe and Gallagher's belief the skeleton could have been female.

Doubting the diagnosis of the backwater doctor, Gillespie and his associates set about to fit the details into a frame that put

Earhart and Noonan on the island. The sextant was described as nautical and therefore unlikely to be the specific model Noonan had with him. However, it was discovered in an old news article that Noonan carried a spare nautical sextant just in case. The presence of an "inverting eyepiece" indicated it was used for aviation. Again, this could suggest the one found on the island was Noonan's spare. During its 1991 expedition TIGHAR had also found the remains of a can labeled "--rower Produce"—which Gillespie deduced to be Grower Produce. The use of "produce" as a noun is an Americanism, he wrote. The tropical leaves on the can were identified as bananas. Gillespie discovered that when Earhart crashed the Electra in Hawaii a tally of the supplies aboard was taken. It included cans of bananas.

For Gillespie, the search now came to finding what happened to the skeletal remains. The purpose: DNA test. "We know that the remains and the artifacts he [Gallagher] found were eventually shipped to Fiji and we are now trying to determine if they may still survive in some official repository there."

Prior to the discovery of Gallagher's report, arguments could remain general, but afterward specifics had to be addressed. Yet the TIGHAR methodology does it none too well. Taken as a whole, Gallagher's report is actually damning to the Nikumaroro theory. It is best to look at the actual exchange of official communiqués.

The exchange began on September 23, 1940, when Gallagher sent to Tarawa the following report:

> Some months ago a working party on Gardner discovered human skull-- this was buried and I only recently heard about it. Thorough search has now produced more bones (including lower jaw), part of a shoe, a bottle and a sextant box. It would appear that
> (a) Skeleton is possibly that of a woman,
> (b) Shoe was a womans [sic] and probably size 10,
> (c) Sextant box has two numbers on it 3500 (stencilled) and 1542— sextant being old fashioned and probably painted over with black enamel.
> Bones look more than four years old to me but there seems to be very slight chance that this may be remains of Amelia Earhardt [sic]. If United States authorities find that above evidence fits into general description, perhaps they could supply some dental infor-

mation as many teeth are intact. Am holding latest finds for present but have not exhumed skull. There is no local indication that this discovery is related to wreck of the "Norwich City."
                              Gallagher.

Gallagher's information was of such interest that the Resident Commissioner on Ocean Island sent a telegram to him on October 1. The High Commissioner on Fiji was already informed and was trying to trace the numbers on the sextant box. Within this telegram, the Resident asks for qualifying information: "(a) How deep was skeleton buried when found, (b) How far from shore, (c) In your opinion does burial appear deliberate or could it be accounted for by encroachments of sand, etc., (d) Is site an exposed one (i.e. if the body of Mrs. Putnam had lain there is it likely that it would have been spotted by aerial searchers)? (e) In what state of preservation is shoe, (f) If well preserved does it appear to be of modern style or old fashioned, (g) Is there any indication as to contents of bottle. Do you know anything of wreck of 'Norwich City'— e.g. when did it take place, were any lives lost and how long were survivors marooned at Gardner Island?"

The Resident's office was obviously well-informed, as question (d) implies. They knew Gardner and the entire Phoenix Group had been overflown starting a week after AE vanished.

Gallagher set out to put the facts down. In his 6th October response, he clarified that the skeleton was not buried at all. Only the skull had been buried, and this had been done by the natives when they discovered it. The coconut crabs had scattered many of the bones. The location was about 100 feet above high water, with ordinary springs about. He replied to (c) with only "improbable"—this is a bit frustrating since the Resident had asked two opposite questions (was the burial deliberate or natural over time). Only a part of the sole of the shoe remained, and it "Appears to have been stoutish walking shoe or heavy sandal." The bottle was Benedictine (liqueur) but no indication of contents. He adds: "There are indications that person was alive when cast ashore— fire, birds killed, etc., 'Norwich City' wrecked and caught fire 1930 or 1932. Number of crew sailed to Fiji in lifeboat, remainder picked up later at Gardner by 'Ralum'. Think Board of Enquiry held Suva— loss of life not known. This information derived from gossip only."

Interest in Gallagher's discovery escalated. The High Commissioner's office now sent an inquiry direct to him on October
15, asking him to tell the Commissioner the "particulars of finding of skeleton in Gardner Island." They wanted to know where
exactly it was found and what his reasons were for thinking it
was the skeleton of a woman. Did he have any anatomical reason? They wanted the dental condition and they wanted him to
measure the skeleton from "vertex of skull to arch of foot." Also,
they wanted to know the approximate "age and condition of
bones and whether any hair found in the vicinity of skeleton."
They wanted him to prepare a suitable coffin for it and keep it in
secure custody "pending further instructions." The telegram
ends: "Keep matter strictly secret for the present. — Secretary,
Western Pacific High Commission."

Gallagher's response on October 17 is illuminating for a
number of reasons. Two of the most important points in it are
the clarifications of the location where the remains were found
and that he reiterates his suspicion the bones are *very* old.

Complete skeleton not found only skull, lower jaw, one thoracic
vertebra, half pelvis, part scapula, humerus, radius, two femurs,
tibia and fibula. Skull discovered by working party six months
ago— report reached me early September. Working party buried
skull but made no further search. Bones were found on South East
corner of island about 100 feet above ordinary high water springs.
Body had obviously been lying under a 'ren' tree and remains of
fire, turtle and dead birds appear to indicate life. All small bones
have been removed by giant cocoanut crabs which have also damaged larger ones. Difficult to estimate age bones owing to activities of crabs but am quite certain they are not less than four years
old and probably much older. Only experienced man could state
sex from available bones; my conclusion based on sole of shoe
which is almost certainly a woman's. Dental condition appears to
have been good but only five teeth now remain. Evidence dental
work on jaw not apparent.

As Gallagher describes it, the southeast of the island meant
the corner of the island, which is not the location that TIGHAR
claims to have found the campsite in 1991. Gallagher also con-

firms his theory it's a woman's skeleton is based solely on the shoe. Interestingly, the "many teeth" of an earlier communique are now only 5. He concludes:

We have searched carefully for rings, money and keys with no result. No clothing was found. Organized search of area for remaining bones would take several weeks as crabs move considerable distances and this part of island is not yet cleared. Regret it is not possible to measure length of skeleton. No hair found. Bones at present in locked chest in office pending construction coffin.

Gallagher

On 26 October the Secretary to the High Commissioner told him that a search should be organized for any other items that can be found. All that he so far has, including the sextant, bones, and shoe should be sent to Suva, the district capital.

On October 27, Gerald Gallagher wrote a formal letter to accompany the remains to the secretary. He wrote that two parcels were on their way. One box was the coffin with the remains; the other package was the sextant box with the other items that had been found.

By an unchancy fate, the Royal Colony Ship *Nimanoa* set in at Tarawa first. Here the British Colonial Medical Officer presumptuously intercepted the parcels. He sent a telegram, a copy of which was sent to Gallagher.

I understand from the Master R.C.S. Nimanoa, that he has certain human remains on board consigned to Suva. As I am in charge of Medical and forensic investigation of such objects throughout the whole colony and have no knowledge of the matter, I presume that the package was intended to be consigned to myself?

Isaac

The Resident Commissioner sent a message to Gallagher. He told him there was no need to respond. He was communicating with Dr. Isaac and giving his position. We do not know what happened, only that Dr. Isaac examined the bones. TIGHAR asserted there are reasons to believe the exchange between the

Resident and Dr. Isaac was "heated."

In any case, on February 11, Isaac cabled to Gallagher:

> For your information remains taken from "Nimanoa" part skeleton elderly male of Polynesian race and that indications are that bones have been in sheltered position for upwards of 20 years and possibly much longer.

Gallagher seems to have accepted the conclusion graciously. The Senior Medical Doctor had confirmed Gallagher's own suspicion that the bones were quite old; and indeed the good doctor may have been correct.

Yet the circumstances were never clarified to Isaac — not by the Resident nor by Gallagher. The tension between the Resident Commissioner and Dr. Isaac, and the fact he had told Isaac nothing, is reflected in the following telegram, a copy of which was also sent to and retained by Gallagher (and thus in the National Library and Archives at Tarawa now). It is dated February 14, 1941. Dr. Isaac states:

> Your telegram 11th February. Confidential. Matter became somewhat tense and complex after guillotine conversation between us. As I had (and still have) no information save presence of remains and therefore .... quarantine from .... no danger infection, I am still wondering how wretched relics can be interesting.

After this, the bones had been sent on to Suva. They did get there, of this there is no doubt. The last remaining telegrams confirm receipt by the Secretary for the High Commissioner's Officer on Suva, the date being April 28, 1941. But though the remains and sextant box came, the High Commissioner was expecting also a sextant. With Gallagher's response, we get our last bit of vital information. "No sextant was found. Only part discovered was thrown away by finder but was probably part of an inverting eyepiece."

Like the Saipan Spy and Die Theory, Gillespie was led to an island by a story. But unlike the Saipan theories, there is tangible evidence to refute the Nikumaroro theory. The first hurdle is to explain why Lt. John Lambrecht never saw anything on the is-

land when he and his mates overflew it on July 9, 1937. They
buzzed the island as low as 400 feet. In contrast to Gardner's
desolation, when they buzzed over Hull Island natives came
running onto the beach waving cloth at them. In addition to
John Lambrecht's overflight there was that visit by Eric Bevington. He had scouted the island only a few months later. He notes
a campsite, but he does not note a decaying corpse. Gillespie is
forced to speculate that Earhart and Noonan were actually still
alive on the island; they were simply away from their campsite
when Bevington visited (October 14, 1937).

Such shaky speculation was made necessary because of cyclical reasoning. He had to get a body back to the campsite in order for Gallagher's planters to find its skeleton in the summer of
1940. For TIGHAR that meant Earhart and Noonan returned to
the camp to live there permanently, killed and ate the birds and
turtle, and left the other remains, which apparently Gallagher's
people never saw (the other shoe, banana can, etc). Yet in light
of Gallagher's report, it is unlikely Bevington even found the
same campsite. Dr. Isaac had confirmed Gallagher's own suspicions that the bones were much older than 4 years. (In fact,
TIGHAR exaggerates somewhat Gallagher's excitement that the
bones could be Amelia Earhart.) It would seem far more reasonable to assume that the campsite Gallagher and Bevington describe are not the same one. Bevington may indeed have come
across what he describes—a one night campout. Gallagher's
planters obviously came across a campsite where someone had
lived for a while and eventually died under the Ren tree.

Bevington's report should have greatly distressed the budding
theory of Gardner Island, but TIGHAR's discovery of a woman's
shoe was tangible. TIGHAR's theory became symbolized by this
artifact. It was, in essence, a contrast to what Fred Goerner had
experienced. His research had become dangerously symbolized
by the generator and then dismissed when the generator was
proven false. TIGHAR's theory became symbolized by the shoe
sole. Since no one was in a position to disprove it was Amelia
Earhart's, it became a symbol to legitimize a search for her fate.

The only one to seriously question this search was, in fact,
Fred Goerner. Always remaining in the loop, he followed Gillespie's evolving thesis. After TIGHAR's first expedition, and

therewith the first presentation of their discoveries on the island, Goerner had written to the editor of *Life* Magazine, Ed Barnes, on October 11, 1991, warning him about Gillespie's claims, evidence, and methodology. After detailing a long list of Gillespie's claims balanced by facts, Goerner asked Barnes pointedly about the linchpin of Gillespie's evidence.

> You should ask Gillespie and TIGHAR where the evidence is that shoes of Earhart's size were found. The truth is Earhart DID NOT WEAR WOMEN'S SHOE WHEN SHE WAS FLYING. She wore men's low-heel brogans, see photos taken the morning before the final takeoff from Lae, New Guinea July 2, 1937.

The challenge went unpublished.

Anyway, specific challenges such as Goerner made could be easily lost in the flood of conjecture issued from TIGHAR. For example, Gillespie brings to bear the story told by an old Guardsman, Richard Evans. When he had been stationed on the island in the mid-1940s, there had been reports of an aircraft wreck on the island. One colonist had also told him that he came across the remains of a water catching device when scouting parts of the island. Putting it all together, it sounded as if there had been survivors of a plane crash on the island before the war. Who else could it be?

Like with Gervais' Hull Island theorizing, TIGHAR's theorizing creates unfathomable contradictions. John Lambrecht had noted (during his overflight) that there had appeared to be signs of recent habitation. He later qualified this to mean crumbling adobe walls, not a survivors' campsite. How could he have missed a plane wreck? Bevington scoured the island in order to assess its probability for colonization. How could he have missed a plane wreck? Why hadn't Amelia and Fred come running out at the sound of Lambrecht's plane motor overhead? If they had already expired in the first week, why didn't Bevington find their bodies only months later?

Another example: Jeff Glickman of PHOTEK also examined some old aerials. He asserted the campsite in question can still be seen in a 1941 aerial photo. This inspired Gillespie to believe that Earhart and Noonan could have survived for a staggering

amount of time on the island. This requires an even more pro-
found suspension of disbelief.

For in November 1939 a team from the USS *Bushnell* surveyed the island. TIGHAR stated, however, that they couldn't
uncover any clear evidence the landing party had surveyed the
southeast area, the location of the campsite. Still, as with Bevington's expedition in 1937, we must assume Earhart and
Noonan never once while ambling over the island noticed the
submarine tender anchored offshore. In Goerner's letter to Ed
Barnes he noted that in 1938 the NZPAS (New Zealand Pacific
Air Survey) also "conducted a full survey" and even cleared
some obstructions from the lagoon.

Various TIGHAR expeditions have searched the island looking for any bones Gallagher believed the crabs scattered. But a
careful presentation of facts in TIGHAR's article "Gallagher's
Clues" reveals pros and cons for accepting which may be the actual site Gallagher had discovered. The only conclusion a reader
can make is that even TIGHAR is not sure if they ever found the
same site. Then to whom did that woman's shoe belong?

Nikumaroro was indeed settled by colonists, remaining popu-
lated until it was abandoned in the 1960s. There is much human
debris remaining on the island. There is little reason to think
TIGHAR found Gallagher's campsite, and equally less reason to
believe the actual campsite described by Gallagher was related
to Amelia Earhart. "We have searched carefully for rings, money
and keys with no result," had written Gallagher. How did they
miss the banana can or the other shoe? "No clothing was found"
means it was indeed an old skeleton. The shoe Gallagher found
was "stoutish," not narrow. It may have belonged to a sandal.
TIGHAR could have found anybody's shoe. TIGHAR's justification to pursue the bones hinges on assuming Dr. Isaac was not
skilled enough to make the judgment about age and sex. Yet
Gallagher's messages prove Isaac's opinion did not stand alone.
He too was "quite certain they [bones] are not less than four
years old and probably much older."

To put it kindly perhaps, TIGHAR had been used to 8 years
of defending their position with highly speculative dissertation,
the exegetical purpose of which was to justify their standing theory. This methodology, although no longer applicable, contin-

ued even in the face of Gallagher's evidence. The solid facts he reports do not allow any interpretation to support the Earhart theory. In some ways the "evidence" is less tangible than the witness testimony on Saipan, for here on Gardner there are tangibles that contradict TIGHAR's thesis.

Without finding those exact bones and getting a positive DNA test, or an identifiable piece of the Electra wreck, Gillespie's rather intricate theory is little different than Gervais' theory—only Gardner Island and not Hull.

Joe Gervais went on to be the supreme loose-cannon theorist and concoct the Earhart Lives in New Jersey Theory, psychologically recovery after a rum go of it with Tojo. Gillespie never went into conspiracies thus perhaps masking that his reasoning was just as fluid and cyclical as Gervais'. Each started with a final resting place and worked everything else in. It is the lack of conspiracy theories, however, that have probably shielded Gillespie from Gervais' ignominious fate.

Using the same methodology, TIGHAR did a laborious study of post-loss radio signals. The purpose of analyzing the messages is simple and to the point: "Clearly, if any reported signal was genuine, the Electra did not go down at sea. A comprehensive and detailed catalog and analysis of the reported post-loss radio signals must, therefore, be an element in any informed investigation of the Earhart disappearance."

Unfortunately, TIGHAR's investigation only convolutes the problem. Three stations did home-in on a carrier wave that triangulated over the Phoenix Group, but each could have been detecting Naval Radio Tutuila to the south in Samoa. The voice messages "from nowhere" did not originate from the Phoenix Group. These were picked up in the USA, clearest toward the East Coast.

Amazingly, however, in their article "The Post-Loss Radio Signals," TIGHAR writes that the only choices allowed any investigator are:

1. Either Earhart and Noonan were making radio calls from the Electra on land somewhere in the Phoenix Group of islands or 2. There was a hoaxer pre-positioned in that region who was able to transmit on Earhart's frequencies, had information about her that

was not known to the public, was able to mimic her voice, and knew [beforehand] that she would not reach Howland.

No voice came with the carrier waves from the South Pacific. Only Nauru's operator, Barnes, heard a voice the night of July 2. Thrice he picked up a woman's voice. He said it was the same as the one he had heard while Earhart passed the island in flight the night before and reported "a ship in sight ahead." *These* are actually the most provocative post-loss radio messages.

There was only one voice message picked up locally by an official US station, and this was the one to which Commander Warner Thompson alludes in his report. He said Navy Radio Wailupe in Hawaii had received it, but the contents are not presented by him.

However, the actual words spoken may have been preserved by Elmer Dimity. While investigating for CBS, Fred Goerner discovered Dimity had tried to get a special search funded to look for Earhart soon after the official one had ended. He was inspired to do so because he believed some of the post-loss messages were genuine. He allowed Goerner to go through his material. Within it, Goerner found a copy of the official log from Diamond Head. On July 7, a woman's voice was heard: "Earhart calling. NRU1 — NRU1 — calling from KHAQQ. On coral southwest of unknown island. Don't know how long we will . . ."

If this is the message that Thompson implies Wailupe picked up, then sadly Wailupe's reception is the third installment in a trilogy of fakes. The first was picked up on Saturday the 3rd by Charles McGill in Oakland. "SOS, SOS, SOS, SOS, KHAQQ, SOS, SOS, KHAQQ. Fred Noonan taking over." Code now commenced: "225 north northwestward off Howland. Battery very weak. Can't last long. Flares all wet. Baks." On the 6th McGill picked up another message: "NRU1-KHAQQ, KHAQQ-SOS, SOS, SOS-KHAQQ. 281 North Howland. Cannot hold out much longer. Drifting slowly northwest. We above water. Motor sinking in water. Very wet."

UPI covered the McGill story, dateline San Francisco July 6, 1937. Dimity was featured in the piece, the article declaring he and GP put faith in the messages . . . yet all this was dashed when it was proven Earhart could not have been transmitting while floating. The July 7 message is merely the culmination of her drift westward onto a sandbank, at least according to this "voice from nowhere."

Although a few have searched (including TIGHAR), no one has been able to locate the July 7 message in Dimity's files in order to confirm Fred Goerner saw an authentic transcript. Sadly, he had made many mistakes when relating messages, and it is likely that when he said he saw "Diamond Head's" message he merely saw another one of Elmer Dimity's worthless clippings. Worse, Goerner could be accurate, and this is truly what Wailupe records— the third installment of a West Coast hoaxer.

Any actual examination of the post-loss radio messages underscores the enigma of the Nauru messages. They are the only instance of locals picking up a voice that suggests Earhart had initially survived. As we know, the operator Harry Barnes identified it as the same voice he had heard when Earhart had passed south of Nauru and reported "a ship in sight ahead." The only difference now was the lack of background engine sounds. Moreover, he reported her voice was over-modulated. This is something Leo Bellarts had also reported while AE had strained to reach *Itasca* that morning. We have two different radio operators reporting the same fault, one unquestionably listening to Earhart during her flight, the other in the most immediate post-loss radio messages received.

The broader context within which these messages occurred is also a powerful clue to their authenticity. It is unlikely that after ditching on a reef or shoreline, with twisted and bent propellers, Earhart is going to be able to turn over her right engine. This would leave her with only battery power. This would allow her up to 8 hours to transmit, if she did so intermittently.[11] Thus she would not be able to send many or strong messages, and she would be limited to short bursts over the first few days. This is the context within which the only locally received messages occurred.

---

[11] Confirmed by telegram July 5, 1937, to GP Putnam by Joseph Gurr in Burbank, who had worked on AE's Bendix radio in preparation for a number of flights.

Within the major theories we see a factor in common. They start from an island, but none of the theorists can explain how Earhart got to said island. Competent fuel estimates don't allow her to have reached the Marshalls or the Phoenix Group. Only Fred Goerner later compromised and believed that Earhart went down on Winslow Reef.

There is something compelling about Winslow Reef, but there is also something beguiling about it. It beckons us because it wasn't found. It's beguiling because if only one post-loss radio message was genuine an uncharted reef becomes necessary. As it turns out, there was more than one uninvestigated reef in the vicinity of AE's fuel range. The clues were followed back then, but forgotten by today. It's time we begin to put things together and find cohesion.

Part III

Back to Earth

Chapter 14

Rumor Hath It

Amelia Earhart's "casual," "happy-go-lucky," or just plain haphazard style of preparation is no more keenly felt than in trying to determine what her alternate plans were if she couldn't make Howland Island. Some vital things are spoken so offhand they are mere rumors.

Rumor hath it first that AE said she would turn around and head back to the Gilbert Islands. Over 20 years later, Fred Goerner put some context to this rumor. "In her discussions with Eugene Vidal and William Miller, she had said, 'If we don't pick up Howland, I'll try to fly back to the Gilberts and find a nice stretch of beach. If I have to do that let's hope I choose an island that has fresh water.'"

Rumor hath it next from George Putnam's own mouth that the Electra had been "fixed" to float, which must mean something to do with securing the fuel dump valves so they wouldn't implode upon a ditching at sea. The inference was, of course, that seawater could not flood the empty fuel tanks; as a result the Electra could indeed float and drift.

"I feel confident that Miss Earhart and her navigator will be rescued," he told the *San Francisco Chronicle* on July 3. "The ship should float for hours. I couldn't estimate how long, as no Lockheed has ever been forced down on the water before."

Rumor hath it that Gene Vidal independently requested the British authorities in the Gilbert Islands to conduct their own investigation. Rumor hath it the request carried the statement they had evidence indicating that after her disappearance Earhart had spent her first two nights on land.

How to verify these rumors? We only have George's word on the dump valves, and his word isn't exactly coin of the realm. Paul Mantz had also echoed GP's words, but he may merely have wanted to encourage the searchers to continue.

Contemporary evidence, however, *does* exist to underscore the Gilbert Islands as AE's alternate plan. During the intense moments of the search on July 11, 1937, AE's personal secretary Margot DeCarie sent a message to Coast Guard HQ in San Francisco. "Conferred with wife of Noonan this day and she states characteristics of Noonan was to turn back when in doubt. This appears a reasonable assumption in view of prevailing wind and apparent sufficient fuel for about 3 hours computed from actual time in air of slightly over 20 hours to last radio contact and establish back that fuel consumption was 42 gallons per hour at cruising of 130 knots." Furthermore, she adds some interesting tidbits about fuel consumption. "Technical advisor for Earhart thinks plane could operate at slow speeds 30 gallons per hour and positively safe that radio could not be used in water. Above indicates possibility plane may be in Gilbert group."

As for the Vidal request, there is a tantalizing reference to it in an old State Department memo written by Frank Sieverts (expert on POWs and refugees) on February 5, 1965, due to all the mania for Spy and Die on Saipan. "The only evidence in the Department's files that the Department had any idea that the two fliers might have survived for even a short period appears in a single telegram . . . involving a special search of a specific area near the Gilbert Islands, which the British government undertook at the request of Miss Earhart's husband." Sieverts only quotes a single sentence from the cablegram ("Evidence which to many sources seems positive indicates that Amelia Earhart was on land the two nights following her disappearance"). He admits, in a rather convoluted way, that Gene Vidal, FDR, his personal secretary Marvin McIntyre, and Undersecretary of State Sumner Welles were involved.

Much has been lost behind closed doors, but I was able to establish a timeline. Two days (July 20) after the search had ended, President Roosevelt's secretary, Marvin McIntyre, wrote to FDR: "Gene Vidal has been in very close touch with the Earhart story, talking several times a day to her husband, Mr. Putnam. He has some very interesting sidelights and some speculations, which are probably true, as to what actually happened. You might find it interesting to spend 15 minutes with him." FDR wrote back: "Mac, I would like to see him for 5 or 10 minutes."

What follows is from fleeting shadows of men on the wall and the murmur of voices before and after the stately doors closed and opened again. Beside himself with fret, GP was telling a worried Gene Vidal that AE had been on a reef for two nights, but now she was drifting. He was skittish about his sources, but Vidal was ready to indulge him.

Elements of confusion will come into play here initially, and I must also seek the reader's indulgence. It is unavoidable because here we are dealing with rumors. It is necessary to walk their path because these rumors came to influence actions and attitudes in Earhart's inner circle. And it was from the inner circle that there rippled out the "conspiracy of silence," which in the hands of interpreters came to influence broader conspiracy theories. Obviously, in our own quest we must know which rumors to ignore and which to follow.

Within all the rumors there is only one substantial one: AE would return to the Gilbert Islands if they could not find Howland. All the other machinations about which direction of the 337/157 line of position she may have followed only serve to dangerously overshadow and obscure this initial truth.

Of the unsubstantial rumors, there is one above all others: the report that a Japanese fishing boat had picked up the dauntless duo. On July 13 the story broke far and wide. The report caused such excitement in Tokyo that it vied for space in the major shimbums with the reports on the war in China, which Japan had invaded only a week before. A day or so later, American dailies reported that Japanese dailies were retracting the story. It had never happened.

Both of the above—Gilbert Islands and Japanese fishing boat— underpin every spoken and unspoken suspicion in the early years of Earhart's disappearance. They came to saturate her inner circle. From later published accounts and released documents, we can piece back together what GP had told Vidal and what Vidal began to confide in FDR only a few days after the search had been discontinued.

These shadows on the wall were set in motion by psychics. In the 1930s, séances and mediumship were respectable enough and indulged in the most be the rich, idle, and erudite. Duke University continued to probe into the reality of ESP and remote viewing. The very fact public opinion was undecided left the door open to at least consider psychic contributions to such pursuits as crime investigation and finding missing persons.

Captain T.K. Johnson was always standing by in San Francisco, ready to act as GP's liaison with the search operation. As early as July 9, Johnson confided in Admiral Orrin Murfin something GP wanted. It was "confidential for pressing reasons he says too intimate to disclose. . ." GP wanted the Navy to branch off the 281 North position and search northwest to the Gilberts. Johnson must have known Murfin wasn't going to budge because of undisclosed information, which sounds too much like whim. On the communiqué to Murfin, he appended at the bottom that "E.C." and "L.S." in Hollywood had heard from "Post, Kingsford Smith, and Noonan. Noonan died Saturday. Messages allege A.E. then in rubber boat 304 miles northwest by west of Howland Island. Call letters given WXAQQ. Message ended with reassured word from K.S. that she would be found."

Sir Charles Kingsford-Smith was a noted Australian pilot who in 1928 flew the Pacific in a trimotor. "Post" must mean Wiley Post, yet another famous aviator, and Noonan was, of course, Fred Noonan. These 3 men had one thing in common: they were quite dead by July 1937— well, Post and Kingsford-Smith were, both having died in aviation accidents. According to the codicil on the communiqué, Noonan had just joined them.

They weren't communicating by shortwave. Obviously, this was psychic, and perhaps the addition of the codicil reflects Johnson's suspicions about the credibility of GP's "intimate" sources.

In any case, according to these sources the Electra was drifting to the Gilberts. The next night "E.C." reported the Electra had remained intact until Sunday (July 4) and then sank. AE (also "they") was now drifting in the rubber raft.

From a more rational standpoint, Captain Johnson encouraged GP to hold on. In a letter sent GP on July 15: "My belief is that the fliers are still somewhere in the area yet to be searched, and that when the search reaches the Gilbert Islands, that something will be found. The belief that the radio signals come from the plane is too strong to give up, and the logical conclusion is that the plane must have been on land somewhere."

Johnson's letter was not probably long in GP's hands when he burst in on Jackie Cochran. In her autobiography *The Stars at Noon* she recounts how she and Amelia agreed to use her psychic intuition to help locate her if she should go down. Then in almost lamenting tones she writes:

> With all this ability and preliminary work with Amelia, why didn't I locate her when she went down? The answer is that I did, or at least I think I did, but can never prove it one way or the other, and besides it was all to no purpose. George Putnam was in my apartment in Los Angeles almost as soon as he could get there after the news of her non arrival at Howland Island. He was extremely excited and called on me for the kind of help Amelia thought I might be able to give. I told him where Amelia had gone down; that with the ditching of the plane Mr. Noonan, the navigator, had fractured his skull against the bulkhead in the navigator's compartment and was unconscious; that Amelia was alive and the plane was floating in a certain area. I named a boat called the *Itasca* which I had never heard of at the time, as the boat that was nearby, and I also named another Japanese fishing vessel in that area, the name of which I now forget. I begged Putnam to keep my name out of it all but to get planes and ships out to the designated area. Navy planes and ships in abundance combed that area but found no trace. I followed the course of her drifting for two days. It was always in the area being well combed. On the third day I went to the Cathedral and lit can-

dles for Amelia's soul, which I knew had then taken off on its own long flight. I was frustrated emotionally and overcome. If my strange ability was worth anything it should have saved Amelia. Only the urging of Floyd ever prompted me to try my hand at this sort of thing again and he hasn't urged me for several years for he knows it upsets me.

Frustratingly, Cochran does not give us the coordinates. However, the only time GP requested the Navy to search a specific location without giving any justification was on July 17. Coast Guard San Francisco sent his request to search 170 degrees East and .09 North. The Navy declined, saying that it was impracticable and all the Gilberts (to the west of this location) had already been searched. No one knew GP's motive, but Captain J.S. Dowell of the *Lexington* Group reasoned within his report that GP must have been inspired by a 2 knot westward drift. Rather GP appears to have been inspired by Cochran and these are the coordinates that she gave him but could not recall in her 1954 autobiography.

Obviously, GP had not burst into her apartment for some time; over two weeks after Amelia had vanished, in fact. Actually, it was the day before the Navy would suspend the search. Seeing this coming, GP might have rushed to her as a desperate last ditch effort. Thus Cochran's recollection that AE drifted for a few days may be taken in this context to mean she drifted until about July 19/20.

I do not list her record of her remote viewing to endorse the idea of its reality. I enter it here because it is only one tile of similar information that GP was putting together from psychic and solid sources to form a mosaic that when viewed full-on could only impress upon him his wife had survived. As a result, he was desperate to tap as many contacts as he could, the hope being to continue the search.

Contemporary written messages preserve how GP is always reticent to admit to his sources. He declared to his contact at the Department of the Navy (Mr. Roper) on July 23 that "confidential and extraordinary evidence seems to exist indicating castaways still living though of such strange nature cannot be officially or publically considered."

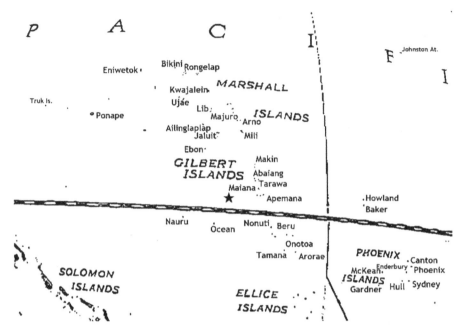

Plotting the coordinates (star) G.P. Putnam asked to be searched reveals the location is just west of the Gilbert Islands.

Around the same time GP wrote to Roper, yet more psychic information had come his way. During séance an esoteric spiritualist group in Canada was receiving messages from the late Captain Hinchliffe, who had vanished in the North Atlantic in 1928 attempting to carry the first woman across the ocean. The spiritualist contact, T. Lacey, had sent GP an interesting summary of their readings. Captain Hinchliffe was materializing regularly, and the following could be gleaned: "The plane was damaged in the forced landing as undership caught on reef. High winds and rough seas later released plane which floated out to sea and sank in deep water." Lacey continued:

It has been definitely given to us that only hope of rescue will come from help of natives of surrounding islands and Japanese fishermen now in those waters. Some of these natives who are very psychic know of the plight of the castaways and by some means of telegraphy have broadcast the news throughout the islands. Noonan was badly crippled in the landing and little hope is held out for him.

Rescue must come long before your expedition can reach those waters or the worst can be feared.

For George, this fit nicely with what Cochran and the other psychics had told him. They had the Electra drifting, and by mid-July all knew it was impossible for AE to have sent any radio message from the Electra unless it was on land. When Lacey told GP the Electra had come down on a reef first before drifting off, it explained it all. As GP wove it together, Amelia had ditched on this reef on Friday, July 2. She had sent the initial post-loss messages. Then she had drifted off on Sunday the 4th and was now in a rubber raft. Noonan was injured.

Soon GP would come to feel he had confirmation of this scenario from the real world. For . . .

. . .Meanwhile, a mariner named L.M. Wilson had gotten in touch with GP with actual coordinates about an uncharted reef in the Gilberts. In 1933 he was sailing on the yacht *Quebec Ptarmigan.* He met an Australian captain named Heyen, master of a Chinese copra vessel. He was told "a reef or low lying island existed one hundred seventy four degrees and ten minutes east longitude, two degrees and thirty six minutes north latitude." From the southern tip of Taritari (Makin) Island the reef should bear 106 degrees true and be about 85 miles away. "Heyen informed me that reef only known to last generation Gilbertese natives who sailed there for turtle eggs." Wilson admitted he never saw the reef and that it was not on his sea charts, but he believed it could exist "as a Butaritari native told me his grandfather sailed there with outrigger frequently."

With the news reports lamenting the end of the search, Wilson reached out again to GP on July 21st, for the news was reporting he was going to continue the search in his own hired yacht. Wilson had found Heyen's home address in New South Wales and included it for Putnam to verify the story. "I also recall talking about this reef to Mr. Maude in Tarawa, the capital of the Gilbert Group. Mr. Maude was governor of the islands when I was there and he seemed to think that the reef existed as it was common talk among older Gilbertese natives." Wilson also suggested that Captain I. Handley of Tarawa could "throw some light" on this reef as he was the commander of the island schooner and had sailed the Gilberts for years. He concluded: "I know that all this information I have passed on to you is but a stab in the dark but if there is any truth to the garbled messages sent out by the fliers (and there might be) the above is worth investigation." And it wasn't long before GP believed the same.

According to a message from GP on July 30, he stated to Sumner Welles, Undersecretary of State: "Confidentially this information astonishingly corroborates the position actually repeatedly given me during last ten days from other sources probably disclosed by Vidal which themselves interesting because their independent unanimity if not necessarily convincing because their nature." GP is, of course, talking about Wilson's coordinates compared to, once again, conduits of information that seem a bit embarrassing for him. He had just had a conference with Vidal, he had declared, and he implies above that Vidal probably had already informed Welles. The urgency was there (for GP) to find the reef and follow the currents of drift.

Exchanges of letters such as these, plus a flurry of telegrams from GP urging Washington to ask London to search, help one to put in order this period. It was the culmination of a few weeks of remarkably consistent psychic claims about the "castaways" added to fragments of more conventional information, especially L.M. Wilson's lost reef. Prodded by a desperate GP, Vidal, McIntyre, Welles, and FDR had moved forward with State.

All this fretting condensed into the following. Undersecretary Sumner Welles acted with permission from the Secretary of State himself, Cordell Hull.

July 30, 1937
7 p.m.

AMEMBASSY
        London (England)
328.

Evidence which to many sources seems positive indicates that Amelia Earhart (Mrs. Putnam) was on land the two nights following her disappearance. In the circumstances we should appreciate your getting in touch with the Colonial Office or other appropriate authority and telling them: (1) that if the authorities could

send a boat from the Gilbert Islands to continue a thorough surface search of those islands Mr. Putnam would be glad to defray
the expenses involved, and (2) that word might be circulated that
there is a reward of $2,000 offered for any evidence leading to a
solution of her disappearance whether in the nature of wreckage
or more positive indication of what happened.

HULL
(SW)

This evidence? Basically, it seems to be faith that the post–
loss radio messages received over the first two nights were really
from AE. This conviction (at least with GP) was strengthened by
the coincidences between the readings of numerous psychic
sources.

Only a couple of days after the above telegram was sent to
London, Gene Vidal quickly informed Sumner Welles the actual coordinates had not been included. Welles sent another message to London on August 2 in order to convey the exact position
in the Gilbert Islands.

GP wrote back to Lacey on August 4, thanking him and:

> I also want you to know a very interesting fact – especially if it
> proves out. From a mariner familiar with that territory I was ad-
> vised the other day in detail of an uncharted island on the eastern
> fringe of the Gilberts. It appears that old time Gilbertese went
> there in their dugout canoes. It is only 85 miles from a village.
> The extraordinary fact is that the detailed position given for that
> island exactly coincides with the position you gave me in an earli-
> er letter. Through local British authorities, I believe that an im-
> mediate search of the location has been arranged.

With an exact position, the British did act upon it. The Colonial Office contacted Tarawa. On August 10, Captain Handley
sailed by cutter to the location. It was a tense rest of the month
for GP. Finally, on August 31 he was told by telegram that Handley had found no reef.

The gist of Wilson's messages, however, proved he was sincere. Captain Heyen could be contacted, and the British in the

Gilberts could verify they had heard such stories. But this was the second reef that could not be located. Unlike Winslow Reef, this reef would never be identified.

Contemporarily, George Putnam only knew that along with Winslow Reef yet another uncharted or mischarted reef had slipped by undetected. This Gilbert one, however, fit with the ocean drift patterns, with the Los Angeles amateur short-wavers hearing what they believed were coordinates near the Gilberts, and then Cochran remote viewing AE as now drifting west of the Gilberts.

Given all this, GP could never be satisfied with the negative response as conclusive. All he could do is accept that the reef could not be found. He believed she had drifted from it after two nights. Until Gene Burns' March 1944 article from the Marshall Islands, this was the final episode. Then Elieu spoke only of a white woman flier. All the psychics had said Noonan had died, but specifically Kingsford-Smith said AE would be recovered. Could the psychics have been right after all? One can only wonder what GP really believed thereafter. He could have come to believe what Amy Otis believed.

She didn't need to tick-tock back and forth between psychic esoterica and news rumors. She remained purely entrenched in her own theory, which in some ways was wilder than the scenario coming from the psychics.

Brief reports of that Japanese fishing boat had stirred her the most. She was down at the Japanese consulate in Los Angeles the next day, demanding information. They knew nothing. Then Gene Burns' March 1944 article about Elieu's story brought back her latent suspicions. He had not written that this American woman flier had been considered a spy. She had merely been taken away. This allowed Amy Otis to put an even darker spin on things. As early as May 6, 1944, mother Earhart coalesced her suspicions in a letter to Neta Snook. Then it would slip out in 1949 in a *Time Magazine* article. She had declared that Amelia had landed on a "tiny atoll" and "was picked up by a Japanese fishing boat that took her to the Marshall Islands, then under Japanese control." She asserted that the Japanese had allowed her to broadcast from the Marshall Islands initially because they "believed she was merely a transocean flier in distress. But Tokyo had a different opinion of her significance in the area. She was ordered taken to Japan. There, I know, she met with an accident, an 'arranged' accident that ended her life."

Part of Amy Otis' impassioned conviction was garnered from a young friend. During that anxious July 1937, this friend drove across Los Angeles to quickly inform Amy Otis she had been listening to a shortwave radio "when a broadcast from Tokyo came in saying they were celebrating there, with parades, etc. because of Amelia's rescue or pick up by a Japanese fisherman." The rest is the result of Amy Otis taking Nina Paxton's statements emphasizing Mili Atoll and the Marshall Islands and then adding them to the Burns story sent direct from the Marshall Islands.[12]

It is only now that Ajima's story comes into play in the sequence of rumors. Coming from the isolated islands right after their liberation, it appears so independent that it becomes the second most substantial rumor in the sequence. And it makes the unsubstantial rumor of the fishing boat look believable. And because that story had been retracted, there is now the halo of a dark conspiracy around daughter Earhart's fate.

It isn't hard to see how these reports weaved together in Amy Otis' mind to create a believable and grim theory. After her rescue, logically, the Japanese should have repatriated AE to the US, but this obviously wasn't done. After Elieu's story independently verified the old fishing boat story, it was easy to believe the Japanese had instead played some sinister hand. There was therefore some greater purpose to AE's flight that made her secret death a necessity.

It would be easy for AE's inner circle to consider there is truth to this aggregate of rumors and sequence of facts. AE did not have the fuel to have flown to the Marshall Islands. But in flying back to the Gilbert Islands, which rumor hath she would, she was in a position to ditch where currents would drift her westward to the Marshalls.

Drifting for weeks is not beyond the bounds of possibility. There was the dramatic case of Eddie Rickenbacker. His B-17 became lost trying to find the airport on Canton Island on October 20, 1942. They ditched at sea in the same area where Earhart

---

[12] The details were also in her May 1944 letter to Neta Snook.

had vanished and drifted in their raft for 22 days before being sighted and picked up.

Thus the three rumors that begin this chapter are truly fundamental to the belief that Earhart had survived. Her Electra may have been capable of drifting. It could have drifted to an island or drifted off an island in the Gilberts and a Japanese ship came along and picked her up. Alternately, it may have sunk; she may have continued in a raft.

There is another piece that might have played a factor in influencing Earhart's inner circle. I cannot prove Amy Otis heard of it— the F.B.I. is never a leaky sieve— but due to the political connections within AE's circle it may have gotten out that a man claiming to be her cousin had been part of the Bataan death march and then taken prisoner by the Japanese and held in the Philippines. Once he was freed after the liberation he made a report. It is contained in a memorandum sent to G-2 in Washington from J. Edgar Hoover on December 27, 1944:

> . . .He was attached to the American forces in the Philippines prior to Pearl Harbor and that on one occasion he and another American were entertained by some Japanese in a hotel in the Philippines. He stated the walls of the hotel were extremely thin and he overheard a conversation in English between two Japanese to the effect that Amelia Earhardt [sic] was still alive and being detained in a hotel in Tokyo. [He] stated that he was never able to forget these remarks and shortly after Pearl Harbor he was taken prisoner by the Japanese along with other Americans remaining at Bataan. . . He stated that he had been in Japanese prisoner of war camps from that time on. He pointed out that at one prisoner of war camp he was given the job of typing statements made by American officers to the Japanese intelligence authorities. He stated that one day after some interviews had been conducted and he was alone in the room with the Japanese intelligence officer, he inquired of the Japanese officer, "Would you tell me frankly if my cousin Amelia Earhardt [sic] is still alive?" [He] stated that the Japanese officer was apparently taken aback by [his] remark but is alleged to have stated that he could not tell [him] anything except "don't worry about her well being. She is perfectly all right."
>
> [He] stated that this caused him to inquire of various Japanese guards at the various prisoner of war camps from time to time re-

garding Amelia Earhardt [sic], and he stated that some of the Japanese stated they did not know anything about it, some stated that they had heard her over the Japanese radio, others that they had seen her in Tokyo, and still others that she was alive and in Tokyo.

Whether the soldier was delusional or not (Hoover warned G-2 his reliability was unknown), there was more than enough reason to advise that he "tell his story to the Military Intelligence Service in order that it might be brought to the attention of the proper officials of the War Department so that it may be run out as a target when the American forces land in Japan."

Paul Briand believed that the Army had done just that. Finding this report is what had inspired him to write his friend Joe Gervais the oxymoron that "hearsay evidence" existed indicating Amelia had been in Tokyo. With the help of Gervais' conspiratorial ruminations, he began to reassess a conundrum involving Jackie Cochran. In 1945, she had gotten into Tokyo *even* before the occupation forces. He strongly suspected Cochran had been assigned to find Earhart.[13]

Apparently Briand didn't want to believe Cochran's own story in her autobiography. During the war, she had been a Lt. Colonel and head of WASPS— Women's Air Forces Service Pilots— for the Army Air Corps. According to her own account, immediately after the war she was only a licensed correspondent with *Liberty*. She wrote she had to pull every string she could to get into Japan. It is only as an aside that she mentions General Hap Arnold had asked her to also look into the role of women in the Japanese war effort. Cochran devoted only one paragraph to it in her book, and her account is quite benign.

> My search of the records found no evidence that the Japanese women had participated in any active war effort beyond factory or home production. I did, however, find numerous clippings and photographs about Amelia Earhart and Jimmy Doolittle and other American pilots, including myself. There were several files on Amelia Earhart.

---

[13] Expressed to Gervais in *Amelia Earhart Lives*. By 1967 Briand was writing a new book on AE's fate entitled *Requiem for Amelia*.

Ironically, Muriel Morrissey added an intriguing tidbit to the whole affair in her 1963 biography of her sister, *Courage is the Price*. "Nothing indicated that Amelia had been a prisoner," wrote sister Earhart. "As the file was still 'open' in 1945, it seems unlikely that the Japanese government had any knowledge of her being 'liquidated' by their order." Although "open file" seems purely to be Muriel's invention, the statement served to feed Briand's and Gervais' suspicion AE *had* survived.

Muriel unwisely wrote up Cochran's examination as ending the whole idea of Spy and Die on Saipan. It's a slim rebuttal that was wiped out handily 3 years later by Fred Goerner's stunning bestseller. Eventually, Muriel also had her doubts. She went to the State Department on May 21, 1970, and inquired about any documents. "Mrs. Morrissey cannot believe that her sister was on an intelligence mission and can see no evidence of the truth of the Goerner thesis . . . but she is obviously distressed by all the allegations and felt she should have a look herself."

There are no references, of course, in the records to any spy mission. And if there was, it's missing the point anyway. Records could only prove AE was on a mission. Any such paperwork could not prove if she had survived. By 1970 that was the object on everybody's mind.

Muriel Morrissey's suspicion her sister had survived was due to more than Goerner's book. It was also the culmination of a long chain of unusual circumstances. . .and unusual circumstances always include GP Putnam. Since he had died in 1950, he had told AE's family the following provocative story before then. Muriel had also written of it in *Courage is the Price*.

After the European D-Day when the collapse of Japanese resistance was imminent, a woman's voice was sometimes heard, broadcasting from Tokyo false information to the American forces. Could this "Tokyo Rose" possibly be Amelia, brainwashed to the point of leading her countrymen into enemy traps? Every fiber of GP's being denied the possibility, but he alone in all that vast area could without question identify Amelia's voice, even though weakened and tense from psychological mistreatment. He made a dangerous three-day trek through Japanese-held territory to reach a Marine Corps radio station near the coast where the broadcast reception was loud and clear. After listening to the voice for less than a minute, GP said decisively, 'I'll stake my life on that is not Amelia's voice. It sounds to me as if the woman might have lived in New York, and of course she had been fiendishly well coached, but Amelia—never!'"

There was more than enough reason for G2 to be curious about Tokyo Rose. In quick succession they had the report on the alleged finding of AE's belongings in the Marshall Islands (which even CINCPAC Chester Nimitz had heard). Then a month after Eugene Burns' story on the Marshall Islands went over the wires (March 21, 1944) *Time Magazine* did a piece on Tokyo Rose (April 10, 1944), declaring she was cultured with a "touch of Boston." Then in December Military Intelligence is told about the soldier's account from the Philippines. A hare must have run through a Washington brain and the point was pondered: could Amelia Earhart be Tokyo Rose? It would be within the natural course of events that GP might be asked to listen, but there is little reason to believe in Putnam's dare-devil story. At best, George may have been asked to listen to a radio *somewhere*. If this did happen, then he was in a cushy office. Of course, the whole story could merely have been his typical grandstanding.

But I digress. . . . The point is that Putnam's story implicitly impresses upon one that officialdom believed as late as 1945 it was possible Earhart could have survived in Japan.

In any case, we are with this chapter basically restarting the quest for AE all over. The rumors that circulated in the beginning, especially the quashed fishing boat story, given impetus by this wartime report from Gene Burns, and even GP's story above, help us to understand why so many within AE's friends and family were willing to accept some form of the Akiyama story in 1960 or some form of Goerner's thesis . . . or something worse.

Whether Gene Vidal believed in the psychics or not, he and a few government officials had believed some post-loss messages could have been genuine. They could have accepted that AE had been picked up or drifted from a Gilbert island after having spent two nights there. Reports of her survival that hinged on this would be more believable, and in the summer of 1937 a very macabre one emerged. And with a specific description, Gene had more reasons than anybody to believe it.

What follows is one root of the "conspiracy of silence." We have to go back again, back to 1937. With the discontinuing of the search, George Putnam put out a $2,000.00 reward for any information that would lead to his wife.

Chapter 15

From Long Island to Long Pig

On August 3, 1937, only a month since his wife vanished, George Putnam was somehow approached by a small man calling himself "Johnson." The timid figure claimed he was a member of the crew of a gun running vessel. While sailing the Pacific en route to Panama they passed an island. Thereon was a ditched aircraft. They came in closer and launched a boat. There was a man and a woman, he told Putnam. The man was dead. The woman was half mad.

The crew took the woman aboard ship. The Chinese doctor tried to help her, but she was hysterical most of the time. It was only at Panama they discovered she was Amelia Earhart. They learned there was a reward. Continuing to New Jersey, they put in and he was chosen by the crew to approach Putnam and get the $2,000.00 reward money. They would then hand over his wife. It had to be done quickly. She needed help.

GP didn't buy it. He wanted proof. Then the little man presented a scarf. It was indeed Amelia's scarf. GP remembered it.

George Putnam agreed to pay him, but he put the man off. He arranged for them to meet and exchange the money. In the meantime he called the F.B.I. and they arranged to mark ten $100 dollar bills to be used. The meeting was arranged and Putnam insisted the little man go with him to the bank and get the other $1,000 outstanding. On the way they were intercepted by New York City police detectives.

Johnson was taken down and booked. His actual name was Wilbur Rothar, a janitor who lived in the Bronx.

The news broke quickly. The August 5 edition of the *New York Times* published part of Rothar's account:

> . . .A few days out of New Guinea the skipper anchored off a small island to take on fresh water. In a cove on this island, Rothar said, a wrecked airplane was discovered. The body of a man was lying on the wing of the plane. On the rock shore a woman was standing in nothing but a pair of athletic shorts. The sharks, he said, had eaten away the lower part of the man's body. The ship's crew buried the man at sea, and took aboard the woman, who was out of her mind, and badly injured.

A few articles followed elaborating on the incident, wherein it was stated Rothar confessed to being a part of a plot to extort money. There was no freighter. AE wasn't stashed in Jersey. Rothar eventually pled not guilty with a specification of insanity. He was remanded to the Sanity Commission for 10 days of study to see if he could stand trial. He was found insane. On October 13, 1937, he was formally declared insane in court before Judge John Freschi. By New York State law at the time this prohibited him from standing trial. He was committed to Matteawan Hospital for the criminally insane. A little filler in the newspaper ended the public story of Wilbur Rothar, alias Wilbur Goodenough, alias "Johnson."

Behind-the-scenes, however, the story continued. Rothar never came to trial and the strange case never saw the light of rational day. Without trial he remained ensconced in various asylums for 25 years until a petition to dismiss the indictment was accepted (in 1962) by then-District Attorney, Frank Hogan.

Major Joe Gervais rediscovered the case and followed up on

it in 1968, drawn to it for quite a different reason than we are here. As usual, he began to flirt with sensational and convoluted conspiracy theories, even speculating that Wilbur Rothar was Fred Noonan, insane and given a new identity. But Gervais actually did admirable work in finding the court documents. Through the references he listed, I was able to obtain many more documents. One document remained restricted. It was the report of the Sanity Commission. In 2013 I was not given this report, but in 1968 by special circumstances Judge Brust allowed Gervais to examine it while a court employee stood over. He was not allowed to take notes, but Gervais tried to remember as much as possible. What I quote now has to be taken in light of this fact.

Police forced Rothar to take the reward money offered by Putnam for information about Amelia Earhart, Rothar told Dr. Lonnardo. Rothar claimed to have been severely beaten on his arrival at the police station after his arrest. This, he said, resulted in a neck injury. . . Rothar described Fred Noonan's body, legs, genitals, intestines protruding from a torso half eaten by sharks, at least a thousand of which were swimming nearby. Noonan and the plane wreckage were lodged on a reef, according to Rothar. . .Dr. Lonnardo noted that Rothar kept asking over and over throughout the examination for his sister, Muriel. Rothar said Muriel wore a brace of some sort when she was younger. . .Then the doctor noted Rothar's description of Amelia Earhart, mad, head bandaged, tied to the bunk of his ship, sheets badly soiled with blood and excrement, out of her mind and raving wildly. . . Throughout the entire examination Rothar maintained that Amelia Earhart was alive, but Fred Noonan was dead. 'The Boiler was blown up by ammunition,' he repeated no less than eight times. . .There on a sheet among the notes of Dr. Lonnardo was a map of an island—drawn by the hand of Wilbur Rothar. On the map of the island was circled an X. It marked the spot on the beach where Rothar said he first saw four colored men cooking something like a leg and eating it. He described in vivid detail how the four men in turn repeatedly raped the woman he later learned was Amelia Earhart. He described in exceptionally obscene language the intimate and perverse acts performed, not only upon her, but upon himself, switching from acts of rape to acts of sodomy so often that the doctor could not be sure which victim of sexual mayhem he was talking about—Amelia Earhart or himself. . .He used vile yet vivid language, portraying acts so repulsive that Gervais developed an instant mental block in discussing what he found in the report. . .Rothar also described seeing a warship, either a destroyer or a minesweeper.

Dr. Lonnardo declared Rothar had been insane during the examination and had also been insane at the time of the crime.

The Rothar incident is quite curious even without any link to Gervais' conspiracy theories. And in spite of a few mistakes in recalling what he had read (Joseph Lonnardo was Rothar's attorney, not the doctor), extrinsic documents exist supporting Gervais general summary of the sanity commission. For example, there seems little reason from our perspective today to doubt Rothar's statement that the police forced him to take the money so they could railroad him for extortion. I obtained a document from the court records. It was the brief questioning Rothar had been given upon arrest. It is entitled "Line up at Manhattan Headquarters." The interrogator was inspector Donovan of the Corrections Bureau. It is dated August 5, 1937.

"WILBUR ROTHAR charged with attempted extortion. Charged by complainant with attempted extortion. Complainant is husband of Amelia Earhart the missing aviatrix, stating he was member of crew of a boat containing Amelia Earhart and demanded $2000.00 for the release. Arrested by Dets. Gleason and O'Neill of the M.O.D."

Q. Is that true, Wilbur, did you make a statement to the District Attorney?
A. (No answer).
Q. Where were you born?
A. I don't know.
Q. Never been arrested before?
A. Never, I don't know.
Q. How much money did you have in your possession when arrested?
A. No answer.

(This prisoner evidently took a fit at the last question).

The very question of the money upset him. There is no reason to disbelieve his statement to his examining psychiatrist that he was to some extent framed.

Why did George Putnam take this seriously enough to agree to entrap the man? Was it the scarf alone? The subsequent investigation asserted that Rothar had found it at Roosevelt Field. He had gone to see AE landing that day. It had blown off Amelia and tumbled away, and he finally picked it up. Apparently it was having possession of such an authentic article that had emboldened him to try the extortion attempt.

But there is something else quite curious here, and it merits some attention. The scarf wasn't the only reason for GP to have believed the lurid story. How did madman Rothar know his wife wore men's athletic shorts? George was certain AE wore his boxers while flying because they were more comfortable for her. Rothar's description was close enough to this fact, at least for someone who claimed to have seen her from afar on an island.

Whatever may have gone through GP's mind, this was the worst time for Rothar to pop up with such a story. Presently, George was fretting with Gene Vidal. He was hoping to get Floyd Odlum involved in a search and trying to get Mac McIntyre to light a fire at the State Department so that State would move the British to search the Gilbert Islands and that uncharted reef L.M. Wilson had told him about. Now this fellow pops up and talks about a reef and mentions men's shorts. Rothar also said Noonan was dead, just like all the psychics had told him. Doubtless GP didn't believe that this ship's crew had his wife in Hoboken. But the kernel of truth could be the crew passed the island and saw these events from afar. GP may have baited Rothar so the police could browbeat the truth out of him.

However, there may have been a more persuasive factor involved. GP may have been urged by Gene Vidal to believe some element of the story. The truth, it seems, is that Gene knew AE wore jockey shorts, *his* jockey shorts. How could madman Rothar have said what he had said unless he had actually seen Earhart? As one might expect, her unmentionables were not in the realm of common knowledge.

In her biography of Earhart (*East to the Dawn*, 1997), Susan Butler only briefly touches on Rothar in a vague way. "Some years after her last flight, it was reported that a Russian sailor had seen a white woman signaling from an island dressed in jockey shorts. George told Gene that the outfit had been wrong— it couldn't be Amelia, because 'she always wore my shorts when she flew, but I wore boxer shorts.' Gene thought that was very funny."

As told by Butler, the story is obvious fiction. It comes from Gore Vidal, Gene's son and celebrated fiction writer. He used it to accentuate a love affair had existed between his father and AE. But his vignette above, uncritically repeated by Butler, is impossible to believe. The Rothar affair actually occurred only a month after AE vanished. Given the circumstances, how could GP minimize such a report merely based on the difference in a boxer short and an athletic short, especially when seen from afar? Moreover, had Gene Vidal loved Earhart as much as Butler evolves it, his reaction would not be musing at having an inside joke on his paramour's husband. Gene would be frantic at the news. He would have said: 'Brace yourself, George; she wore my jockey shorts. That Russian said something he could not have made up. We must find that island and go search.' But in Butler's carbon recounting of Gore's fantasy no such logical reaction is required because it was "years" later and thus there was no viable lead they could pursue.

Anyway, AE probably did wear jockey shorts, for Katherine Vidal (Gene's second wife) corroborated that Gene bought *new* athletic shorts for AE.

Whether AE and Vidal were lovers or not, the Vidal family stories implicitly tell us two things: AE wore Gene's jockey shorts and we can accept that Gene never did confess to being the benefactor of AE's unmentionables while GP lived.

Yet the Rothar affair did occur, and it happened within a short time of AE's disappearance. Rothar's specific statement would have cut to Gene's core, and he could only have reacted in a serious way.

Outside of George, Gene had been the most active in trying to make heads or tails out of Amelia's disappearance, even proving the critical link between GP and Washington to get the British to search for a reef. Then as State is transmitting the request, the Rothar story breaks about Amelia being seen in jockey shorts on a reef. Gene may have viewed the Bronx janitor, albeit mad, as having had some truth in his story, perhaps even put up to the extortion by those who had actually been the witnesses.

Vidal had two choices. Over time he had to accept that AE had drifted free from a Gilbert sand trap and the Japanese fishing boat had picked her up, or he could have believed the basics of Rothar's story; that she had died at the hands of libidinous Gilbertese and the actual eyewitnesses attempted extortion through madman Rothar.

Clues suggest Vidal believed the latter for quite a while, and these clues seem concentrated around transportation department members—those with access to Gene Vidal's Bureau of Air Commerce. (Though he no longer worked there, he maintained all his old contacts.) One such example was recorded on May 13, 1938. Henry Morgenthau, head of the Treasury which ran the Coast Guard, was interrupted in a meeting. Malvina Scheider, Eleanor Roosevelt's secretary, was on the phone. Eleanor had heard about a written report on Amelia's loss. Paul Mantz wanted a copy, and Eleanor wanted to know if that was possible. The Dictaphone stenographer continued to type away while Morgenthau chatted. It is clear from the transcript below that two stories are being conflated. Morgenthau at first is alluding to Earhart breaking down and going hysterical, as related by Warner Thompson, and then another fate gets mixed in.

Henry Morgenthau (on White House phone)
Oh, hello— Oh, thanks. Hello, Tommy (Malvina Scheider). How are you? This letter that Mrs. Roosevelt wrote me about trying to get the report on Amelia Earhart. Now, I've been given a verbal report. If we're going to release this, it's just going to smear the whole reputation of Amelia Earhart, and my. . .Yes, but I mean if we give it to this one man we've got to make it public; we can't let one man see it. And if we ever release the report of the *Itasca* on Amelia Earhart, any reputation she's got is gone, because— and I'd like to— I'd really like to return this to you.

(continuing) Now, I know what the Navy did, I know what the *Itasca* did, and I know how Amelia Earhart absolutely disregarded all orders, and if we ever release this thing, goodbye Amelia Earhart's reputation. Now, really— because if we give the access to one, we have to give it to all.

The above revolves around Earhart's last communications and her failure to respond to the *Itasca's* radio requests, her ignorance of how long it takes to get a minimum, and her inability to get her own minimum on the *Itasca*. But there is now something else. Morgenthau continues:

> And my advice is that— and if the President ever heard that somebody questioned that the Navy hadn't made the proper search, after what those boys went through— I think they searched, as I remember it, 50,000 square miles, and every one of those planes was out, and the boys just burnt themselves out physically and every other way searching for her. And if – I mean I think he'd get terribly angry if somebody – because they just went the limit, and so did the Coast Guard. And we have the report of all those wireless messages and everything else, what that woman – happened to her the last few minutes. I hope I've just got to never make it public, I mean. –O.K. – Well, still if she wants it, I'll tell her – I mean what happened. It isn't a very nice story. –Well, yes. There isn't anything additional to something like that. You think up a good one. – Thank you.

The phone conversation over, Morgenthau turned to another member present, a Mr. Chauncey, and continued their previous line of conversation before he touched on the phone call all present had been probably been quite engrossed with.

> Morgenthau: (to Chauncey): Just send it back.
> Chauncey: Sure.
> Morgenthau: I mean we tried— people want us to search again those islands, after what we have gone through. You [meaning Gibbons, another member] know the story, don't you?
> Gibbons: We have evidence that the thing is all over, sure. Terrible. It would be awful to make it public.

What are they talking about?

More than one thing seems certain. From starting with Earhart's behavior in the cockpit, the conversation leads into inferences that the search of the islands had not been diligent enough. Then the terrible things AE went through in the last minutes. Gibbons infers they have proof it "is all over" anyway.

From our perspective today, the conversation runs together because we don't hear what "Tommy" Scheider is saying on the other side. But it seems evident the conversation wandered onto more than one aspect of Earhart's fate. And it is obvious that Morgenthau believes they know her final moments. "It isn't a very nice story."

Gene Vidal had been head of Air Commerce, and it is unlikely that Morgenthau or Gibbons hadn't heard of the Rothar affair from him or members of his former bureau.

What we don't know, of course, is why Vidal accepted elements of Rothar's tale. Was it the statement of athletic shorts only? Or, eventually anyway, was it with GP's tacit encouragement?

It is quite impossible to believe that GP hadn't heard Vidal's boast that his wife wore his looms. Butler's muddled vignette based on Gore's memory implies there was some reason for George to make a point contradicting the assertion. And he's not going to do so in the context she presents— based on the distant observation of a sailor. Therefore he disputed she wore jockeys for another reason. We can assume it was to refute Gene's gauche claims. What we do know is that George spun the Rothar story with several lies, and we really don't know if spite led GP to convince Gene that Rothar's obscene story was true.

One of GP's versions was eventually repeated by Muriel Morrissey. In her biography of her sister, *Courage is the Price* (1963), she touches on the Rothar affair.

> GP was subjected to a cruel extortion hoax. . . An ex-seaman had found one of Amelia's bright scarfs left in the hangar at Wheeler Field in Hawaii, probably at the time of the Electra's ill-fated crash. Using the scarf, which GP recognized as belonging to Amelia, as a token of the authority of his information, the man demanded five thousand dollars for disclosing the name of the island in the Caroline cluster where Amelia was marooned and held prisoner by smugglers. Under the astute questioning of Mr. Black, who had observed the Navy's prodigious search efforts from the cutter *Itasca*, the fake informer was caught in such a maze of contradictions that he soon admitted he had no information to sell, but was looking for 'easy money.' Mr. Black urged George Putnam to have the man indicted, but he refused.

"No, I'll not press charges," she has George say grandly. "I know Amelia would not want it that way. Why, I remember she wouldn't even let me fire the houseman whose negligence was responsible for the fire at our Rye home, because she said anybody could be forgetful once in a while."

Muriel continues:

> Then, turning to the shame-faced and frightened young man, he said, 'No, I won't have you jailed. You must be pretty hard up to try such a low-down trick as this. Here is fifty dollars for my wife's scarf. Now, get out of my sight, but try going straight for Amelia's sake.'

Until the discovery (and then for me, the release) of the court documents, the slant George Putnam put on the whole Rothar affair to AE's family went unchallenged. Aside from outright prevarication, he is pathetically self-serving in his account. The write up is a joke compared to the truth of the matter and the extent that GP helped to entrap Wilbur Rothar.

The poor madman remained in various asylums trapped within the system and never tried in court. The Indictment against Rothar was dropped only in 1962, probably when Muriel was penning that utter rubbish above. It was dropped because logically and legally he had served far more time already than he ever would if he was now declared sane, stood trial and was convicted for a first offense of extortion. He was released into the care of his sister Mary Rago and son Edmund Rothar. (New York has since changed its laws. Someone declared insane can stand trial first.)

There was no truthful clarification of the Rothar incident until 1970 with the brief publication of Gervais' and Klaas' outlandish conspiracy theory. Then I followed up and got the actual paperwork myself.

Yet in 1938 there is evidence that a number of people within Washington D.C. believed in parts of Rothar's story; that essentially Noonan and Earhart wound up as long pig in the hands of libidinous Gilbertese. The Morgenthau Transcript gives us a date that implies almost a year after-the-fact those around Commerce in Washington believed AE's final moments were ghastly.

How much really could be true here? Some of it actually could be. But everybody's take on it, then as now, is based only on deduction. There are enough facts only for inference and we all must draw our own conclusions. This present writer cannot believe GP was sincere, but it is certainly true that Putnam fed the rumors that AE could have survived. His supposedly harrowing trek through enemy territory to listen to Tokyo Rose is a case in point. Maybe he had believed some of Rothar's story, but his adventurous journey to Tokyo Rose could just be the machinations of a shameless self-promoter.

Reflected glory from Earhart's increasingly lily white reputation was no doubt a very good thing both when GP spun his tales and in 1963 when Muriel repeated them. In the Rothar affair he told Muriel he admonished the hustler in the name of Earhart to go straight.

Be all above as it may, there is something enigmatic about a handful of witness testimony on Saipan. Equally there is something disturbingly intriguing about "Zuse" Guerrero's belligerence. Despite Goerner's and Gervais' mutual antagonism of each other, neither would whitewash "Kumoi's" character. As the first to investigate officially, Elias Sablan encountered Zuse's shadow right away. As soon as word got around there was such an investigation underway he had intimidated the people from talking. He had not just been a head detective, as Goerner had written; he had essentially been chief of police of Saipan under the Japanese. He survived the war to ingratiate himself to the US Naval Administration and was appointed Sheriff of Saipan. He was fired in 1952 for nearly beating a man to death with a rubber hose. "Zuse" was good at intimidation, and the earliest witness stories squarely fingered the insular police at the center of the stories of this mysterious white woman flier.

The concept AE had survived begins with Gene Burns and his article in March 1944. This fact was easily lost to history because his article never captured the mind of the public. A year into his investigation in 1961, Fred Goerner had yet to even hear of it. When first told, he wrote: "The development did not amaze me; I was by then inured to the unusual." Yet it had caught on with Earhart's inner circle, and they had been the ones leading Goerner to believe in AE's potential survival, though obviously not declaring the source of their influence.

By his stories, GP also fed the believability of Burns' article, and AE's inner circle also knew of an undeniable action on his part that more than anything laid the foundation to believe in Burns' report. As soon as he got the negative reply from the British (August 31, 1937) regarding the existence of the turtle reef, GP was in action with the Japanese, asking them to search the Marshall Islands and asking what it would cost him. All he could tell AE's family and friends was that finally he got a reply. It had come from Admiral Yamamoto himself, the Minister of the Navy, assuring him they would search, but George Putnam never knew what constituted the Japanese search. It wasn't until 1944 and via Burns' article that he and AE's inner circle get the first feedback. Why should they not believe there had been truth to Burns' dispatch? And therewith why then not believe in some of the accounts later coming from Saipan?

It is time to go back to the beginning . . . and the beginning is not Amelia Earhart's disappearance. The beginning is the publishing of Gene Burns' story from the Marshall Islands, dateline March 1944.

Chapter 16

Marshalling the Facts

Over the decades, Fred Goerner came to refine his own theory. In the end he opted to believe that Earhart and Noonan had ditched on Winslow Reef. Yet during the course of his journey there was something he said in *The Search for Amelia Earhart* that was undeniably true. "The first tangible evidence that AE and Fred had been held by the Japanese came with the February 1944 invasion of the Marshalls. The information could have been held in the hope that they might later be found alive; the information was probably only fragmentary."

Today, it remains fragmentary and the tangible evidence is only alleged. But thanks in part to his sleuthing we can put these fragments together and refine the quest. The "tangible" evidence was on the island of Namur on Kwajalein Atoll. The personal items linked to Earhart were a diary and a suitcase. They were found in a barracks, in a room supposedly still done up to accommodate a woman. This discovery was made by Marines and the rumor that some of her belongings were found went through their channel to the highest level of the Pacific Fleet.

Independent of this channel there was the information provided to the Navy command on Majuro Atoll by a native named
Elieu Jibambam. Before the war he had been told by a local Japanese trader named Ajima that an American woman flier had
come down near Jaluit, another Marshall Islands atoll. Put together with the Marines' discovery this explains how these items
allegedly belonging to Amelia Earhart got to Kwajalein.

It would be wonderful if it was that simple. Unfortunately, it
is not. And authors ready to pursue and expand upon the conspiracy theory of Spy and Die on Saipan never sought to unravel
the problems. Goerner was actually the first to complicate
things. He never quoted Gene Burns' March 1944 article. The
news story had actually said that Elieu had been told "three and
a half years ago," so about autumn 1940. This is over 3 years *after*
Earhart and Noonan disappeared. The way Elieu's story is presented to us by Goerner, Ajima could be sailing between the islands on business when he comes across the Japanese ship that
picked her up, or alternately he came across someone in-the-
know soon after the event. Given the ring of a recent occur-
rence, it is understandable that he tells a native friend. But as
the original story goes, Elieu is told over 3 years later.

For anyone truly seeking to bring order to chaos, Goerner's
avoidance of clarifying this significant point takes on the air of
intentional negligence. He took the extreme effort to finally
reach Majuro Atoll (along with Ross Game), but he never quali-
fies this vital point. He doesn't ask Elieu to confirm *when* he was
told. In addition, he doesn't ask *why* he was told. What prompted such a conversation? In fact, Goerner pursues no context
whatsoever. We have no motive for why Ajima told Elieu of this
event 3 years after-the-fact.

In addition, Goerner has Elieu add: "He said she was a spy
and that she was taken away by the military." This assertion
stems solely from Goerner's personal visit to Elieu in 1962. The
wording of Burns' March 1944 article actually contradicts this.
"A Jap trader named Ajima three and a half years ago on Rita island told me that an American woman pilot came down between
Jaluit and Ailinglapalap atolls and that she was picked up by a
Japanese fishing boat and the trader Ajima heard that she was
taken to Japan." Burns underscores Elieu's honesty by implying

there is no embellishment. He quotes Lt. Bogan, stating: "Elieu, the 30-year-old native, limited himself to these statements and stuck to them."

Based on Elieu's account, Fred Goerner handily worked the Marshalls into his theory. Yet years later when he modified his theory and adopted the angle that Earhart ditched on Winslow Reef, Goerner basically had thrown out Elieu's account of Earhart having gone down near Jaluit. According to his compromised theory, weeks went by while AE and Fred sweated it out on Winslow Reef. The Japanese ship then came by and took her to the Marshall Islands.

Dots must be connected, but the lines drawn between them by the Spy and Die theorists don't form a logical outline. For instance, if Earhart was found on Winslow Reef there is no reason for the Japanese to consider her a spy. This location was nowhere near any Japanese possessions.

It is Josephine Akiyama redux. Elieu's story has become compote, as did hers. First it is molded to fit new facts and then eventually thrown out altogether. Yet like her story it was the signpost that led to ever-elaborate theories that contradict it.

Elieu's story fits much better if we just throw out Fred Goerner's questionable quote from 1962. Remove "spy" and we are left with the Japanese recovering the American woman flier and taking her away. We are only left to ponder why Ajima tells Elieu over 3 years later.

The most impressive bit of information coming out of the Marshall Islands is actually what the Marines heard on Kwajalein: that a suitcase had been found with Earhart's belongings inside. The story in a nutshell, as Goerner relates it: three Marines find the suitcase in a barracks and bring it back to camp rejoicing. Another Marine, Jackson, realizes what it could mean and tells them its significance. The last he sees of them, they are headed to HQ. A day or so later, through his interpreter Rudy Muller, Captain Maghokian hears that grunts found something that could have belonged to Amelia Earhart. Rudy Muller is now told by Kwajalein natives that a white man and woman (not specified as fliers) had been on the island before the war. Along with everything else he heard this is what Captain Maghokian reported to G-2. But he never could trace the items found.

Truth be told, Goerner's recounting of this event has gaps too. The gaps once again surround motive. From his retelling, Captain Maghokian and Rudy Muller hear from Marines first. Then Rudy Muller hears from natives. But we are not told if Maghokian set him to specifically investigate if AE and Noonan had been on the island. Thus the islanders might have been innocently led in their replies; some assert a white man and woman had been on the island. But where is the evidence? Apparently the suitcase never even made it to G-2.

There is no secret that the G-I's of World War II engaged in the ancient rite of conquerors and pillaged what they would and, moreover, that their 90-Day-Wonders could be real thieves (even of their own men), but it is odd that none of these belongings have ever surfaced.

As far as this goes, what the Marines found in the barracks could originally have been flotsam or jetsam retrieved near or on a Jaluit or Ailinglapalap beach. This might then explain why Ajima had heard only of a woman flier, no man aboard. If he did tell Elieu in late 1940, the stuff could recently have been found.

There is therefore great need to have contextualized Elieu's information, especially when and why he was told; also, to clarify whether Muller was asked to investigate and what questions were put to the natives. What we do know is the story ends here.

By the 1980s, other authors had added more witnesses in the Marshall Islands to the point their collective story becomes unbelievable. Those who tell of encountering Amelia Earhart and Fred Noonan sadly reveal they received their inspiration from Goerner's book and not from firsthand encounters. They mention the duo beached at Mili Atoll and that Noonan had a severe knee injury— rubbish inspired by the talkative shortwave crank Nina Paxton insisted had been Earhart. Yet in 1962 when asked if there were others who could relate information about this American woman flier, Elieu tells Goerner: "No one around Majuro anymore." Jaluit was also wiped out by a storm and many of the people there moved to other islands. Goerner was banned from Kwajalein due to top secret missile testing.

As is obvious, the biggest problem in springing forward from the Marshall Islands juncture in the legend of Earhart's fate is determining the context of the facts. Without context Elieu's story can lead anywhere, and indeed it has.

To help place Elieu's comment in context we must understand that the Marshall Islands were not as cut off from the outside world as was often promoted. The South Seas mandates were the one exception to Tokyo's ban on shortwave radios. Here private ownership was encouraged so Japanese residents (at least) could tune-in to propaganda broadcasts. Radio reports from Tokyo of Japan's involvement in the search for AE seem a certainty. After all, the major shimbums had reported Earhart had been picked up by a Japanese fishing boat before, that is, the retractions. How much did Ajima hear, and when did he hear it? Without knowing the context of why he tells Elieu over 3 years later, we really don't know, but the possibility is very real that he is relating embellished gossip based on Tokyo broadcasts.

Tokyo was anxious, to say the least, to get involved in Earhart's search and make some good PR of it. In fact, the US never reached out to Japan for assistance. It was Tokyo that initiated contact through the Japanese embassy in Washington with an "urgent telegram" on July 5, 1937. Mr. Hayama immediately informed Mr. Joseph Ballantine, of the State Department's Division of Far Eastern Affairs. The Japanese government wanted to help. Tokyo's big edge in the search for Earhart, as they put it to Washington, was the fact "Japan had radio stations and warships in the Marshall Islands." State was grateful. The Japanese were told of the 281 North Howland message, and they in turn said they would conduct a search. The survey ship *Koshu* would organize it with the Japanese fishing fleet. The search expanded on July 10 when AE's family "expressed the opinion" her plane could be drifting to the Gilbert Islands. State asked the Japanese government "because of the generous offer" and "because of the continuing interest the Japanese government has taken in the search for Miss Earhart's plane" if they could search the Gilbert Islands. In response State was told by Mr. Hayama that many "Japanese fishing craft in and to the east of the Marshall Islands have been instructed to be on lookout."

Records prove the *Koshu Maru* was at Ponape on July 2, and on July 9 proceeded to the Marshall Islands on orders to search for Earhart. The vessel arrived at Jaluit on July 13. The ship obviously didn't do much, perhaps steaming far enough east to maintain some radio coordination with those Japanese fishing boats that had radios. On July 19, the day after the official search was terminated, it departed to Truk.

Tokyo's eagerness to help may have been motivated by the fact they intended to essentially invade China within the week. Making a show of searching for Roosevelt's missing buddy could only demonstrate friendly relations with the USA. . .But, *but,* Tokyo possibly had another motive. They didn't want to be in the unwieldy position of blatantly denying US Naval access to search the Marshall Islands, if the US should ask first. The solution? Offer to search first.

There is no question that the Japanese were secretive about their mandates. As early as July 7, Consul-General Fukuma in Honolulu cabled his bosses in Tokyo: "It has already been five days since the Earhart plane was first reported missing, and the fate of the missing plane is today generally thought to be pessimistic. Despite this, however, the fact that the United States Navy has set up such an exaggerated search plan raises a suspicion that they may be trying to collect materials for strategic study under the pretense of such an air search."

At this juncture in the Marshall Islands Theory, one can take one of two paths. The first takes us along the most negative vantage via which to view the matter. It is to assert Ajima had heard nothing of substance but radio embellishments, and the elusive suitcase could have been jetsam. This path ends here. The other now unfolds before us.

Earhart would not have been a spy, but was the search for her used as a massive reconnaissance expedition? It is the plot of *Flight for Freedom.* Yet in this case it is suggested in a cable from the Japanese consul in Honolulu only a few days after she vanished. A chain of events occurred over autumn 1937 that could prove disturbing when fitted into the quilt of these known Japanese suspicions.

It started in September. After GP got his negative reply from the British on August 31 regarding the existence of the lost turtle reef, he wanted to believe AE and Noonan had drifted to the Marshall Islands. He wanted to pay for a search there too. On September 7, Consul-General Shiozaki in San Francisco sent in his request. On September 10, Vice Minister of Foreign Affairs

Horiuchi also relayed the request. Noting that Putnam would pay, he requested an estimation of what it would cost. Admiral Yamamoto, who would become the architect of the attack on Pearl Harbor, responded to Horiuchi on September 17. "In regard to the search for the remains of the Earhart plane in our mandate territory, our Imperial nation will have all the vessels and fishing boats in the area make every possible effort to search for the remains." It was the very polite Japanese way of saying it won't cost you anything. But, of course, there was no way to determine what constitutes the "search."

Nevertheless, it may be at this time that they actually scouted their own islands. They had not done this before. They had instructions to be on the lookout, but the only search coordinates they were ever given were in the Gilberts or to the east in the area of drift from 281 North Howland. It is only now, in response to Admiral Yamamoto's instructions, that they would have come across anything in the vicinity of Jaluit or Ailinglapalap, the heart of the Marshalls. Now would also have been the worst time to find Amelia Earhart.

By mid-October 1937, Australia was stirring the pot of Pacific war tensions. *Smith's Weekly* published an article confirming the worst Japanese suspicions. It stated the US Navy used the search for spying. In part, the article read: "So when Amelia Earhart went down. . .the search for her gave the pretext that was needed." After searching the Phoenix Islands, "they circled on, covering the area in which the Caroline and Marshall islands are to be found. . .Naval flying men are admirable observers. It is their profession. . . .It was an opportunity not to be missed, a real excuse to fly over Japan's islands-by-mandate, to observe what the waters contain." The real kicker came when the article stated: "Today, the Australian government has been apprised of some of the knowledge gleaned." American magazines were reprinting or quoting the *Smith's Weekly* article. Foreign Minister Hirota in Tokyo immediately told Consul-General Wakamatsu in Sydney to get a copy of that magazine and send it on.

As Yamamoto's response to GP Putnam indicates, the IJN had its own command link to the Marshalls and vice versa to Yamamoto, the then-Minister of the Navy. If Earhart and Noonan drifted to the Marshalls in a rubber raft and were picked up, sent to Kwajalein, Yamamoto would soon know of it. The story would have come to a very public conclusion. However, if it is true that the Electra could float and was picked up in mid-ocean between Jaluit and Ailinglapalap or beached on a Marshall island, a surprising discovery could have changed matters.

Fred Goerner heard the story from that skittish man who admitted to John Day, retired VP of CBS, that he had worked on the Electra before the flight and installed belly cameras. His inference was "spying." That deduction could merely have been his own, exaggerated by the vagaries of memory and popular theories. Nevertheless, the Electra may have carried belly cameras for more commercial motives. There is an inference in the radio traffic to the *Itasca*. Putnam asked Richard Black to send along (in his wife's plane) the negatives of the film he shoots of her landing on Howland Island, plus any still pictures and other motion pictures on board. This was for a story in the *Oakland Tribune*. He then added: "Suggest you emphasize desire she secure air views of island. If possible remind her bring available photos from Lae."

Whether the plane had belly cameras or more than one handheld camera inside, the Japanese would become curious about what she had been up to. This suspicion would have been magnified if her pick-up on a Marshall island was actually after the publishing of the *Smith's Weekly* article.

The fact Elieu only hears of the white woman flier in 1940 indicates the search for Earhart in 1937 wasn't big news *within* the Marshall Islands. This is understandable since concurrent with the search in July the Japanese had concentrated east of the Gilberts and then within the Gilberts. But there was no indication they searched within their own islands or were even led to believe she could have been near the Marshalls. It is only in response to GP's request to search the Marshalls, due to drift, that Yamamoto said they would. And it is possible the Minister of the Navy was good to his word. It is at this time that the Imperial Navy searched and didn't alert the local civilian vessels. It is equally possible a Japanese fishing boat by chance came across the Electra.

Finding Earhart and Noonan in these circumstances isn't going to be island news. In fact, the Japanese have no immediate reason to blow a trumpet about finding her. And considering the cables that must have been sent to the Marshalls from Tokyo during the search, it is hard to imagine any authority in the islands would have been ignorant as to whom she was. They would be polite, and no doubt ship her off by seaplane in stages to Japan (via Saipan) rather than by slow freighter. Burns' article actually reflects this context. Conspiracy theorists invented Earhart as having been taken away as a spy, but Burns' original article never implied that: the white woman flier was merely taken away to another island or to Japan.

We now come down to cases. "Spy" is the objectionable word. It is also *the* vital clue. It could only have been loosely hung on AE by her IJN handlers *after* the *Smith's Weekly* article. This would mean autumn, and this would also mean it happened during transshipping. It is only at Saipan that "spy" as a moniker is first attached to some white woman and man, not in the Marshall Islands.

Being painted with the spy brush could never have happened in the summer. Conspiracy theorists wanted to believe that between July 13 and July 19 the *Koshu* picked up AE and Fred on Mili and then took them to Truk, then Saipan. Of all ships, the *Koshu* would know who Fred and Amelia were. If it is true that AE and Noonan got to Saipan under the cloud of espionage, the *Koshu* and the summer of 1937 had nothing to do with it.

But by autumn. . . ? And indeed there are a few witness accounts on Saipan that suggest the white man and woman flier had languished quite some time before having been picked up. They are described as grizzled, weak, frazzled, suntanned, and all around suffering from exposure. Saipan could figure in the shipping stages if intelligence agents were coming from Tokyo to talk to her, however discreetly. It was also the closest island to a US possession. Thus repatriation would eventually follow to nearby Guam. Why did it not happen?

Every theory from year aught one is based on trying to answer this question. Fred Goerner was not the father of Japanese treachery theories. Already by 1945 they were well established, but a motive for the Japanese holding onto AE and Fred was never a coherent, integral part of any because Gene Burns never mentioned espionage. Going back to this year reveals a great truth, and it is best we go back now.

Gene Burns' 1944 article had a snowball effect within the core group of Earhart's most ardent followers. Brief though it may have been, it naturally excited those who had maintained a lively interest in her legacy and mysterious fate. None of them had been satisfied with the official conclusion of drowning. And because Burns' story was so paltry on facts, each could take her disappearance as far as they could and with what motive they wanted. And within this core group there was a network of shortwave enthusiasts anchored by Walter McMenamy.

A shortwave radio expert, he was quite involved along with Karl Pierson in the preparations for AE's final flight. They were going to trace her radio messages as she traveled around the world, thus providing a sort of cocoon of protection in case she went down. Pierson and McMenamy's joint reception of post-loss radio signals indicating Earhart was southwest of Howland was widely reported, and some still rely on their report today as proof Earhart survived.

Although Pierson was regarded as a very reliable character, McMenamy apparently went over the edge. The post-loss radio messages about a woman on a sandbank, Paxton's Mili Atoll claimant, and then the 1944 Marshall Islands news report, sent McMenamy weaving. By 1945 he was casting his shortwave web over the Pacific and trying to enlist those within his network to help investigate Amelia and Fred still being alive and in Japan.[14]

We have a pretty good idea of what buzzed over the Pacific airwaves, for some of those involved in the shortwave klatch condensed it to theory and took it to officialdom in long letters. One exquisite lunatic was Seward Sutton of St. Helena, California. He wrote to GP first. "Recourse is had to signals heard unofficially." His grammar "Recourse is had" means 'I was listening to radio broadcasts' and the rest is how he puts together the chatter he has been hearing. "Allowance is made for irresponsibles among amateur radio men; some persons of these would have fictitiously reported—possibly sent, some signals. Underlying indication, regardless of outwardly chaotic reports, is clear: (a)

---

[14] McMenamy had contacts from Hawaii to Brisbane, Australia. He also had access to W6NNR, one of the most powerful stations on the West coast.

plane on reef or atoll remote from Howland." The gist of what he puts together is a massive conspiracy on the part of the Japanese to conceal they have Earhart. He analyzed the 281 North Howland message ("281 North Howland--- cannot hold out much longer—drifting southwest--- we above water—motor sinking in water-- very wet ---"). It was sent by Japanese as a red herring. "This is glaringly obvious in Japanese language structure, regardless of any assumed errors. It is less probable as an amateur's fabrication than as a purposely deceptive message from Japanese source. It would have been sent had the flyers been picked up and had noted military evidence." The purpose of the post-loss radio messages, forged we are led to believe by the Japanese, was also to "fend" off the American search craft from noticing "Japanese military craft and evidence throughout whole region of Marshall Islands." But, he wrote Putnam, there was another message, one of great significance. "Sending of a further and ironical message, after Japanese officers were sure that searchers had derived no significant intelligence. This message was: '- -alls well at 5 degrees south latitude, 173 degrees west - -'. This was to add to the confusion and also to express the ironical feelings of the Japanese officer. This fits as a Japanese act . . ."

Starting in January 1946, Sutton would contact the Australian Intelligence Director General in Canberra, Lt. Colonel Longfield Lloyd, and then field agents in Japan. He revealed details about where Ajima and Elieu lived on Majuro, how Noonan was alive in Japan, how he and Earhart had possibly been marooned during the war on the Kerguelan Islands in the South Indian Ocean, and he asserted the US Navy played a conspiratorial hand involving Captain Takagi (of the *Koshu*) during the search.

This last assertion was based on that "significant" and "ironical" message above. He couldn't understand why it was sent to American ships. It grated on him. Reactivated by all the Spy and Die hoopla of the early 1960s, Sutton wrote to Senator J. William Fulbright on November 25, 1961. He wanted to know the name of the Japanese official who denied the execution of Earhart on Saipan. He baited the Senator with what festered on his scattered mind. "During the search in 1937, a brief innocuous message was received by U.S. Naval craft, from Comdr. Hanjiro [sic] Takagi of the Japanese Navy. This was totally suppressed.

Thirteen innocuous words. No more is mentioned at this time."
Because we have Sutton's letter to GP in April 1946, we know
the 13 words: "All is well at five degrees south latitude, one seven
three degrees west," which Sutton proposed was a Japanese code.
Over time it came to imply a conspiracy with the US Navy.

It's not hard to deduce that in 1945 Sutton had been getting
juiced over the shortwave. There are obvious nuances between
his conspiratorial ramblings and those of Walter McMenamy.
We get that shortwave addict's version in stages. First, the most
unfiltered view: "Walter McMenamy is a ding-a-ling," Fred
Goerner declared in a 1971 letter (to Fred Hooven).
"McMenamy claims AE flew directly to an island and landed on
time. They broadcast from the island for several days, and they
were picked up by the U.S. Navy. Noonan, he says, 'is probably
still living.' He says he saw Noonan in 1949 or 1950. That he had
changed his name and was 'still with Navy intelligence.' AE, he
adds, was alive until November 6, 1945, when she was killed in a
headon crash of a pair of Navy planes near Guadalcanal. He said
he got his info regarding AE from the FBI."

Had Goerner understood that McMenamy was the original
sire of Japanese treachery theories he should perhaps not have
been so infected by the concept. McMenamy had inspired Amy
Otis, Muriel Morrissey, Margot DeCarie, and most anybody else
whose writings or personal contact had implied to the CBS
journalist more must have been afoot in AE's flight.

This domino effect is easy to see when McMenamy finally
speaks for himself. Randall Brink used him as a source in his
1994 book *Lost Star: The Search for Amelia Earhart*. We get direct quotations of post-loss messages McMenamy claimed he actually heard over shortwave. Brink writes:

> "He must be at least an admiral," Amelia exclaimed in her final
> message that day. According to McMenamy, she was describing a
> Japanese shore patrol that was nearing the crashed Electra just be-
> fore her radio fell silent at last.

Put together with what he told Goerner, we can deduce that the
admiral above is actually the captain of the *Koshu* (Kanjiro Takagi). He then sent a message to a US Naval ship which then

picked up Amelia and Fred and a remarkable conspiracy began that reflects Sutton's spate of letters (1946, 1961) claiming the U.S. Navy was in cahoots in some way with the disappearance.

Shambling through the theories begun in 1945 reveals that great truth I enticed the reader with a couple of pages previously. Nobody in this shortwave klatch had ever heard of Saipan. For 15 years they had brewed the stew works they made from Burns' 1944 article. The great truth is found in an unflattering comparison. After Akiyama's story achieved traction in 1960, the same thing happened, only a lot more theorists were now involved and getting published. All they did was add Saipan to the equation and then convolute the conspiracy and yet give no believable motive for the conspiracy.

And, remember, there never had been a motive. Amy Otis could only infer. She had said the local Japanese "believed she was merely a transocean flier in distress. But Tokyo had a different opinion of her significance in the area. She was ordered taken to Japan. There, I know, she met with an accident, an 'arranged' accident that ended her life." Margot DeCarie titillated Goerner about where the Japanese found AE: "All I can tell you is that it was within moderate range of Howland Island." Now alarmed, Goerner asked:

"Did she intend to land at Howland?"

"In the beginning, she did."

"Beginning of what?"

"I mean that was her intention after the first change of plans but before what really happened."

"I'm sorry, I don't understand."

"That's all I'm going to say. I've already said too much."

"Your suggestion then is for me to talk to Vidal?"

"There are a lot of people who can tell you part or all of the story. Your problem is to open them up."

That was all I could learn from Amelia's secretary.

Had the KCBS journalist followed through, he would have learned nothing from Gene Vidal. There was nothing to learn. But we have discovered something here. DeCarie had certainly been listening to McMenamy. "Captain Takagi's mysterious" 13 word message has degrees— 173° W Long. by 5° S Lat. This is smack dab in the Phoenix Group between Hull and Nikumaroro. Before Winslow Reef's rediscovery this could easily have implied the location of the "mythical reef." DeCarie certainly implies Winslow Reef in her own comment to Goerner. Eventually the redoubtable KCBS journalist gave up his Marshall Islands theory to come back to Winslow Reef, partly based on DeCarie's conviction without realizing, once again, from whom it was ultimately coming. Anchored by McMenamy, shortwave chatter had set all in motion in 1945 in response to Burns' article, shifting back and forth from Winslow to Mili per the tastes of the theorist as to where AE was calling from.

To put back only the original facts is to reveal how sparse and what secondhand facts they really are. The evidence in the Marshall Islands isn't really fragmentary. It is only two fragments— what Elieu told the Navy and what Rudy Muller got from the natives at the behest of Captain Maghokian.

Upon these two fragments anybody can build anything they want with the limited building blocks they have. But the most damning component of all Spy and Die theories has always been their basis in *popular* information. Whether the theories stem from 1945 or 1960, they are based on believing Nina Paxton's shortwave crank and then inventing thereon more details. None are based on the possibility that Earhart and Noonan were picked up *months* after they had effectively vanished. Yet if only fragments of witness accounts in each location (Marshalls, Saipan) are true, then there is no other option. It isn't until late September or October before the Japanese would have received notices to be on the lookout in the Marshall Islands proper.

Saipan, *if* a genuine fragment, becomes a puzzling clue. Put with the other two fragments it is proof, of course, that AE and Noonan survived. Yet with the knowledge we have today about how the Japanese colonial empire was administered, Saipan really doesn't fit in the scheme of things.

The Mariana Islands were only one of 6 sectors of the Japanese colonial empire. Saipan was its major civilian administrative center, but it was a link in a chain that did not lead to Tokyo. As things stood politically in 1937, a civilian government known as the South Seas Government governed the mandated islands and was based in Koror, Palau Islands. The South Seas Government reported directly to the Minister of Colonial Affairs

How it really worked—civilian capitals (5 point stars) would report to Koror; Imperial Navy bases (4-point stars) report to Truk.

in Tokyo. If these two white folk were transshipped through civilian authority, Jaluit would ship them to Koror, thence to Manila for repatriation. If trans-shipped via the Imperial Navy, then Kwajalein would likely have informed Truk, Japan's premier naval administrative base, the "Gibraltar of the Pacific;" thence to ship her and Fred Noonan.

There are only two conceivable ways to slip through this system and get straight to Saipan. The first has already been mentioned. Because she was ill, the IJN flew her by seaplane to Saipan for repatriation on nearby Guam. There they would question her. But, being ill from exposure/dysentery, she died on them. Months later why stir an already explosive pot and try and explain it? Mum's the word.

The other way is far more convoluted.

Within the Japanese structure of their mandated islands, there was confusion at times between the jurisdiction of the civilian authority, the Imperial Navy, and the trading companies. Within the Marshalls the Nan'yo Boeki Kaisha (South Seas Pacific Trading Company) had the concessions, and within the Marianas the powerful Nan'yo Kohatsu Kabushiki Kaisha— the NKKK— had powers that sometimes rivaled and overlapped with the civilian authority. The company had become so powerful that at the end of the war the Allies insisted it be abolished.

Saipan fits within the scheme of things if the N triple K was at the center of it all. Both Saipan and Tinian were huge bases for them in the exploitation of sugarcane. Aside from a small Imperial Navy administrative liaison, authority on Saipan would have been local and probably not that supervised. This would mean AE and Fred would be in the hands of the insular police under Zuse "Kumoi" Guerrero.

That the Saipanese natives and the brutal "Kumoi" in particular were the ones on the case is found in the letter of Brother Gregorio to Joe Gervais. Now stationed on Yap, he remembered that kids came to him at the vestry shortly after the "spies" were apprehended near Garapan. They said one was "an American woman who wore long pants like a man and had a haircut like a man. The Japanese police held these two Americans as spies." Of the man, he wrote: "The woman's companion's face is very suntanned like Spanish people's faces." Later he wrote, however, that "Kumoi spoke to me a few days later about these two American intelligence spies" and he told Brother Gregorio, rather boldly, that if they paid him enough he would show them what they wanted.

This could be pure braggadocio on Guerrero's part, but it doesn't sound like this white man and woman came to Saipan with much military escort.

Alone of the Saipanese, it was Guerrero who was upset by the investigation on Saipan. "Galvan," as Fred Goerner referred to him, was prepared to make trouble. Joe Gervais and Bob Dinger also learned in what contempt Guerrero was held on Guam by the native law enforcement officers there. They were told he had been Sheriff of Saipan under Navy administration until 1952 when he was fired for nearly beating a man to death with a rubber hose. "Kumoi's theory always was," declared his successor Sheriff Manuel Sablan, "if you beat a man long enough and he tells you nothing, it proves he is not lying." He had been the head cop during the Japanese period.

De-fragmenting a bloated conspiracy theory requires we reconstruct it with the most reliable fragments. To begin—

1 All evidence indicates AE and Fred had agreed to re-

turn to the Gilbert Islands if they could not find Howland.

2 Earhart undeniably believed she was on time over Howland, as testified by her own comments at 7:12 a.m. (by her clock). Subsequent weather reports indicated much stronger headwinds. Therefore she had to be much further out and closer to the Gilberts. Her total silence after switching to 6210 also indicates she was much further out from Howland than Thompson and those following his theory wanted to accept.

3 The garbled messages picked up by Nauru the first night indicate AE and Noonan were closer to the Gilberts and on land for the first night. If this was a reef, they elected to drift with their plane rather than stay or they took to their raft. The current would take them to the Marshall Islands. It could be weeks at sea (20 mile drift per day).

Naturally, the next fragments are those stories gleaned in the Marshall Islands in 1944.

4 The original source is Ajima. In late summer 1940 he tells the native Elieu that a white American woman flier was picked up near Jaluit. She is taken to Japan, no inference of espionage.

5 Marine Captain Victor Maghokian, through interpreter Rudy Muller, discovers and reports that two white people (man and woman) were on Kwajalein briefly in 1937 before being taken to another island, no inference of espionage.

6 Date uncertain, mode uncertain, a white woman flier arrives on Saipan. She is supposedly considered a spy. She dies in a week. No one knows what becomes of her male companion.

Just in and of himself, Ajima is a clue. He is, after all, a trader and thus no doubt worked with the trading companies. Where else could he have gotten his information except from the grapevine in the company? What if in response to Yamamoto's "alert," a trading company vessel found Earhart and Noonan beached or drifting in the Marshalls? How close to the vest would the company play it?

Obtaining— "rescuing"— Amelia Earhart would have been a publicity boon for Nan'yo Kohatsu. She is housed at the hotel in

Garapan. Zuse de Leon's detectives watch her here. "Spy" may have been bandied by a few administrators in response to the *Smith's Weekly*. She is dead a week later. N triple K's headquarters were also in Koror, and it could be that any message sent to Koror went through in the company name. But the NKKK could also have sat on the information. If Earhart was severely ill or that brutal Zuse had tortured her, the last thing they would need internationally is Amelia Earhart admitting the latter or . . . dying on them. When she did, the silence began.

The picture is one of a largely native affair, with little Japanese military influence. And this, once again, means the South Seas companies and the insular police.

During his visits to Saipan in the 1980s, Vincent Loomis picked up on a story that may be of help here. "Olympio and Florence told of another incident involving a Japanese policeman before the war. He had been having dinner with his thirteen year old daughter when he was interrupted by a number of drunk Japanese police officers. They proudly boasted of killing two Americans, a man and a woman. This upset the policeman, who told them their act was wrong and kicked them out of their house. He told his daughter never to say a word about the visit. She kept the secret until her father died, and then began to tell the story."

This appears to be a muddled version of what the daughter of Jose Pangelinan had told Goerner in 1961. They had been told many times, she had said, of a white couple whom the Kempeitai had killed. However, when the CBS journalist spoke to her father direct, his story was almost identical to Matilda San Nicholas' story. The woman had died of dysentery and the day after the Kempeitai had beheaded the man by samurai sword.

It is thin like all the other stories coming from Saipan. Yet like all the others it does follow a predictable pattern. It is tailored to vilify the Japanese rather than the local insular police. But what if there is an element of truth to this? If the NKKK kept such a tight lid on their guests' identity, someone like "Zuse" may not have known their significance and believed the rumors of "spies."

The legend relied on conspiracy theories that in themselves hinged on the Imperial Navy controlling everything. This simplified it by giving us the antagonist. The Spy and Die Theory invented the military doing away with Earhart and Noonan as spies. Historical context doesn't allow that. The Japanese Navy had known Earhart was lost. No one on Saipan could execute anybody without orders, and these had to come from Tokyo through Koror or Truk.

Thus we are plunged back into nothing but any theory based on three fragments, the last of which—Saipan— doesn't really fit. And we have been led there from an improbable story from Josephine Akiyama that everybody eventually threw out anyway.

"Spy" is the objectionable word and seemingly impossible context. If we can remove it and execution from the equation we can formulate something that has a better chance of including Saipan.

I have offered:

The IJN flew her there for questioning and then repatriation on Guam. But she was quite ill and died. Too hard to explain all the circumstances months after-the-fact, so just keep quiet instead.

The South Seas companies, in particular NKKK, rescued her and shipped her to Saipan. Ill, she died. Even the Japanese government was not fully aware of what had transpired.

I offer the above two scenarios as working hypotheses only. To pursue them would be another matter. It means looking for cables and messages sent to Koror and Saipan between the NKKK, NBK, or the civilian government. These could date as late as October to December 1937. Similarly IJN cables at this time would be of most interest. If the suitcase found on Kwajalein was jetsam, it means looking for cables sent around late summer to fall 1940, the time Ajima told Elieu.

Supposedly, tons of World War II era documents still survive and many untranslated were returned to Japan from the USA. There may reside within these stacks of parchment the cablegrams with questions or hints, bare hints. Their brittle, faded pages may contain the only clues as to what happened.

However, in sum, the bare snippets of facts, these fragments, allow us no more than what is a more amorphous compromise of a very elaborate modern legend.

Its chief authors created this legend out of the shortest snippets of rumors, which they then discounted, out of elaborate
theses whose purpose was to steer readers around points that critically compromised their evidence, such as when and why did
Ajima tell Elieu so long after-the-fact, and a lot of imaginative
speculation based not upon the dots of known facts but upon the
blank space in between. Within all of this static, there is potential for a white woman flier to have been on Saipan for about a
week. She then died, ostensibly of the effects of severe dysentery
and exposure. So much more provocative is the legend that this
single potential fact is lost. Confronting this fact should really
overwhelm the serious student of Earhart's life, but its poignancy
and its proof is lost to the span of time and the squelching
amount of embroidered legend.

To paraphrase Amelia Earhart: 'There are some things which
should be writ before we conclude— things that have been
talked about by others.' Today, Amelia's reputation has suffered.
It is not because of an alleged relationship with Gene Vidal or
her fluid commitment to marriage. It has suffered primarily for
one reason: her hand-in-glove association with George Putnam.
His publicity contacts were the reason she engaged in a largely
reluctant marriage to further her own career. Determined to
make her the image of women's aviation, he stepped on several
other female pilots— from Elinor Smith to Lady Mary Heath.
Reservations about her image orbit this central pole: how much
of her reputation is deserved by merit and how much was the
byproduct of the ruthless publicity machinations of GP Putnam?
    For the last 15 years the mire has been stirred. As a result I
had great difficulty writing and arranging this book. Authors
previous could write up a glowing biography for AE and then
follow it with the mystery of her disappearance and then the results of their own personal investigation. A condensed but glorifying biography section only helped set the stage the authors
wanted. It built Earhart up into a plaster saint and expert pilot
who could easily have been entrusted with a daring spy mission.
The execution of a national symbol doing her duty tore at the
hearts of their readers.
    Given the developments of the last decade, the luxury of

such a layout I could not afford. The other option was to devote the first part of this book to a critique of Earhart's reassessment. Obviously, this defeats the purpose of the book. No reader, having acquired the ennui that comes with a character study, would give a figue as to her fate, the intrigue of mystery notwithstanding. I do not believe the negative appraisal of Earhart is accurate, but beginning a book with an objective critique and then counter-balance of the arguments is simply not going to help matters.

This I have reserved for an appendix. In the truest sense what follows is not strictly ancillary. In order to get to the bottom of the theories about Amelia Earhart's ultimate fate, one has to dispassionately assess her abilities and stability as a pilot. Would she have been considered good enough by the powers-that-be to undertake a spy mission? Could she have pulled off a ditching at sea? Her abilities bear on determining which theories we can faithfully accept or finally once and for all reject.

Appendix

An Agnostic Looks at Amelia Earhart

At anyone who attains the level of mega-fame there is an effort by some to adulate them for what they come to symbolize and by some an effort to denigrate them for being less than the symbol. Quite critical of AE, Judith Thurman (*Missing Woman*, 2009) writes: "The abuse of the term 'icon' incites iconoclasm, or ought to. Earhart was saint-like only as a martyr to her own ambition, who became an object of veneration and is periodically resurrected— her unvarnished glamour, like a holy man's body, still miraculously fresh. Embraced by feminists, she was featured on a 1976 cover of *Ms.*, which promised a story 'better than the myth.' Read closely, however, Earhart's life is, in part, the story of a charismatic dilettante who lectured college girls about ambition yet never bothered to earn a degree." Thurman admits that her flights were "feats of courage," but "compared with the achievements of the women in her [Earhart's] scrapbook their significance was ephemeral." Thurman's final quote above reveals the lynchpin of iconoclasts' arguments.

"Overrated" is a frequent criticism of those who achieve outsized publicity because of their charismatic personality rather than because of their accomplishments within a network of equally qualified though less captivating peers. Today the iconoclasts contextualize AE as a "second rate" pilot who achieved her pioneering image because of the sleight-of-hand of the first true über-promoter, her influential husband George Putnam.

This attitude has two enormous flaws. The first presupposes that a flier's proficiency is the standard of judging Amelia Earhart's fame. In truth, this does Earhart a great injustice. AE became famous for little substantive reason, which is something she admitted. She called herself nothing but a "sack of potatoes" on the Atlantic flight in 1928 that catapulted her to stardom. The second flaw doesn't understand that success at promoting is two-sided. The combination of promoter and subject is jockey and horse— every bet knows both have to be tiptop to win. AE remained famous because of something entirely unique to herself— those qualities of *Fun*, adventure and virtue. She was also an oddity— erudite, polished, yet packaged in an androgynous body with a blushing, tomboyish face, hair that looked cut by a cropper's shears and set in place by a careless breeze. George Putnam projected these, like any film projector would, enlarging and casting a small image as a giant onto the silver screen, where Earhart would explicitly or implicitly encourage people to follow their dreams. As a result, she became the center of a personality cult and not a footnote for the history of aviation.

Putnam's bigger-than-life projection, as all projections, is only a two dimensional silhouette. The real Amelia Earhart was a complex individual, equal measure a prisoner of GP's publicity spin as well as a beneficiary. Iconoclasts may be able to justify their attack on her legacy by reminding us she was a willing accomplice to GP marketing her as the "premiere aviatrix." But they must admit, as does Thurman, that Earhart's flights were "feats of courage." Contemporarily, that was actually enough. That was the fad: individual courage that highlighted progress. Though perhaps not as technically impressive as others, this tomboy's flights made her a mascot of progress and an irrepressible example of the budding unstoppable womanhood.

Over and over again, this is what Earhart tried to project. With time, this was forgotten and she became an icon of aviation. But contemporarily she preferred the image of *Fun of It.* Progress, so it appeared, was merely an incidental result to her quest for adventure. During the grand receptions and blaring MovieTone praises, self-effacement always projected this formula. For example, after achieving her trans-Atlantic triumph she declared: "I realize this flight has meant nothing to aviation." And: "If science advances and aviation progresses, and international good will is promoted because of my flight, no one will be more delighted than I— or more surprised." This is Earhart.

However, what George Putnam was doing is another matter. He unquestionably was facilitating and monetizing the image of pioneer and AE didn't stop him. "[Putnam] was so proprietary that a rival of Earhart's described him as her Svengali," wrote Thurman. When next conceding that "she, however, was the real mesmerist," Thurman is declaring that even Earhart's projected personality was false, leaving us with the iconoclast formula— imperious ego instead of humility, wandering infidelity instead of virtue, manipulator rather than motivator.

The abuse of iconoclasm always leads to the damaging of the character of the real person who inspired what later became twisted veneration. Just in answer to a point presented, one can clear Earhart of having been hypocritical in her lecture of students. She never believed a degree applied to what she did. As to who was the actual Svengali, if there was one, this requires a deeper and more protracted look between the public and the private lives of Amelia Earhart.

A truer image of the private Amelia can probably be gained from her "prenuptial" letter to GP Putnam.

Dear GPP

There are some things which should be writ before we are married— things we have talked over before — most of them.

You must know again my reluctance to marry, my feeling that I shatter thereby my chances in work which means most to me. I feel the move just now as foolish as anything I could do. I know there may be compensations but have no heart to look ahead.

On our life together I want you to understand I shall not hold you to any midaevil [sic] code of faithfulness to me nor shall I consider myself bound to you similarly. If we can be honest I think the difficulties which arise may best be avoided should you or I become interested deeply (or inpassing) in anyone else.

Please let us not interfere with the others' work or play, nor let the world see our private joys or disagreements. In this connection I may have to keep some place where I can go to be myself, now and then, for I cannot guarantee to endure at all times the confinement of even an attractive cage.

I must extract a cruel promise and that is you will let me go in a year if we find no happiness together.

I will try to do my best in every way and give you that part of me you know and seem to want.

A.E.

Judged against the image she wished to project, there is little at odds here with her goal of *Fun*. But it is hard to deny there is quite a bit more here for the iconoclasts than the expression of *potential* infidelity. "Gravity was uncongenial to her," Thurman had noted, "and she made light even of grave things." This trait obviously was not a mere projection on Earhart's part for public consumption. It is here contained in a private letter. Her light-hearted nature introduces the letter, but it really masks its dark-ness. The lack of expression of, or even the desire for, love is sti-fling. There is only the air of calculated relenting. She consid-ered it enlightened to not express any faithfulness to her oath of marriage. She would not hold GP to account for infidelity, and likewise it worked the other way around, even to mere passing fancies. Is this "modernism" or is this someone who truly did not understand the gravity of the subject matter?

The letter does tell us the truth of her priorities. Work above all was the most important to her. So much so she could admit to others that her marriage to Putnam was a "marriage of con-venience," and what made him convenient were his promoter skills. Her career was everything, she wrote, and it would be a better approach (though harder) for the iconoclasts to assess and finally agree exactly what AE's career was.

At her stride AE preferred *The Fun of it* image and that progress was merely the byproduct. But when asked by journalist Carl Allen if she missed her social worker days, she declared she had never left the very honorable profession. Apparently for her inspiring others by her feats and then the subsequent lucrative motivational speaking was still social work. This was certainly the formula that dominated the era of *Fun* that followed the Atlantic conquest. As Susan Butler writes: "'It's a routine now,' she once said. 'I make a record and then I lecture on it.' That was certainly true— lecturing paid the expenses, made the records possible, took most of her time, and were best attended when she had just done something newsworthy."

When in 1934 women could not partake in the Cleveland Air Meet (National Air Races), she boycotted the race. The newspapers reported she would not fly movie royalty Mary Pickford to the event. This was certainly very glitzy social work, but it could fit within the *Fun of it* concept.

The projection of *Fun of it* was so dominant that the business element behind AE's *Fun* was diametrically at odds with her image. Because of this the controversy over the $10,000 Hawaii money caught her off guard. In an interview at the Hotel Seymour in New York, a reporter brought it up and Earhart was eager to explain why she accepted money for these flights. There had to be a commercial aspect, she asserted. Being brutally honest, she declared: "Flying with me is a business. Of course, I make money. I have to or I couldn't fly. I've got to be self-supporting or I couldn't stay in the business." Her intent was to dissuade people from believing the Hawaii money was essentially the motive for her flight (and a bribe for an ulterior reason). However, this was perhaps not the best clarification, as it revealed the ultimate monetary necessities of her flights.

Paying for your hobby as you go is rather standard procedure for all hobbyists. But this simply was not the public's image of the girl who did things for *The Fun of It.* It was a sensitive enough answer that even decades later Susan Butler tries to qualify its meaning in her biography. "But the 'business' she was referring to was the lecture tours, magazine articles, and books she had written." If this is the correct interpretation, AE had basically admitted in glaring contradiction to her usual "I do it for fun" and "Adventure is worthwhile in itself" that in order to maintain her value—i.e. public demand— she basically had to engage in stunt flying. Butler even itemizes Earhart's earning power: $300 per lecture amounting to $40,000 dollars a year. Since these stats were for 1935, they reflect her increasing demand because of her highly publicized flights. Butler notes this was Earhart's most hectic year. She had 126 lectures @ $300 per.

For the depression when the average income was paltry by comparison, Earhart was pulling down the equivalent of ¾ of a million in today's dollars. Aviation firsts had made this possible, but once again so had her charismatic personality. She was socially elite, catered to, and followed slavishly by the press, so much so that the first negative publicity she received before a flight caused her to respond in ways that perhaps revealed too much that was contingent on her having *Fun.*

And the most critical contingent was GP Putnam. She only gave him "that part of me you know and seem to want." He, in turn, monetized her brand as aviation pioneer and gave this to the public, and AE needed him to do so. The iconoclasts quibble with Earhart marketing, and it is ironic they cannot see that Earhart never claimed to be anything more than a thrill seeker.

There is much of the true Amelia Earhart in the rough draft of her article "Thrill." She revealed how she loved experiencing uniqueness. While flying to California from Hawaii she describes the Pacific in the darkness of night. She wanted to cry out words to describe it, but there were no words— "only a thrill." She then clarified: "I never use the word thrilling to describe trivial sensations." There were a few things she felt should be thrilling in one's life— beauty so awesome, self-revelation (the "light that breaks after years of darkness"), sudden "consciousness" of one's own hidden powers, challenges of the future, and "freedom of self." She writes: "When I undertake a task, over all protests and in spite of all adversity, I sometimes thrill, not with the task but with the realization that I am doing what I want to do and that all men and women can do what they want to do if they will."

She realized a sense of inferiority is not unique to women, but was also among men. She thrilled that people who are scared can be courageous. They can open their eyes and see the vision they have for themselves— "if they will!" She also thrilled at progress. Machines now took the burden of toil off mankind's back, and new knowledge lifted the load of ignorance. We can be free "if we will," and this meant to follow our dreams.

Exclusive experiences also caused her to thrill, such as flying high over the Pacific (en route from Hawaii) and seeing the sunrise. For the rest of the world it was darkness. Even birds still nested peacefully under their wings. "It was night for them. Morning had come only to me. And then I thrilled." She wanted to learn to relive this moment always.

She concluded by basically using her experience in flying as a metaphor for progress. A narrow sky we can rise over and then look below to see the star drift; if the night is too long, climb over it and "outstrip the darkness, and meet the sun." Wings of understanding will lift us from the abyss. "Man has found wings! That is the thrill— the challenge— of this new world."

Cynically, one could say, I suppose, she repeatedly included her readers "if they will" merely to fulfill her income as a motivational speaker. But Amelia also truly thrilled at being an influencer. In this role, she was being introduced to many exclusive thrills. Obviously, she was more strategy than logistics, as all motivational speakers are. Few of her audience could truly change their life course anymore.

There is nothing to condemn in AE monetizing her hobby with Pollyanna enthusiasm, but the observer of her life must understand the pecking order. *She* truly chased her own dreams of exclusive experiences, but motivating her readership was her bread and butter. Thrill inspired her expensive hobby, and she had to monetize it in order to continue it. George Putnam was good (and necessary) toward this end.

From her brief stint of Los Angeles fame, AE knew flying in and of itself didn't have sustainable monetary value. Lucrative endorsements for doing "firsts" were a very new fad, thanks largely to Charles Lindbergh's publicity flight because it showcased individual courage. AE was a *courageous* individual. This fad was made for her. And she was lucky enough to get involved at the cusp due to being a passenger. Thanks to GP and the uneven playing field he helped landscape, AE's subsequent flights stood out and she broadened her influence and with it her appeal. This gave her the pioneering image to sustain the reiteration of "world's foremost aviatrix," and her captivating personality did the rest.

To her detractors, using or outright relying on George Putnam inspires another criticism: her feminism was hypocritical. Feminism to Amelia Earhart, however, meant doing what she, a woman, wanted to do. She always wanted to make money. She always wanted to live the good life. She *needed* to experience thrills. She craved that intense pleasure. The first line in her own poem "Courage is the Price" somewhat reflects this compulsion: "Courage is the price that Life exacts for granting peace." She got satisfaction by following the intense pleasure of her thrills. If she were alive now to confront her traducers, she would have a witty, tongue-in-cheek reply about how last time she noticed she was a woman and she was doing what she wanted— reaching for her dreams. She would probably declare that she could not imagine anything more feminist than that . . . for a woman anyway.

What AE's feminist detractors don't appreciate is that George Putnam truly fell at the feet of her genuine charisma. He did not control Earhart nor influence her personality. If he had, he would have made her perfect flying— her "in" to this celebrity world— a lot sooner than she did.

It is really quite remarkable how long she took to finally refine and even broaden her limited aviation skills. She had a cross-country flight, which was disastrous but unobserved. A highly overproduced air race— the Powder Puff— and then she settled into an editor's life in New York City. In this the iconoclasts have the correct answer: AE was a dilettante. Ever devoted to her romanticized image, Paul Briand writes up her dabbler nature the most charitably:

> In her fever of activity, Amelia now turned from competitive flying and magazine writing to developing airlines. With a characteristic burst of initial energy, she plunged into first one and then another aspect of air-line operation, first with one organization

and then with another. But, as with nursing and medicine, and as at Columbia when she was too impatient to follow a prescribed course of study, she soon tired of the new activities.

Briand graciously attributed this to her yen for flight. "There was no occupation on the ground that could hold her interest for long." Frankly, the occupation that held her attention most was thrill, no matter where it was. Now her appetite for excitement's crave was being sated by the zest for her new influential career— i.e. she was enjoying her glib Madison Avenue acronym.

As far as I can define her elusive career, she was an amateur thrill seeker who became an influencer who had to become a professional thrill seeker in order to remain an influencer. The influencer "career" was so lucrative that after her tremendous debut she essentially learned flying in baby steps within the protective medium of GP's publicity spin.

It is from this era that most of the criticism emerges about Earhart being a mediocre pilot. It stems from the fact that she had trouble handling her grunting pig of a Vega, a true bruiser aircraft for the era. She had a pilot fly her to most of her engagements, Putnam explained, because she had to dictate her speeches, etc., to her secretary while riding in back. Iconoclasts don't believe the spin, for the pilot GP hired was Captain Bill Lancaster, a British pro pilot. He would be billed as "mechanic," an unusual job title for such an esteemed pilot as Lancaster.

There are clues that suggest Lancaster was indeed doing most of the flying at this time, thus accounting for AE's lack of progress. The Powder Puff Derby is a case in point. The race was to begin in Santa Monica, California, on August 18, 1929. All pilots had to get there no matter where they were based. AE seems to have gotten there from New York without incident, but in flying the race, when there was no doubt it was Earhart flying the Vega herself, there was more than a single landing mishap, which never happened when Lancaster was aboard as "mechanic."

Before Earhart had settled on buying the Vega, she had tested a Bellanca (March 1929), with Elinor Smith as the instructor pilot. Smith was the very young (19 years old) and gifted test pilot for Giuseppe Bellanca, and in substance would rise to become one of the true female pioneers of aviation. She had a very negative opinion of Earhart's handling of the plane.

Former *Flying* editor Stephen Wilkinson joined the iconoclasts in his January 2010 article in *Aviation History*, noting of
this period:

> If she had a fault, it was that she would never have admitted
> such a lack of flying talent. With one exception, when she
> acknowledged planting a Lockheed Vega on its nose due to "over-
> application of the brakes," accidents were never her fault. They
> were always due to a hidden ditch, "spectators say a whirlwind hit
> me," landing gear weakened by another pilot's bounced landing, or
> a mechanical failure.

It is arguable whether Smith overstated Earhart's poor ability
at handling the Bellanca, but the context is really not that significant. She was, after all, testing a very different model over the
puddle jumpers she had been used to. The same argument can
mollify Wilkinson's observations. The Vega was a brute. The autogiro was a nightmare. Earhart had piloting skill. What she
lacked was experience. This word is the key. I understand the
criticisms of pilot mediocrity, but they are only applicable to this
narrow window in Earhart's career. But her lack of experience
continued far beyond this narrow window.

Compare this moment in Earhart's career, now known as AE
the spunky *Cosmo* aviation editor, to the endeavors of those like
Lady Mary Heath, who by spring 1928 had already flown from
Johannesburg to London over the then-Dark Continent. This
took skill, experience and *endurance* (it took her a couple of
months) and in turn this fostered those much needed skills for
long endurance flights.

Compared to what other women pilots had undergone, AE's
flights were anemic, though highly publicized. Because of her
image her flights were good for continuing her career through
paid speeches and articles. Because of her fame they were good
for promoting tourist trade. Viewed from this cynical perspective, her flights had been those of a flying mascot. Mexico City
to Newark; Hawaii to Oakland— both had symbolism for air
commerce; and the CONUS speed records showed how fast
travel could be coast-to-coast for business. Air Commerce was

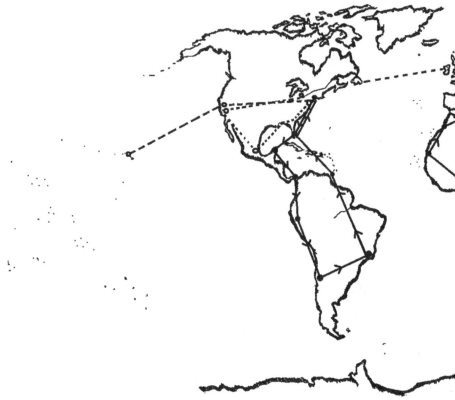

Solid line London to Melbourne, Australia— the MacRobertson
the route of Amy Johnson, first woman pilot to fly solo from
Solid line—Africa: Beinhorn's route and stops on her flight across
Cape Town to London, 1928. Solid line—Americas: Laura Ingalls'
1934, a total of 17,000 miles making it the longest solo flight by a
Amelia Earhart. Broken lines are token of numerous cross-country
Jersey 1935.

even the ultimate message of her triumphant Atlantic flight. Sounding like a corporate commercial for the budding airlines was probably an agreed part of the promotional package, with George's professional or Gene's private tickling. Thanks to George, everything else was promotion for products that came from the publicity she garnered for these overproduced firsts.

AE's detractors see only this disproportion today. They take the breathtaking exultation of MovieTone announcers declaring Earhart's grandeur and contrast it to the substance of her actual flights. Perhaps put most politely, Lane Wallace summed in the

*"Great Air Race," October 1934. The route somewhat exemplifies
England to Australia, May 1930, and Elly Beinhorn in 1931.
Africa, 1933. Broken line—Africa: Lady Mary Heath's route from
flight from New York and around South America (and back)
woman. Broken lines North America/Atlantic/Pacific: flights of
flights, then North Atlantic 1932, Hawaii 1935, Mexico-New*

Atlantic (*Enough of Amelia*, October 20, 2009) that "there are so
many other really accomplished women pioneers who get lost in
Amelia's disproportionate shadow. Women in Aviation, International has a Hall of Fame that lists the bios of dozens of women
who were Earhart's contemporaries. Interestingly enough, Earhart herself was not inducted into the Hall of Fame until five
years after its inception, and her entry is not as compelling as
some of the others."

Such a summary is neither personal nor capricious. It is more
polite than the iconoclasts, but it comes down to the same thing.

Free today of Earhart's contemporary glory, one is able to assess her actual accomplishments in aviation. The result: "overrated."

Compressed within the narrow context of aviation, perhaps the iconoclasts have the high ground. But actual accomplishments in aviation and piloting skill are not the same thing. What is important to this assessment is her competence as a pilot to conduct the world flight. This assessment must also be of those aspects of her career and character which may help to understand her disappearance and the mysteries and theories that have arisen thereafter.

Pilot competence to pull off the flight seems obvious. By this time, she had truly become a very good pilot. Had her radio receiver not clunked, and had she attended the Bendix radio instruction, she would have worked out the problem with *Itasca* and followed **A** on 500 kilocycles to Howland Island.

It is in her character that a problem is found. The sloppy, "happy-go-lucky" if you must, flight preparations are a direct reflection of her dismissive, fatalistic attitude toward her quest for thrill. They are also the result of another trait. Thurman was right when she noted: "Gravity was uncongenial to her, and she made light even of grave things."

To an extent the limited viewing angle of critics today hides a criticism that is most relevant to Earhart's disappearance: the superficiality that was behind her motives.

AE *was* a dabbler and a thrill seeker. It is the latter that drove her to some level of consistency in aviation more than a missionary zeal for progress. She truly believed in her *Fun of It.* She was doing this for herself, for that intense pleasure she got from the thrill of flying and the grand prospects of a new and exclusive experience. Public adoration eventually became gravy and it was needed to fund her fix. But when alone at high altitude her poem again speaks to us: at mountain heights "bitter joy" can hear the "sound of wings." Excitement's crave was a two-edge sword of danger from daring and joy at success. This was Amelia. The courageous pilot venturing out is her Dr. Jekyll; the stubborn, inexperienced planner her Mr. Hyde. And because of her stubborn fatalism, and indeed because "gravity was uncongenial," her Mr. Hyde had his moments in hasty preparations.

Susan Butler, in her venerating biography, gives us a vignette of her Mr. Hyde in action. This played out at her luxurious Rye house before her Atlantic conquest. It reveals much of AE's mental focus on flights. After Ruth Nichols had recovered from her crash in New Brunswick, AE had invited her over for dinner. Amelia was friendly and helpful, but didn't seem interested in Ruth's gratuitous advice. According to Butler: "Ruth was always looking for support and help and good ideas, and it didn't occur to her that Amelia wasn't too, but Amelia, made of sterner stuff, was looking for none of those things. Ruth described the modifications just being completed on *her* Vega, and particularly the safety factors that had been added, sure that Amelia was focused on safety considerations as she was, but Amelia was confident that she and Bernt had thought of everything. She just didn't think in terms of negatives. 'I don't bother to go into all the possible accidents that might happen,' Ruth remembered her saying." Butler accentuates AE's self-confidence by noting that she wasn't going to pack a parachute for her own Atlantic flight nor did she even inquire of Ruth the conditions at the Saint John airfield where Ruth had cracked up because "so supremely confident was she that Bernt was right and that the problem had been Ruth and her plane."

Butler may find laud in this, but actual history has shown us that AE was really only interested in the epoch making leg of the flight and not its preparations, for it would be Bernt who flew her to and landed her at Saint John and then Harbour Grace. Earhart need only takeoff and maintain a course to land, any land, opposite the Atlantic for success.

Butler gives us another valuable vignette. GP had given AE 20 bucks for her Atlantic flight. When she landed in Ireland she broke it to send the telegram to him about her success. She later borrowed pounds sterling to retrieve the bill. She then signed it and gave it to GP; according to Butler it was one of his most treasured souvenirs. "It is hard to reconcile this gesture of Amelia's with anything that went before. By retrieving it, Amelia shows she knew how epochal her flight was, how significant and valuable that twenty-dollar bill was, or she wouldn't have thought of doing it— and then signing it."

To fully appreciate why I have used this vignette, Earhart's actions above must be set against the backdrop of her public comments. After the applause at the awards ceremony in Constitution Hall: "I think that the appreciation for the deed is out of proportion to the deed itself . . . I shall be happy if my small exploit has drawn attention to the fact that women, too, are flying."

Put together, the above reveals to what extent Earhart knew that her image was based on publicity and not accomplishment. Here the iconoclasts have some traction. From her actions with the 20 dollar bill it is clear that her public humility and GP's media spin were to some extent the acts of a Svengali giving us a pioneering yet diffident heroine. Behind-the-scenes, however, she knew how significant it was that *she* flew the Atlantic. The flight was epochal only because of publicity. The crowds cheered not because she was the first woman to do so, but because she was fulfilling her promise. She became famous for being the first woman passenger. Piloting the Atlantic herself was a particular personal triumph she had long vowed to make behind the megaphone of her fame.

As the map indicates, the Atlantic crossing was a triumph of symbolism, but the flight in itself was the "small exploit" Earhart called it. It was not an arduous endurance flight anymore or even required excessive skill. The Atlantic flight was a milestone of publicity, and it created her into a lasting celebrity. But in substance her execution of it fell short. In fact, she had barely surpassed John Alcott and Arthur Brown of 13 years before. They were the first to fly nonstop over the Atlantic. Taking off in June 1919 from St. John's, Newfoundland, in a Vickers Vimy, they eventually landed in Ireland. Mistaking a bog for a field, they upended on landing. Basically, Earhart excelled them in that she stuck her landing. Yet the enormous positive publicity caused everybody to overlook that she had not only missed her intended destination of Paris but the entire European continent. Indeed, she had almost missed Ireland.

Even her critics saw only her publicity and not her compromises. In response to her Atlantic triumph, M.E. Tracy had written in the New York *World-Telegram*: "Amelia Earhart has given us a magnificent display of useless courage. . .the interest in such performances is one great weakness of the present age."

Insulated by her public self-effacement, the few humbug critiques didn't make an impression. And from this point forward they could never go far. Her new public image was *The Fun of it*. And who could criticize this motive as being pretentious when progress (apparently) was the result? Challenging the dangers of flight, this scrawny, androgynous yet charming tomboy typified courage rising over adversity. Weakness for the current fad, once again, existed because it represented progress. Its cornerstone was individual courage, and AE had much of this.

Nevertheless, Amelia Earhart really did not have endurance skills. In fact, her mettle for endurance was challenged the most within the relative safety of the United States. Her longest hop would be her first speed record (1932) at 19 + hours. Second was her Pacific flight. It came in slightly short of this at 18 hrs., 16 min., only an hour longer than her second speed record in the US (17 + hours) in 1933. Her international flights, including the trans-Atlantic, fall far short (Mexico-Newark at 14 hours, 19 minutes; and the Atlantic flight at 14 hours, 56 minutes).

The continental speed records were given such coverage because of the publicity generated from her personal fame. Otherwise they were fairly straight line speed runs.

Nothing that she was doing really tested her endurance or honed her navigation skill. Asked why she didn't fly to Hawaii instead of hauling her plane there on a ship's crane, she herself said: "It's easier to hit a continent than an island." Such is the truth. Her self-deprecating manner often hid the biting truth: lack of experience. She was not a great navigator, and even after 6 years of being hailed as the premier aviatrix it is unlikely she would have found Hawaii in January 1935. Indeed, on her next flight she would have missed Mexico City had she not landed at Nopala first. She apologized at Mexico City for not making it there nonstop, but from the cheers no one seemed to care.

As rare as they were, her critics only responded to her publicity. They did not objectively assess her accomplishments. Even an academic institution like Purdue made this mistake. They saw AE's intrinsic charisma as the most important.

After Laura Ingalls shattered AE's speed record, Purdue set out to buy Earhart her dream machine. A bulky Vega could no longer convey the 38 year old brand acronym to any significant challenge of young women and sleek planes. Like the complex union of soul and body, AE's charisma still needed the spirit that haunted the veneer of "pioneer." No sooner had she got the Electra when she was planning her world flight, and GP was planning her income.

Her spontaneous and ambitious response to Purdue's gift set in motion that most dangerous component of her character—the Mr. Hyde of sloppy preparations. A true admirer, Paul Briand spun this as "happy-go-lucky." Lack of attention to detail Butler promoted as stern confidence. AE's failure reveals both assessments as glossing foolhardiness.

This is the only attribute that can explain her accepting Fred Noonan with a shrug. He was not the best navigator, but after Manning packed up he was handy. Jackie Cochran writes:

> I had plenty of hunches about that flight and none of them was on the optimistic side. I questioned whether the navigator she had employed, although an exceedingly fine man, was up to the high-speed celestial navigation in a plane. I asked her to take him out to sea for quite a distance from Los Angeles and then, after flying in circles for a time so that he could no longer be oriented, to ask him to give her the course back to Los Angeles. She told me they reached the shore line halfway between Los Angeles and San Francisco.

Briand wrote that AE was "undisturbed by the navigation error, even in view of the irrefutable and just demonstrated fact that a mistake of one degree on the compass could, on a long flight, take her miles off course. That she still engaged Noonan, knowing as she did that Howland Island was just two miles long and only three-quarters of a mile wide, a mere fifteen feet above sea level, and more than 2,550 miles from Lae, New Guinea, is testimony to an unshakable confidence in her own ability."

Once again, Briand's statement was the product of a filtered 1960 assessment of Earhart's image. More than anyone AE should have had trepidation at relying on her own navigation. Her own final notes prove that. Before she vanished, she mailed off much of her early jottings on her world flight. Flying over the Bahamas, she wrote: "I certainly have a sissy trip. The Sperry Gyro Pilot does much of the flying and Noonan navigates. Were I alone I should be hopping along shore line I think." It is hard

to believe that the choice of a subpar navigator was based on being confident, as Briand interprets it. The hasty Mr. Hyde of her
preparations took over. Mr. Hyde had always been with her, and
she had always had success. Why worry now?

In other words, she believed she was good enough to rely on
homing beams now. Flying the Bahamas she jotted she was more
interested in listening to the radio for weather and local commercial programs rather than the "airway beam." There were
more than enough homing signals and she knew how to follow
them. She must have felt that two ships in the Pacific were more
than enough to guide her to tiny Howland Island.

Conspiracy biographers tried to avoid Noonan's inadequacies
as a navigator because AE's choice of a subpar navigator didn't
build a picture of her entrusted with a top secret spy mission.
But hints of his inabilities snuck through even these biographers. Fred Goerner only writes in passing how Mantz conveyed that Noonan could have made a radical navigational mistake that directed them straight to Saipan (in order to accommodate Akiyama's story). Goerner's tender friendship with Mary
Bea Noonan no doubt caused him to spin: "Fred Noonan was a
talented and handsome man. Only one major flaw disturbed the
image. He could drink a bottle of whiskey in the afternoon, and
get through the better part of another in the evening. 'Boozer,'
'drunk,' 'lush'—are hard words, and none of them fit Fred. He
was hooked on liquor, yet somehow always managed to function.
He fought his adversary with courage and conviction, but sometimes he lost, and those defeats were costly. One of them caused
Pan American to let him go." When William Van Dusen, senior
vice president of Eastern Airlines, told Joe Gervais that "Noonan
couldn't navigate his way across my duck pond" Gervais became
a twit with his conspiracy theories and thought Van Dusen
might have been Noonan (after plastic surgery) trying to throw
him off the scent.

The fact is that only those who wanted to portray AE on a
derring-do spy mission wanted to project Noonan as more than
he was, but those around AE at the time knew very well there
could be problems and few were silent about it. Therefore the
elements within her character that allowed her to select Noonan
are relevant here. It was her hasty, fatalistic Mr. Hyde.

Über-GP can't be blamed for this aspect of Earhart's character. When they did that bit for the camera before her world flight, they played her headstrong character for fun. She blushed, giggled and they chuckled together. . .yet it was obvious this 118 pound "slip of a girl" could push George through the hoop when she wanted.

Colonel Hilton Railey was witness to another main event. George had thought up many money-making schemes to cash in on her name, including an Amelia Earhart hat.

She looked at it, turned it over in her hands: "This won't do at all. You'll have to cancel it."

GP replied that he couldn't. The contract was signed and they are already made. AE fumed. She had foolishly given him power of attorney. "Then tell the manufacturer to unmake them. Tell him at once— right now!" Then pointing to the phone, she commanded him: "Phone him!"

GP went into a flailing ambit of the room.

AE: "Since I can't very well sue the manufacturer, and you had my power of attorney, then I most certainly shall sue you— unless. . ."

Railey intervened and was able to cancel the deal.

AE's choice of men, which had reluctantly included GP, was never stellar. After her return from the world flight, she and Paul Mantz were going into business together (a training field and perhaps even an air circus). Butler writes that Mantz had "a penchant for brilliant ties, loud sport coats, gold jewelry, cigars, frosted martinis, and women," and he was "according to fiction writer Irving Wallace, empty-headed and shallow, a man of no real perceptions or sensitivity."

More than anyone it was Paul Mantz who fostered the idea Earhart could have been on a secret spy mission. He had pumped Fred Goerner full of the notion there were extra fuel tanks aboard that could carry the Electra over 4,000 miles. Goerner came to accept that Mantz had a keen sense of publicity, but he really didn't seem to understand he was an outright prevaricator. In that telegram sent by Margot DeCaric on July 11, 1937, she mentions she gleaned her information on the Electra's fuel endurance and potential adjustments from the "technical advisor," which had to be Mantz. DeCarie informed them there was "sufficient fuel for about 3 hours computed from actual time in air of slightly over 20 hours to last radio contact and establish back that fuel consumption was 42 gallons per hour at cruising of 130 knots. Technical advisor for Earhart thinks plane could operate at slow speeds 30 gallons per hour. . ." He knew perfectly damn well the Electra had about a 23-24 hour fuel endurance and 3,000 mile range at normal fuel mixture.

The era that gave us Earhart as I Spy conveniently chose to abide by the legacy GP had sculpted during her life. Being the world's foremost aviatrix allowed theorists to promote Earhart as having been commissioned to engage in a dangerous heroic mission that ultimately failed. Within this failure there is weaved some element that is responsible for the "conspiracy of silence."

But today we know GP shielded from the public more than AE's early poor flying habits. He shielded her imperious stubbornness. Goody two-shoes sells. Earhart could wear it. Her tomboyish zest for adventure sold it. It pumped a product— anything from furniture to hats. She drew the line only at cheating children. Her image was a trademark. This image was of the pioneering "world's foremost aviatrix." Kind, generous, brave, intellectual. Goody two-shoes with epaulets.

In death her family and friends wanted this image preserved religiously. The sanctimonious rubbish stemming from George Putnam in *Courage is the Price* is a good example of the image Amelia Earhart's family and friends wanted to preserve for her. This desire probably inspired Muriel to believe the ghastly piety of GP's involvement in the Rothar affair.

This was also the kind of stuff GP churned out in life for the press. Nothing tarnished Earhart in life, and so long as GP lived nothing would in death either. *Last Flight* preserved her image—she was calm, self-effacing, always cautious, never overly confident. Putnam's biography *Soaring Wings* in 1939 was her glorifying epitaph.

But twenty years is a long time, and the Miss Rosy-Ducks image of Earhart wasn't a commodity anymore. Putnam too was long dead. It was an era that could reassess the past more objectively, perhaps even more critically the era that led to the devastation of World War II. It was at this time that the vault creaked from rusty hinges as Paul Briand opened the doors and subtly felt the "conspiracy of silence." He got suspicious, but his suspicion could only see a phantom and not lay hold on a solid form.

What was it about? We followed his and Goerner's and even Gervais' imaginations and accepted something diabolical. It was easy in the wake of World War II to believe the Japanese had been capable of anything nefarious.

Today, however, it becomes harder to accept the spy mission and Japanese internment theories. But the conspiracy of silence was real, and since it has been used to underwrite so many lurid theories, such as Earhart having been Tokyo Rose or Hirohito's mistress, or even brought back to a life of quaffing tea in New Jersey, it has to be addressed again. It remains integral in navigating possible theories in the search for her actual fate.

There's a roulette of options. One is the fear her trite morality would be uncovered. It was certainly sensitive enough for Briand to redact it. When he quoted from her prenuptial surprise to GP, he removed the paragraph where she stipulated adultery, even for passing fancies, was going to be all right. Was the conspiracy of silence in response to the belief her end had been ignoble long pig? Most likely, it was knowledge of Warner Thompson's report. Some within her inner circle must have heard it was bad.

Understanding the silence begins with understanding the era of her fame. In the 1938 movie *Angels with Dirty Faces*, the priest-friend encourages Jimmy Cagney's character to lose his tough guy gangster image before he goes to the chair. It will save many a young man from walking in his criminal path. He hesitates, but in the end he feigns being afraid to fry for his life of misdeeds. His admiring young disciples see this and turn from him and, as we are led to believe, they will not turn to a life of crime. Cagney has, to some extent, redeemed his character before parting to meet the great judge.

Citing a movie is not giving a vain example. It does reflect the era. To fall from grace in the 1930s was to fall really low. It was an era of real life heroes. The fad, once again, had been individual courage. A hero's image was the hero, and the press would not tear them down. It sold because it represented the symbol of progress and, for the Depression, hope for the future.

By 1930s' standards, the cool, courageous image of the tomboyish "wisp of a girl" Amelia Earhart would have been ruined, Henry Morgenthau was certain, if it got out she disregarded her radio instructions and then went hysterical in the last minutes of her flight. He wanted to spare this image, though personal PR for a private citizen was really not the duty of a minister of government. His instinctive desire reflects the double standard of the era's concept of public image. He believed she had, in fact, ruined her reputation, but he wanted to preserve the glorified public image, though he believed it was now false.

Morgenthau really is the first member of the conspiracy of silence. From him it went to Tommy Scheider, then Eleanor, and she no doubt told FDR. Eleanor was probably the most forgiving. But the conviction Morgenthau conveyed must have extended to others within AE's close circle of friends, and even 20 years later they would have shared his personal view that AE's reputation was shot. Perhaps they didn't know the details, but they remembered the certainty it had happened.

For many it was perhaps easy to keep silent. None wanted to lose their reflected glory. Others like the compassionate Eleanor were forgiving and perhaps just chose to forget— one reason perchance why AE's memory went into deep freeze so quickly.

For those within her inner circle who had heard the damning whispers, Amelia Earhart's reputation wasn't "gone" by this single slip-up. They may have feared a domino effect. AE herself always seemed to worry about a closer, more critical examination of her image. Her actions with the $20 dollar bill reveal she understood her fame rested on the raw celebrity of her character rather than accomplishments. Her self-effacing comments, and choosing *Fun of It* as her *weltanschauung*, seem wisely predesigned to insulate her from the criticism that could come from any appearance of pretention.

Wilkinson was right about Earhart always having some excuse to defer attention from her mishaps. "When Earhart crashed an autogyro heavily in 1931, she climbed out of the wreckage and in a moment of candor said, 'It's all my fault.' But she later explained that, heavens, what she actually *meant* was that it was her fault that her husband, George Putnam, had tripped and broken a rib while rushing toward the wreck." She landed in Ireland because of mechanical issues. She landed at Nopala because a bug or dust got in her eye. Excuses were short and sweet until the crash in Hawaii. Initially it was Mantz's fault for his earlier hard landing. From the cascade of excuses that followed, the fear of a reassessment of her "career" seems evident.

The stretching and pulling is obvious in *Last Flight*. Reflecting back on how she was swamped with news at Miami, she had to explain for her readers the complete lack of fanfare via which she left California.

> So much was written before and after the March 17 takeoff at Oakland, and following the Honolulu accident, that I thought it would be a pleasant change just to slip away without comment. The extent of the publicity accompanying the first start was unsolicited and doubtless more than the flight deserved even if it had been successful.
>
> The fact is that the career of one who indulges in any kind of flying off the beaten path is often complicated. For instance, if one gives out plans beforehand, one is likely to be charged with publicity seeking by those who do not know how difficult it is to escape the competent gentlemen of the press. On the other hand, if one slips away, as I have generally tried to do, the slipper-away invites catcalls from those who earn their living writing and taking photographs.

When she would return, she felt the pros and cons, the "merits and demerits" can be thrashed out.

In truth, the above has many demerits. It spins a fear of having her accomplishments examined independent of her lucrative charisma. Much media *had* been solicited by GP, and in a typical formula AE plays it down by saying the publicity was more than the flight deserved.

So stealthy was the beginning of her second attempt around the world that nobody is really sure where the historic flight began. It is often said today that the world flight began at Oakland and *not* Miami. Oakland was a great PR locale for Earhart, but she really only flew there to get the 6,500 postcards from Elmer Dimity. Then she flew back to Burbank.

AE could not avoid qualifying things in *Last Flight*, but she puts some saving spin on it. "Technically," she wrote, "the journey from Burbank across the country was a shakedown flight. If difficulties developed we would bring the ship back to the Lockheed plant for further adjustments."

By the time she wrote her next chapter, "The Start," things became more certain. She recorded her takeoff from Miami at 5:56 a.m. on June 6 "with Fred Noonan aboard as navigator and I as pilot bound for California by about the longest route we could contrive." With her plane passing its maintenance checks at Miami, it became advantageous to say California was the start now and thus the final destination, though whether she meant Oakland or Burbank is not clarified.

Yet at Puerto Rico—1,000 miles from Miami— she logged in her notebook: "First thousand miles of the flight."

Minus the spin, the truth is she had crept out of Oakland or Burbank because she didn't need another mishap toward the beginning of a flight. A reassessment, especially of her beginnings, would ponder why Bernt Balchen had been the crutch that got her safely landed at Newfoundland, and why Mantz had flown the first leg to Hawaii. The book was essentially explaining why the (anticipated) lavish triumph had been at Oakland.

But the inevitable (and somewhat harmless) spin of PR is not really at issue here. It is what it had to cover up. It not only had to cover mistakes. It had to cover the increasing span of distance between Earhart's "career" trajectory and that of the aviation industry. She had seen the writing on the wall. She had chosen the "Fun of it" pragmatically, but it was also the truth. The aviation industry had advanced beyond her ability to continue to affect the appearance she was a part of its progress. Those within the industry long knew it. On the very day she was declared lost at sea, the whispers began. One example (*Salt Lake Telegram*):

> Many long range flying experts smiled wryly when Miss Earhart last spring announced plans for a 27,000-mile air jaunt around the equatorial regions. They asked privately:
>
> "What will that prove?"
>
> Unwilling to be quoted, they argued that Miss Earhart was years behind the times so far as ocean flying was concerned.
>
> They contended that ocean aviation had become a matter for big business— fleets of planes, chains of bases and radio stations, and many technicians operating as a coordinated unit.

Miss Earhart, they said, was still flying in 1927 mode, with a single plane and only limited facilities for such a difficult job.

This was perhaps the politest way of saying the actual airline industry knew her flight was merely a cumbersome stunt for image and income.

AE's fame was such that more than one in the industry did not wish their name associated with a negative comment about her motives. However, as the years went by, Hilton Railey had no choice but to agree.

Long before she mentioned it, I knew that next, and perhaps fatally, must come her globe-circling adventure. Why— when even to her it must have seemed a stunt without constructive benefit to the aeronautical industry— did she attempt that hazardous expedition?

She had to. She was caught up in the hero racket that compelled her to strive for increasingly dramatic records, bigger and braver feats that automatically insured the publicity necessary to the maintenance of her position as the foremost woman pilot in the world. She was a victim of an era of "hot" aeronautics that began with Colonel Lindbergh and Admiral Byrd and that shot "scientific" expeditions across continents, oceans, and polar regions by dint of individual exhibition.

When Railey penned that, he gently made Earhart both a victim of a racket and a willing co-conspirator. She gladly went along with the false "science" behind the purpose of the "Flying Laboratory." The carnival preparations for the flight make it plain there was no science or academia behind it. It was a racket without constructive benefit that had one purpose: image and then income. She had a fast new airplane thanks to Purdue's superficial concept of modernism. She immediately employed it to the most self-aggrandizing carnival purpose but research. It would be difficult to beat Railey's assessment, but rather easy with time to fall short of its politeness.

Railey does not elaborate why he feared the world flight could prove fatal. We can only accept that as a friend he knew both AE's character and the spin that was employed to cover mistakes. He dances admirably around character flaws, but he knew the Mr. Hyde of sloppy preparations was yet another factor. He manifested himself in strobing radio preparations, negligence in getting briefed on her radio equipment and, perhaps, even at the end in pushing Earhart over the edge.

Going to pieces and being overheard to do so would not be something her inner circle would want made public. This is evident in Henry Morgenthau's reticence to release the final report. Thanks to Warner Thompson it was truly believed by Morgenthau and many around him that her last actions and words "smeared" her legacy, to use his own word. And from his expressed attitude, he was capable of protecting her reputation, which could have included redacting *Itasca*'s radio log report.

It is not a suspicion that exists only in a moment in time when the Morgenthau Transcript was jotted down in 1938. The belief Earhart went berserk and the report was redacted entered officialdom, was written down, and continued.

About January 1950 a summary was written by Raymond A. Kotrla of the Department of the Navy. It was written in response to an official inquiry on December 13, 1949, one inspired probably because mother Earhart had gone public about wanting the government to inquire of the Japanese if they knew anything of Amelia. This kind of news collects within the in-and-out boxes on official desks. Someone will want a summary of the context in order to know how to draft a response, if it is ever officially necessary. The idea that Earhart destroyed her reputation in the last minutes of her flight and that the Coast Guard covered-up was preserved somewhere in order for Kotrla, a Naval Intelligence administrator himself, to access it and put it in his summary. In paragraph 1.f he quotes an earlier report:

On 6 October 1943, ONI summarized the circumstances of Mrs. Putnam's disappearance as follows: "Gilberts were searched and British authorities there assisted in checkup on all inhabited islands in vicinity. Mandates were not searched but Japs were cooperative (or appeared to be). Coast Guard cutter at destination (Howland Island) copied Earhart's transmissions and were convinced that she made emergency landing at sea within about 100 miles of Howland Baker. (Her last transmissions were tragic and

near-hysterical—impounded by Coast Guard Command at Honolulu). Studied conclusion at end of exhaustive search by *Colorado*,
Swan, *Itasca* and *Lexington* planes (900,000 square miles) was
that plane landed at sea and most likely went down with a rush
and with crew inside. 20 km headwind throughout flight from Lae
and Earhart's inability to "get a minimum" on her radio compass
bearings of *Itasca*'s transmissions appeared to be the direct cause
of her failure to reach island. Best data available from plane manufacturer convinced me that she did not have any margin of fuel
whatever."

The ONI agent could have been reading Thompson's report,
then still restricted, but he may have had other written documents that alluded to the redacting of the Coast Guard tran-
scripts, which he believes were "impounded" in Honolulu.

True, there is no direct evidence that Thompson's report was
redacted. However, there is an interesting glitch that indicates a
mental breakdown could have been "impounded" from the report. The radio transcript log contains specific times for radio
messages except in the last Earhart message. This is logged as
coming in between 0800 and 0803— a gaping span for a message
only a few seconds long, suggesting something quite juicy was
excised from the report.

Warner Thompson's verbal report was apparently so vivid it
made a deep impact on Henry Morgenthau. His written report
can be interpreted one way or the other, but there are some indications Earhart was bending under strain. Without being able
to pick up their homing signal (which was not dependent on her
receiving antenna), she asks them to take a bearing on her to
lead her in. Articulating Dah-Dah-Dah for only a few seconds
must have struck the crowd in the *Itasca* radio room as truly incredible. And AE most certainly knew the amount of time for
obtaining a radio bearing. She had personally sent the message
for the *Ontario* to transmit **N** for 5 minutes when requested. She
had prepared *Itasca* she would make a "long call" when close.

In his written report Thompson had toned down his ire and
he was genuinely unaware of the cascade of events that created
the radio problems. But he was also unaware of something
else— the sloppy Mr. Hyde of slapstick preparations. And it is

Mr. Hyde or, at least, the fear of him which brings us to his unique advantage in her last flight. She had never had a real endurance flight before. Being the guinea pig of long endurance effects was natty PR, but there was an element of truth to it. In this respect, this flight was true pioneering, at least for AE. And she may have pushed herself beyond breaking point.

Public acknowledgment that AE had cracked under strain would have been disastrous for another reason. It would call into question many of her lively, robust adventure writings. We come back to the fear of GP Putnam and his quill dancing with truth like a duck on ice. For example, there is that glitch between her log entry in Puerto Rico and in her posthumous book. When was "The Start" actually written?— certainly after Puerto Rico. In *Last Flight*, thanks to his publishing skills, we also have AE's recollection of a particularly harrowing moment over the Atlantic in her epoch-making flight.

> And one further fact of the flight, which I've not set down in words before. I carried a barograph, an instrument which records on a disc the course of the plane, its rate of ascent and descent, its levels of flight all coordinated with clocked time. My tell-tale disc could tell a tale. At one point it recorded an almost near vertical drop of three thousand feet. It started at an altitude of something over 3,000 feet, and ended— well, something above the water. That happened when the plane suddenly "iced up" and went into a spin. How long we spun I do not know. I know that I tried my best to do exactly what one should do with a spinning plane, and regained flying control as the warmth of the lower altitude melted the ice. As we righted and held level again, through the blackness below I could see the white-caps too close for comfort.

There is no time for warmer temps to melt ice on a plane spiraling almost vertically downward for a mere 3,000 feet. Being so unperturbed within the context of abject peril seems a false construct anyway, but if put next to her going "hysterical" at the end of her world flight it would truly make any reader question the veracity of AE's reputation as anything more than a musing PR image written at the typewriter for public consumption.

We can blame (or suspect) GP for some of the questionable

vignettes in *Last Flight.* Yet what does even a pure corpus amount to? Judith Thurman was correct: "Her unique experience might have yielded a memoir that would still be read, yet she published only three slight books, one of them posthumous, which were rushed out, for commercial reasons, in weeks."

Twenty years after her disappearance when the enormous interest in her fate resumed, her reputation was potentially more fragile especially that one image she could no longer maintain from the grave: "foremost woman pilot in the world." What Briand failed to uncover, and what Spy and Die theorists misinterpreted, are probably those negative kernels that have since emerged in the hands of other authors: how GP hindered the careers of other women pilots, and Warner Thompson's report. This is what really does attack image more than any (alleged) infidelity with Gene Vidal or a Gilbertese apple in her mouth.

The need for a plaster saint creates a medium in which the roots of the conspiracy of silence can find sustenance. The prospects above would have been enough to make Earhart's former inner circle skittish to talk to anybody going about trying to open doors to the past. Each had basked in the divine light of this uniquely famous individual. Diminish the brightness of the wick and the moth at its fringes is plunged back into obscurity.

But the conspiracy of silence also seems based on another fear—guilt by association. No one liked GP, and no one was really sure what all he had been up to in AE's brand name. Jackie Cochran felt the need to politely draw a distinction: "I was never too fond of George Putnam. . .but I loved Amelia with a deep, true and loyal affection. She was a great flyer and even greater woman."

GP was nicknamed the "lens louse" by photographers for a reason. He was the man who liked publicity and catered to it. George seemed to be a natural grandstander and the penchant never left him. For publicity's sake (and $25,000.00) he was involved in a fake lawsuit against his friends the Odlums when RKO released *Flight for Freedom* (the movie implied a love affair between "Tonie Carter" and her navigator). In May 1939 GP had also been involved in some strange kidnap scheme in which two Germans wanted to prevent the publication of his book on Germany. They snatched him from his North Hollywood driveway and took him to Bakersfield. It netted him a lot of publicity.

Eventually all of the above melds into the ultimate foundation for the "conspiracy of silence," at least from what I can detect. As the newspapers noted on July 19, 1937, at the conclusion of the search, there was that wry smile from those within the aeronautical industry regarding her career. "What will this prove?" Knowledge from within verses perception from without seems the cornerstone of the conspiracy of silence. A reassessment of her actual contributions was perhaps the greatest fear in her inner circle, even 20 years later. Just what was her "career"?

This is not vilifying Amelia Earhart. However, when compared to sister Earhart's halo-fringed *Courage is the Price*, one can see why the conspirators of silence weren't interested in Earhart's past being dredged up or in AE being reassessed.

Her friends within aviation, those who would become the conspiracy of silence, weren't beguiled by MovieTone flickers. What the phenomenally exponential leap of her last flight instilled in them was trepidation— Cochran called her ill feeling about it a hunch; Railey dreaded it would come.

It was not nor is it about pilot deficiency. AE was a confident pilot. It is a character issue. Mix this confidence with her Mr. Hyde who said "I don't bother to go into all the possible accidents that might happen" and this created a formula for disaster.

Amelia Earhart was not the material for a secret spy mission, and her inner circle seems to have known such an assertion could not stand the test of time. Despite the Spy and Die Theory giving her an heroic epilogue a la *Flight for Freedom*, those within her inner circle wanted an amorphous end for her, a primitive transcendence into nature: "Count her amongst the beautiful and brave, her turquoise mausoleum in each wave," as poet Nathalia Crane wrote.

Viewed from a mindset that could embrace such a syrupy epitaph most every peccadillo put forward by her detractors today could inspire a conspiracy of silence in 1960.

Only one fact is pertinent to this study. She was in the hero racket, bound to prove (and monetize) the image of being the "premier aviatrix." Probably AE could not see a compromised image—she had always been truthful about inspiring acolytes to follow their dreams. This is exactly what she did. She ennobled

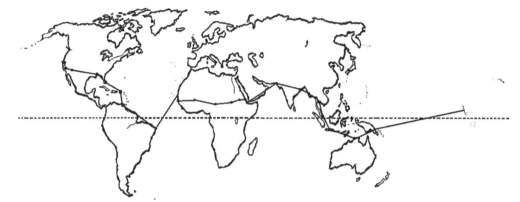

Compared to the map on pages 224-225 the exponential leap of Ear-hart's world flight is evident. She had never come close to requiring such endurance before.

her flights' purposes at times, when necessary, and at triumph was self-effacing. Both were needed in walking the tightrope dividing pretention and substance. She did it smoothly because she was sincere in chasing her intense pleasure, and with GP's spin the audience felt they were included as witnesses to pioneering. They didn't realize they were merely watching someone very idiosyncratic enjoying her life. A lot of spin was involved and in the end it unwound revealing a clear distinction between a charismatic dabbler and a stubborn, inefficient thrill seeker.

For 9 years she had lived this heady life, and now the excitement level seemed to be fading. Publically, she declared she was getting too old for these "long flights," but she really meant her excitement and therewith her dabbling interest was fading. She also understood and no doubt had many times seen that "wry smile" from the actual aeronautical aficionados. She could no longer affect the pretense of progress. She wanted out. And few have taken this into consideration as the ultimate motive for her last flight. She wanted to go out on top— with a world flight no one had done. It was an exponential leap from her previous flights. Now at 39 years old, she was afraid of getting old. We can well imagine that a world flight would secure her image, and her image was really all she would have for retirement.

The world map on pages 224-225 upon which are illustrated Earhart's flights and the flights of other contemporaries makes for a sobering comparison. Billed as pioneering firsts, Earhart flights are centered on America only, where the publicity garnered endorsement and speaking money. This may better explain why she hung on the American apron string. Only here was there a means to cash-in on them (Lady Mary discovered she also did best financially on the American lecture circuit).

Within these confines she became a *very* good pilot, but what is relevant is that by the time she vanished she was not an experienced pilot. She had had long hops, but not long endurance flights.

As the maps reveal, AE wasn't experienced enough to be given such a spy commission. Yet in terms of a personal feat she managed the world flight well until she got to the most dangerous leg. Here her inexperience was fatal. Her preparations had been far worse than "casual," as Thompson mollified his opinion in his written report. He had feared she had receiver problems, and it seems probable now that her receiving antenna snapped off on takeoff at Lae, New Guinea. With the brittle pulse of radio waves broken, AE's subsequent failure can be explained by the maps and in the history of her hasty preparations. She should have gone to the briefings on her Bendix radio. Even with a failed receiver antenna, she would have been able to detect the *Itasca* homing beacon on 500 kilocycles. She would have brought the Electra to Howland Island.

Through Goerner, Gervais, Briand, the Spy and Die theories had made Earhart incredibly famous again, and it was not a nostalgic, historical fame. She was relevant again through the controversy of her new proposed fate. Did it lead to greater conspiracies and national secrets? Formal biographers may like to downplay the legends of her disappearance, but it is really these that gave Amelia Earhart lasting fame unto the present, not her 1930s glamourous *Fun of It* image.

The enormous and glorifying fame Earhart achieved through the Spy and Die theories only underscores that the "conspiracy of silence" could not have surrounded any hush of a whisper that this had truly been her fate. There was nothing ignoble about it, nothing that reflected negatively on Earhart's image; on the contrary. This brings us back to a potential (though unlikely) love affair with Gene Vidal, main course at a Gilbertese luau or, very possibly, Thompson's assertions and the domino effect this would have on reexamination of her public image.

All the evidence points to Amelia Earhart and Fred Noonan being on a publicity flight, but this reality doesn't preclude some of the legend of her fate. If AE and Fred were picked up months after their public disappearance, that *Smith's Weekly* article would have given devastating coincidence to the moment of their retrieval by the Japanese. She would not have been executed. Yet if ill she may have died as she was being transshipped for questioning and (hopefully) eventual repatriation. Diplomatically, it was best to just let it drop.

In the age of iconoclasm, many judge Earhart in the sense of condemning. I judge only in the sense of assessing. Fame based on accomplishment is easy to assess: just recite the litany. But fame based on something intrinsic is almost impossible to easily circumscribe. Noted theologian/philosopher Francis Schaeffer said there was nothing divine about Greek and Roman gods: they were rather amplified humanity. This is also true of anyone mega famous. To be the quintessence of some laudable trait or attribute is a rare thing. It is easier to apply these traits to an inanimate thing like an idol and worship. But how rare is it to find a person who truly embodies something that connects with an entire generation, or several, and thus becomes a symbol of something people wish to adulate? Whatever the combination of ingredients is, it is what makes an icon or a divo or diva. It is the difference between a movie star and merely an accomplished thespian. "There was ether in the very sound of her name," declared Thurman. "Physically, too, she seemed like an airy spirit—Ariel, impatient to be set free." And this spirit combined with the quest for adventure created Amelia Earhart into that rare living idol for a generation and perhaps for many more to come. It may sound tongue-in-cheek, yet that is not my intent— but truly it was harder for Earhart to be what she was than to be merely an accomplished aviation pioneer.

No final assessment of Earhart can overlook reading between the lines of her statements and actions throughout her career in the public eye. She understood that her fame was based on her own charisma and GP's promoter skills. By 1932 it is clear she understood she could not maintain an image of progress for much longer. "Fun of It" was a wise rubric. By 1936 it is also perfectly true that she wanted to give up these stunt flights. Yet like with her race to conquer the Atlantic, glory urged her on more than the accomplishment in itself. When a plane she thought she never could have afforded was given to her on a silver platter, the carnival preparations began. It is not disparaging to say that. She had her way out now, soon, and a plane that could take her around the world. It was a megalomaniac leap over what others had done, and she almost succeeded.

She has indeed obtained the enduring fame she sought, though not in the way she wanted. It is the mystery of her disappearance rather than her accomplishments which has given her the immortality she desired. No successful world flight could ever have given her the lasting fame that the mystery of her fate has given her.

Bibliography

Briand, Paul,   *Daughter of the Sky,*   Duell, Sloan & Pearce,
1960.

Brink, Randall   *Lost Star,*   Norton, 1994.

Butler, Susan,   *East to the Dawn,*   Addison Wesley, 1997.

Campbell, Mike,   *Amelia Earhart: The Truth at Last,*
Sunbury Press, 2016

Cochran, Jacqueline   *The Stars at Noon,*   Atlantic, Little,
Brown, 1954.

Earhart, Amelia,   *Last Flight,*   Orion Books, 1988.

"   "   *20 Hrs 40 Min.: Our Flight in the Friendship,*
Martino Fine Books.

"   "   *The Fun of It*   Academy Chicago
Publishers, 2006.

Friedell, W. L.   Resume Earhart Search by U.S.S. *Colorado.* Passage to Pearl Harbor, Honolulu, T.H., July 13, 1937.

Goerner, Fred, *The Search for Amelia Earhart,* Doubleday, 1966.

Klaas, Joe   *Amelia Earhart Lives,*   McGraw-Hill, 1971.

Long, Elgen M, and Marie K.,
Amelia Earhart: Mystery Solved,
Simon & Schuster, 1999.

Loomis, Vincente V.   *Amelia Earhart: The Final Story,*
Random House, 1985.

National Archives of Kiribati:
Telegrams between Resident Commissioner, Gilberts and Ellice Islands Colony, Officer-in-Charge Gardner Island, Phoenix Scheme,

and Senior Medical Officer, Central Hospital, Tarawa.

Pan American High Frequency Directional Stations Bearing:

Ambler, K.C., Pan American Airways System Memorandum, July 10, 1937.

Angus, G.W., Reports—Special Amelia Earhart Flight, New Guinea to Howland Island July 1 and 2, 1937, July 10, 1937. Chief Communication engineer, Division Communication Superintendent, Pacific Division.

Hansen, R.M., Earhart Flight— Wake Deductions, Division Communication Superintendent, Operator in Charge, Communications, Wake, July 11, 1937.

Miller, G.H. Earhart Flight Activities, Division Communication Superintendent, Operator in Charge, Communications, Midway, July 11, 1937.

⸺⸺⸺

Paxton, Nina L.   *I Heard Amelia's Earhart's SOS,*
                    The Courier-Journal Magazine, 1962.

                    Letter to George P. Putnam, July 30, 1937
                    Letter to G. P. Putnam August 5, 1937
                    Letter to Mary Bea Noonan July 22, 1937
                    Letter to Time Magazine July 14, 1937
                    Letter to Walter Winchell July 30, 1937
                    Letter to (Rep) Carl Vinson August 14, 1937

Putnam Papers, Purdue University.

Rothar, Wilbur, case of:

Beary, Patrick J., Attn at Law, letter to DA Frank Hogan, May 29, 1946 Re: Wilbur Rothar – Ind. No. 214079.

Court of General Sessions New York County: The People of the State of New York Against Wilbur Rothar alias Wilbur Goodenough: Motion to Dismiss.

Court of General Sessions County of New York: The People of the State of New York – against—Wilbur Rothar alias William Goodenough, Recommendation for Dismissal under Section 671 of the Code of Criminal Procedure.

Court of General Sessions of the County of New York, The People of the State of New York—against—Wilbur Rothar otherwise known as William Goodenough, defendant. William Copeland Dodge, DA.

Hogan, Frank, District Attorney's Memorandum in Opposition to Motion For Dismissal of Indictment. Court of General Sessions, County of New York, People of the State of New York Against Wilbur Rothar alias Wilbur Goodenough.

O'Donnell, Leo P., director Harlem Valley State Hospital, August 26, 1960, letter to DA's Office RE: Wilbur Rokar [sic].

Rago, May,   Letter dated June 9, 1945, to DA Frank Hogan.

"   "   Letter dated July 14, 1952, to DA Frank Hogan RE: Wilbur Rothar.

Rothar, Edmund,   Letter to DA Frank Hogan, Oct. 11, 1943 RE: People vs Wilbur Rothar.

Rothar, Wilbur, Request to Dismiss, April 20, 1958, Matteawan State Hospital, sent to DA Frank Hogan.

State of New Yok Department of Corrections Matteawan State Hospital, Letter of Superintendent to DA Frank Hogan, April 18, 1960.
———————

Records of the Department of State and Related Correspondence, 119 pages.

Report of the Search for Amelia Earhart by the U.S. Navy and U.S. Coast Guard, 2-18 July 1937, O.G. Murfin, Admiral, July 31, 1937.

Report of Earhart Search *Lexington* Group, U.S.S. *Lexington* Flag-ship, July 1937, including Narrative of Earhart Search, 20 July 1937, J.S. Dowell.

Report of Earhart Search Operations, 3-18 July 1937, Leigh Noyes, Captain U.S. Navy, Commanding U.S.S. *Lexington.*

Thompson, W. K. Report on the Search for Amelia Earhart, Honolu-lu, T.H., July 29, 1937, with Enclosure Dispatch File.

"   "   Annotated Transcript Log of Itasca Excerpts June and July 1937, Honolulu T.H. 19 July 1937, 106 pages.

Thurman, Judith,   *Missing Woman:*
                              Amelia Earhart's Last Flight,
                                         September 2009, New Yorker.

Wallace, Lane,   *Enough of Amelia,*
                                         The Atlantic, October 2009.
Websites:
https://tighar.org
earharttruth.wordpress.com

Index

Printed in the USA
CPSIA information can be obtained
at www.ICGtesting.com
LVHW090438081223
765728LV00061B/1303

9 780988 850576